Withdrawn

50 CLASSIC HIKES IN NEVADA

9/26/06
$18.95
B&T

AS

50 CLASSIC HIKES IN NEVADA

FROM THE RUBY MOUNTAINS TO RED ROCK CANYON

MIKE WHITE

UNIVERSITY OF NEVADA PRESS

RENO & LAS VEGAS

University of Nevada Press, Reno, Nevada 89557 USA
Copyright © 2006 by University of Nevada Press
Illustrations copyright © 2006 by Mike White
All rights reserved
Manufactured in the United States of America
Design by Kathleen Szawiola

LIBRARY OF CONGRESS CATALOGING-IN-PUBLICATION DATA
White, Michael C., 1952–
50 classic hikes in Nevada : from the Ruby Mountains to Red Rock Canyon /
Mike White.
p. cm.
Includes bibliographical references and index.
ISBN 0-87417-629-8 (pbk. : alk. paper)
1. Hiking—Nevada—Guidebooks.   2. Backpacking—Nevada—Guidebooks.
3. Trails—Nevada—Guidebooks.   4. Nevada—Guidebooks.   I. Title: Fifty
classic hikes in Nevada.   II. Title.
GV199.42.N3W45   2006
917.9304'34—dc22   2005029653

The paper used in this book meets the requirements of American
National Standard for Information Sciences—Permanence of Paper
for Printed Library Materials, ANSI Z.48-1984. Binding
materials were selected for strength and durability.

First Printing
15   14   13   12   11   10   09   08   07   06
5   4   3   2   1

DISCLAIMER: The author has made a reasonable attempt to ensure that the information
contained in this book was accurate at the time of publication. However, a guidebook cannot
guarantee the safety of any individual or group while hiking on trips described within its pages.
Be aware that conditions may change at any time. You are responsible for your own safety and
health while in the backcountry, which may include such precautions as attention to road, trail,
terrain, and weather conditions, as well as the capabilities and competence of your companions.
Staying well informed and exercising common sense and good judgment will assist you in
having a safe and enjoyable experience.

▲ ▲ ▲

To ED GUSTAFSON,
who first introduced a prepubescent lad
to the wonders of the natural world

CONTENTS

ILLUSTRATIONS

TRAIL PROFILES

PREFACE

The state of Nevada comprises a large area of wild landscapes and diverse topography within the basin and range environment, from lofty mountain summits to deep slickrock canyons. Much of Nevada rarely sees the footprints of men, beckoning those who place a premium on solitude and serenity to explore roadless backcountry that few ever experience. Some of Nevada's wild lands can be appreciated with the aid of a fine network of trails, ranging from little used paths in remote regions to well-maintained trails near urban centers. This guide to fifty of the state's finest trails provides an introduction to the awesome wonders accessible to those who prefer to experience the natural world on foot. Those with a limited view of the state as nothing more than casinos and sagebrush will be stunned by the natural beauty of the area after hiking just one of the trips described in this guide.

Far from a comprehensive evaluation of Nevada's trail system, *50 Classic Hikes in Nevada* is designed to give readers an overview of premium hiking routes that span the width and breadth of the state, spurring interest toward further wanderings. The rapid growth of the state's population in recent years, along with an increasing tourist base, has brought many to the state who may be unfamiliar with the natural beauty found within Nevada's backyard. May this book provide the key that unlocks many exciting adventures in one of America's most picturesque regions. Those souls fortunate enough to have hiked a number of the trails described in this book will come away with an excellent appreciation of the diversity and beauty of the stunning landscape that makes up Nevada.

ACKNOWLEDGMENTS

I would like to thank the staff at University of Nevada Press for their assistance in turning my manuscript, maps, and photographs into completed form. Margaret Dalrymple deserves special mention, as she was the one with whom I worked most closely throughout the duration of that process.

Many individuals graced me with their presence along the trails and byways of Nevada during the fieldwork phase. Many thanks are extended to Kathy Baldock, Keith Catlin, Dave Miller, Dan Palmer, Dave Peterson, Bob Redding, and Dwight Smith for their company, pleasant demeanors, and faithful friendships. The most important person in my universe who deserves untold credit is my wife, Robin, who not only provided the manuscript with some much needed review but also is largely responsible for the existence of anything I produce.

Lastly, but perhaps most importantly, I would like to thank God for blessing me with the privileged opportunity to enjoy His creation and for the gifts, talents, and abilities necessary to make this book a reality.

50 CLASSIC HIKES IN NEVADA

CHAPTER ONE
INTRODUCTION

Nevada is blessed with an outstanding array of natural features, varying from rich sandstone formations to alpine summits to just about any other landform imaginable. Far from any major population centers, remote mountain ranges offer sweeping vistas through the clearest of skies. In stark contrast to the surrounding lowlands, alpine lakes, flower-filled meadows, and gurgling streams grace the slopes of the highest ranges. Solitude and serenity, characteristics sorely lacking in more heavily used regions of the West, are easily attained within the wildlands of the Silver State. Visitors unfamiliar with Nevada's natural riches are often awestruck at their first glimpse of the state's majestic topography.

Despite declining budgets that have resulted in the deterioration of some trails within Nevada, hikers can choose from a fine assortment of excellent ones to enjoy while pursuing their avocation. This guide offers fifty of the state's best routes, from short and easy hikes suitable for families with small children to full-scale assaults on the highest peaks. May the reader find the trips described in this book to be as awe inspiring and wonderful as the author found them during his fieldwork.

FLORA

The breadth and diversity of Nevada's vast landscape defies any attempt to accurately classify the flora within the state into exact groupings, but some general classifications are valid. The following biotic zones are presented in descending order.

ALPINE ZONE The alpine zone is the smallest vegetative zone in the state, occupying the lands above timberline. Conditions within the upper elevations of the mountains are extreme—intense sunlight, periodic drought, limited growing season, and high winds. The ground-hugging plants of the alpine zone rarely exceed a height of more than a foot, with many plants developing a mat-like structure. Where moisture is in ample supply, as in the Ruby Mountains, the alpine flora thrive, with individual species numbering almost two hundred. In drier areas, the alpine zone is much less prolific, oftentimes harboring a hybridization of alpine and desert plants. This zone contains a fine variety of flowering plants, including mountain sandwort, rosy pussypaws, whitestem

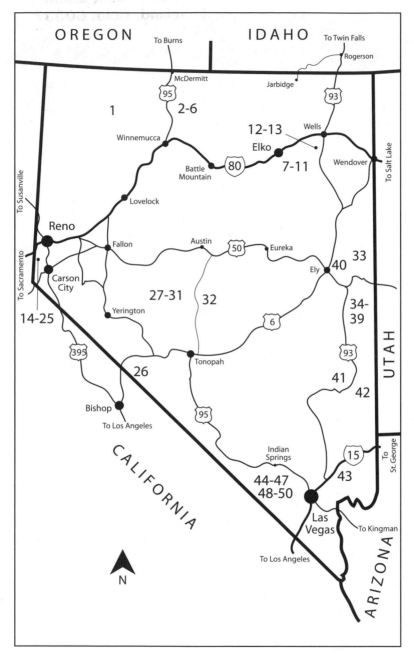

MAP 1 | Hike Locations

goldenbush, and cutleaf daisy. Common wildflowers include western mountain aster, monkshood, arnica, shooting star, subalpine fleabane, elephantshead, bog orchid, and American bistort.

MONTANE FORESTS The composition of the zone below the alpine heights varies significantly across the breadth of the state. The most biologically diverse ecosystems are found along the fringes of the Great Basin; traveling toward the center of the Great Basin is a journey toward less diversity. While some mountain ranges harbor relatively dense forests, the typical Nevada mountain range is made up of rather sparsely wooded slopes of limited species.

Where soil conditions are favorable, the one tree found throughout the Great Basin is the quaking aspen. Aspens flourish in riparian areas, and often intermix with conifers of the mid-elevation forest. Pure stands of aspen are frequently seen sprawling across the canyons of many Nevada ranges. Typically growing at elevations of 6000 to 8000 feet, quaking aspens may extend as high as 10,000 feet under the right circumstances, as is the case on the broad plateau of Table Mountain in the Monitor Range, for instance. The brilliant golden-yellow leaves of the quaking aspen create a dramatic texture to the Nevada landscape in autumn.

Classified as outside of a true Great Basin environment, the Carson Range near Lake Tahoe is biologically distinct from its eastern neighbors. This sub-range of the Sierra Nevada contains the most varied flora of any range in the state, with fifteen species of conifer inhabiting the region. Four species of conifer occur within the pinyon-juniper woodland: Common or dwarf juniper, Western juniper, Utah juniper, and singleleaf pinyon. Ponderosa pine, Jeffrey pine, sugar pine, white fir, incense-cedar, and Douglas-fir are found between 5000 and 7500 feet. From roughly 7500 to 9000 feet, stands of red fir dominate the slopes, with smaller amounts of white fir, lodgepole pine, Jeffrey pine, mountain hemlock, and western white pine. Above 9000 feet, whitebark pine intermixes with lodgepole pine, western white pine, and mountain hemlock.

The majority of forests in Nevada's mountains can be roughly categorized into upper elevation and mid-elevation forests.

UPPER ELEVATION FOREST Below timberline, at elevations roughly between 9000 and 11,000 feet, a trio of conifers composes the upper elevation forest— limber pine, whitebark pine, and bristlecone pine. Limber pine and bristlecone pine are the two most dominant conifers, with limber pine most prevalent in the northern part of the state and bristlecone pine in the southern part. Many of Nevada's mountain ranges contain two or three species of pine, but some ranges have only a single species. Although Great Basin National Park is perhaps the most noted area for bristlecones, the Spring Mountains contain the most extensive stands of bristlecone pine in Nevada.

MID-ELEVATION FOREST   A traditional coniferous forest is absent from the typical Nevada mountain range, as a zone of shrublands often extends from the pinyon-juniper woodland below into the upper elevation forest. This situation is particularly apparent in the Toquima, Toiyabe, and Monitor Ranges of central Nevada. Aside from aspen groves and pockets of mountain-mahogany, mid-elevation slopes are often devoid of trees. However, defying an absolute, across-the-board classification, some Nevada ranges do have a significant mid-elevation forest.

With the exception of the Carson Range, the Snake Range in eastern Nevada (which includes Great Basin National Park and the Mt. Moriah Wilderness) has the most diverse mid-elevation forest in the state. Four species of conifer are found in this zone of the Snake Range, including white fir, Douglas-fir, subalpine fir and ponderosa pine. The Jarbidge Mountains have the most significant mid-elevation forest, with densely covered slopes of subalpine fir common throughout the range. The Spring Mountains also have a fairly significant mid-elevation forest, harboring extensive stands of white fir and ponderosa pine.

PINYON-JUNIPER WOODLAND   Generally, the pinyon-juniper woodland is a zone composed of pygmy conifers spanning the area between the montane forest above and the sagebrush zone below, usually between the elevations of 5000 and 8000 feet. The pinyon-juniper woodlands form the largest forested zone in the Great Basin, exceeding all other coniferous zones combined. The woodland usually has a dominant species of either singleleaf pinyon (*Pinus monophylla*) or one of four types of juniper: Utah, western, Rocky Mountain, or California. Rarely achieving a height over thirty feet, these trees display rounded, spreading crowns—squat forms not usually associated with the correct shape for the perfect Christmas tree.

Since the pinyon-juniper woodland is generally an open forest, a number of shrubs are commonly found either intermixed with the conifers or in extensive clearings. These shrubs include sagebrush, serviceberry, bitterbrush, snakeweed, snowberry, elderberry, gooseberry, rabbitbrush, and wild rose. In southern Nevada, a number of additional shrubs flourish in this zone, such as blackbrush, cliffrose, and Apache plume. A mixture of grasses is also common to the woodlands understory; Idaho fescue, Great Basin wildrye, and squirreltail are the usual species. Cheat grass has become problematic across the state, forming pure stands after fires.

Many trails in Nevada spend much of their initial mileage passing through the pinyon-juniper zone. In bygone days, Native Americans spent a good deal of time in this area collecting pine nuts from the pinyon pines, which were one of the few staples of their rather Spartan diets. Nowadays, pine nuts are frequently found in the gourmet section of grocery stores.

SAGEBRUSH ZONE No other plant is more associated with the undeveloped lands of Nevada and the Great Basin than the big sagebrush (*Artemisia tridentata*). Rightfully so, the yellow bloom of the big sagebrush is honored as Nevada's state flower. Not surprisingly, this zone covers more acreage than any other vegetative zone in the state. The ubiquitous sagebrush seems to cover everything in sight, but before the advent of livestock grazing in the Great Basin, this zone was three-quarters covered in native grasses. Since cattle and sheep eat grass and shun sagebrush, native grasses have dwindled in the Great Basin, with sagebrush and non-native grasses the beneficiaries.

Sagebrush appears in pure stands, but also intermixes with a number of other shrubs. Bitterbrush, desert peach, ephedra, rabbitbrush, and spiny hopsage are common associates. Grasses prevalent in the pinyon-juniper woodland are also found in the sagebrush zone, where cheat grass is problematic as well. Wildflowers frequently seen in the sagebrush zone include Indian paintbrush, lupine, milk vetch, penstemon, and buckwheat.

SHADSCALE ZONE Named for its principal shrub (*Atriplex confertifolia*), the shadscale zone occurs at lower elevations, where soils tend to be alkaline and precipitation is low. Although shadscale is the dominant member, and one of the three most prolific plants in the Great Basin, saltbush, rabbitbrush, bud sagebrush, spiny hopsage, Mormon tea, greasewood, and horsebrush may appear in this zone as well. Shadscale is important winter forage, palatable to domesticated grazing animals, as well as to small rodents, rabbits, and deer.

MOJAVE DESERT ZONES At lower elevations in the southern part of the state, Great Basin vegetation transitions to vegetation of the Mojave Desert, which can be demarcated into two principal zones: the blackbrush zone and the lower Mojavean zone.

BLACKBRUSH ZONE Replacing the sagebrush and shadscale communities of the north, the blackbrush zone within the Mojave Desert is defined by a predominance of the namesake shrub (*Coleogyne ramosissima*). This open scrub community is dotted with Joshua trees and Mojave yucca. Additional shrubs that may be present in this zone include creosote bush, desert almond, and boxthorn.

LOWER MOJAVEAN ZONE   In the lower Mojavean zone, white bursage replaces blackbrush as the principal shrub. This zone is less diverse than in the blackbrush zone, and plants tend to be more widely spaced. Joshua trees are absent, although some Mojave yucca is still present.

RIPARIAN ZONES   Riparian zones occur across the spectrum of previously mentioned plant communities. Thin, green ribbons of vegetation straddling the streams, creeks, and rivers of Nevada spill from the mountain heights to the basin floors. The addition of significant moisture to the various zones within the high and low deserts of Nevada creates pockets of thick foliage resulting in the highest diversity of plant species in the state. Approximately 75 percent of the plant species within Nevada depend upon riparian zones for their survival, in spite of the fact that only 1 percent of the state's lands are classified as riparian. Typically, these areas are dense thickets of brush, grasses, flowers, and trees, forming the most verdant environments in the region. Many of Nevada's trails justifiably follow paths through or near riparian areas adjacent to waterways. Hikers, as well as animals, find relief from the glaring sun of a hot afternoon in the cool shade of the riparian zone.

Cottonwoods tend to be the most dominant tree along Nevada's streams and rivers, although between the elevations of 6000 and 8000 feet, quaking aspen may appear to be the most prolific species. Willow is generally the most common shrub, but alder, birch, dogwood, elderberry, serviceberry, chokecherry, and wild rose may also be present. A vast array of wildflowers usually lines the banks in early spring.

FAUNA

The island sanctuaries of Nevada's mountain ranges hold an interesting and diverse population of animal species. Cooler temperatures and more dependable water sources in the mountains support a rich and concentrated variety of animals, birds, and fish. Although opportunities to observe wildlife in the state abound, most animals living in remote areas remain wary of human contact.

The one large mammal characteristically associated with the mountain West is virtually absent within Nevada; aside from the Carson Range and other areas at the extreme western edge of the state, black bears were either unable to migrate from the Rockies or Sierra to the interior ranges or, if they could successfully make the migration, their populations were too small to be sustained.

In contrast to the black bear, mountain lions seem to be doing quite well sustaining their numbers in the backcountry of Nevada, so much so that a limited hunting season is allowed. Bobcats, smaller cousins to the mountain lions, are also present in healthy numbers. Most likely, hikers will rarely see a bobcat or mountain lion in the wild. These elusive cats pose little threat to humans but generally remain mysterious and misunderstood residents of Nevada's backcountry. As a precaution, don't hike alone in cougar country, and never leave small children unattended.

Another species of big mammal that seems to be faring well is Nevada's state animal, the desert bighorn sheep. After being decimated in the 1960s by diseases passed from herds of domesticated sheep grazing on nearby public lands, bighorn sheep were reintroduced to several former ranges and have recovered nicely during the intervening years. In the mid-1960s, a dozen mountain goats from Washington State were released in the Ruby Mountains and eleven more into the neighboring East Humboldt Range. Today, the Ruby herd is estimated at 250 individuals and the East Humboldt herd at 100. Recovery of the bighorn sheep and introduction of the mountain goat has proceeded so well that a limited hunting season is in effect for both species. Both the sheep and the goats prefer high and inaccessible country near rocky terrain.

Rocky Mountain elk, mule deer, and pronghorn antelope are all big game species that are commonly seen in the wildlands of Nevada. Elk reside within several areas of Nevada, including the Jarbidge Mountains, Monitor Range, and Spring Mountains. They are relatively easy to locate during the rut of autumn, when bugling males inadvertently reveal their position and the position of their harems. Mule deer are migratory, spending winter in the valleys and following the snow line up the mountain in summer. Pronghorn antelope prefer the wide-open grasslands and sagebrush community.

Coyotes are perhaps the most adaptable mammals in Nevada, resisting just about every practice aimed at reducing their numbers. No other animal, with the possible exception of the horse, seems so inextricably linked to the American West. You're apt to see a coyote in just about any locality, and no campfire would seem complete without hearing their evening yelps.

Nevada is home to a wide range of smaller mammals. Beaver, badger, kit fox, striped skunk, western spotted skunk, weasel, and ringtail cat are common mammals one might hope to see in the wild, in addition to the pica, seven species of squirrel, and four of rabbit. Around lakes and wet meadows, watch the sky around dusk for bats in search of an evening meal of insects.

The generally clear skies of Nevada provide a splendid opportunity for bird watching. Golden eagles are the largest natural winged creatures in the state, often seen in pairs rising on thermals above deep canyons. Bald eagles may be seen near waterways in Nevada, but usually only during the winter months. Much more common than either species of eagle, red-tailed hawks are frequently seen patrolling the skies above ranchlands and other areas rich in small rodents. Peregrine falcons, great horned owls, and burrowing owls are other raptors.

In addition to raptors, Nevada has over three hundred species of smaller birds, including the state bird, the mountain bluebird, an azure-colored cousin of the robin. Significant game birds in Nevada include chukar, partridge, Hungarian partridge, Gambel's quail, California quail, blue grouse, ruffed grouse, and sage-grouse.

The lakes, creeks, and rivers of Nevada provide a sanctuary for a diverse population of fish. Due to the isolation of the vast majority of Nevada's waterways, sixty-seven endemic species of fish are found within the state. Unfortunately, due in large part to the diversion of many of these water sources for agriculture, Nevada has the highest number of threatened and endangered fish species of all the states. Despite this shortcoming, anglers in search of a challenge can test their skill on a wide variety of game fish.

For more information on the wildlife of Nevada, check out the Nevada Department of Wildlife's website at www.ndow.org.

GEOLOGY

Any attempt to generalize the geology of a state as large and complex as Nevada is fraught with oversimplification. Lay readers might appreciate the nontechnical description John McPhee provides in his well-written guide to the origin of Nevada, *Basin and Range*. Perhaps no other term so accurately captures the essence of the state's geology as "basin and range," as rows of narrow, linear mountain ranges separated by broad basins march in continuous succession across the breadth of Nevada and the Great Basin.

Geologists theorize that at some time in the distant past extensional forces began to pull apart the crust of the Great Basin in an east-west direction. Vertical cracks formed in the thin crust perpendicular to these forces, producing valleys where the land dropped and mountains where the land rose, creating over two hundred ranges across the Great Basin. Most of these mountain ranges trended on a north-south axis.

Erosional forces continued to shape the topography of the area. Ice-age glaciers sculpted the peaks and upper canyons of the highest mountains. A remnant glacier from this period still exists in the cirque below the steep eastern face of Wheeler Peak in Great Basin National Park. Many of the highest ranges in Nevada exhibit some evidence of past glaciation in the landforms of cirques and U-shaped canyons.

Rock and mineral composition of the mountains of Nevada is highly variable and often unique to a particular range. All three rock types—volcanic, sedimentary, and metamorphic—occur in a wide variety of localities within the state. A geologic map of Nevada is quite colorful.

CLIMATE

Nevada is the most arid of all the United States. As the seventh largest state, at 286,367 square miles, Nevada's climate can vary considerably from one end of the state to the other, particularly from north to south. However, the relative lack of moisture remains constant. The Sierra Nevada presents a massive barrier to Pacific storms approaching Nevada from the west. As storms move east, their moisture-laden clouds rise, cool, and drop most of their water on the western slope of the range before passing into Nevada. The relatively little moisture that remains from these storms is sprinkled across the mountains and valleys of the Great Basin, with some mountain areas receiving over fifteen inches of precipitation annually and interior valleys as little as four inches. Most of the mountain precipitation falls as snow in the winter with smaller amounts as rain from summer thunderstorms. Precipitation amounts vary considerably across the state, as seen in the table below.

The immense size of Nevada allows for significant variations in the climatic patterns across the state. For example, each year a number of winter storms dip down from the Pacific Northwest to brush the northeast corner, completely missing the remainder of the state. Ranges such as the Ruby, East Humboldt, and Jarbidge mountains benefit from the extra moisture that waters some of the most diverse plant communities in the region. On the opposite end of the spectrum, southern Nevada must get by on a fraction of that precipitation.

Not only does precipitation fluctuate across the scope of the state, but temperatures can be quite different as well. Desert conditions often ensure that wide temperature swings occur over a twenty-four-hour day in the same location. An abundance of sunny days may produce hot afternoon temperatures,

TABLE 1. PRECIPITATION

LOCATION	AVERAGE ANNUAL PRECIPITATION	AVERAGE ANNUAL SNOWFALL
Las Vegas	4.13	1.2
Lamoille	14.06	61.5
Reno	7.48	24.3
Glenbrook (Lake Tahoe)	18.15	91.8
Great Basin National Park	13.10	70.7
Jarbidge	20.20	105.5
Austin	12.56	58.0
Montgomery Maintenance Station	7.27	49.9

TABLE 2. TEMPERATURE

LOCATION	JANUARY AVG. HIGH	JANUARY AVG. LOW	JULY AVG. HIGH	JULY AVG. LOW
Las Vegas	57.3	41.1	105.9	86.9
Lamoille	37.3	14.6	85.1	47.6
Reno	45.5	20.4	91.2	50.0
Glenbrook (Lake Tahoe)	41.4	23.9	79.8	48.7
Great Basin National Park	40.8	19.1	85.6	57.2
Jarbidge	37.7	16.5	83.9	45.9
Austin	40.2	18.8	86.5	53.9
Montgomery Maintenance Station	41.3	14.0	83.2	46.8

but the thermometer can plunge by as much as seventy degrees before the sun rises the next day.

HISTORY

EXPLORATION TO STATEHOOD For the pioneers, Nevada's vast landscape was a major obstacle on their westward migration to the more hospitable lands along the coastline and interior valleys of California. The tale of the ill-fated Donner Party is perhaps the best-known struggle of these pioneers, although their disaster occurred just outside of the state in the Sierra Nevada. Once the various pioneer routes became established and well traveled, much of Nevada was caught up in gold and silver mining crazes that swept across the West. In modern times, as the state experiences unprecedented population growth, the backcountry of Nevada is receiving an increased focus on recreation.

The area that would one day be delineated as the state of Nevada was home to three principal groups of Native Americans, the Paiute, Washoe, and Shoshone. Due to the harsh environment, these groups never achieved the stature of the surrounding tribes of the plains and coastal areas, which enjoyed a better concentration of resources. The original residents of Nevada sought the mountains for cooler climes in summer, along with the perennial streams and the higher concentration of game. The discovery in 1978 of an archaeologically significant encampment high on the tablelands of Mt. Jefferson in the Toquima Range underscores this concept. Certainly the Native Americans knew of what many in the current age are unaware—that the mountains of Nevada harbor vital and thriving ecosystems above the sometimes inhospitable basins below. On the whole, the tribes within Nevada were peaceful and not much of an obstacle to the eventual exploration of the region.

The Great Basin, which contains most of Nevada, was the last remaining area of North America to be fully explored by Europeans outside of the Arctic.

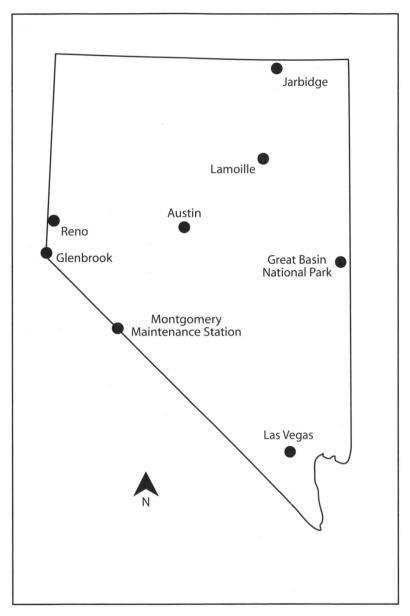

MAP 2 | Weather Data Stations

The interior drainage patterns, harsh environment, and distribution patterns of surrounding settlements all combined to discourage substantive exploration until the mid-1800s. Without much direct information on the Great Basin's geography, the region was shrouded in mystery, leading to an erroneous belief that an inland waterway connected the Rocky Mountains to the Pacific Ocean. The concept of such a river came to be known as the San Buenaventura, birthed by dreamy cartographers and furthered by the fanciful notions of fur trappers.

Alexander von Humboldt (1769–1859) was a famous statesman, explorer, and cartographer who never actually set foot in the Great Basin but greatly influenced the physical conceptions of the region. While visiting the New World between 1799 and 1804, von Humboldt prepared a map of the American West incorporating two major errors that would be perpetuated for several decades—Lake Timpanogos and the San Buenaventura River. Subsequent influential explorers, including Lewis and Clark and Zebulon Pike, would perpetuate these myths of an inland waterway connecting the Rocky Mountains to the Pacific Ocean, and of a vast freshwater lake in the midst of the Great Basin.

Fur traders were the first group of Europeans to make serious excursions into the Great Basin. Having played out many of the bountiful rivers in the Rockies and Pacific Northwest, fur trappers turned their attention to other areas that potentially were rich in pelts. Jedediah Smith (1798–1831) became the first American to cross the Great Basin. After leaving California and scaling the mighty Sierra Nevada, Smith made a lightning dash across the center of Nevada to the Salt Lake area in 1827. Due to the hurried nature of the trip, he obtained scant geographical information.

Peter Skene Ogden (1794–1854), while employed by the Hudson's Bay Company, led his Fifth Snake Country Expedition of 1828–29 into the northern part of the Great Basin, crossing the present-day boundary of Nevada near the town of McDermitt. Traveling south, the expedition reached the Humboldt River and then journeyed upstream to near the site of Elko. Leaving the river, the party crossed the Ruby Mountains at Secret Pass and continued over a southern spur of the East Humboldt Range before returning north to the Snake River system for the winter. The following spring, Odgen and his men returned to the Humboldt and followed a circuitous course to the Humboldt Sink. Heading back up the Humboldt River, the expedition veered north and exited the state west of the Santa Rosa Range.

Ogden's Sixth Snake Country Expedition (1829–30) returned to the Humboldt Sink and continued south to the Walker Lake area. Heading southwest, the expedition passed the present site of Hawthorne on the way to Owens

Valley. Winter weather forced the party south across the Mojave Desert to the Colorado River and then probably into California. After Ogden left his post, John Work assumed his position, leading another expedition into similar terrain in 1831. The explorations of both Ogden and Work proved invaluable in the initial understanding of the topography of the Great Basin, particularly of the true nature of the Great Salt Lake having no outlet. However, the idea of the San Buenaventura was still alive and well.

The next few years saw a flurry of activity by fur trappers exploring vast areas of the Great Basin in search of a major stream that would support their livelihoods, although their efforts largely proved to be unproductive. Both British and American fur trapping companies ultimately found the Great Basin to be inhospitable, suitable only for a subsistence level of existence.

As the coastal areas began to prosper, a viable overland route to California became a necessity. In 1833–34 the Walker-Bonneville party established a significant part of what would become the Overland Trail. Heading west from Salt Lake, the expedition crossed the East Humboldt Range and then paralleled Ogden's previous route along the Humboldt River to the Humboldt Sink. Following the course of a seasonal stream, they crossed into the Carson Sink and proceeded west over the Sierra Nevada into California. Crossing back over the Sierra, Joseph Walker and his men entered the Great Basin near Owens Valley, eventually rejoining the approximate alignment of their original route to return to Salt Lake. Although Smith and Work had traveled along the Humboldt River, the Walker expedition was the first group of Europeans to record their journey into the Carson Sink, up the Walker River, and over the Sierra.

In 1841 the Bartleson-Bidwell party became the first migrating group to employ covered wagons in the traverse of the Overland Trail, as well as the first party to transport white women into the region. Many more wagon trains would follow in the westward migration. Despite the increasing numbers of pioneers crossing the region, a complete understanding of the topography of the Great Basin continued to elude the thoughts of men. Only after John C. Frémont visited the region would the mystery be solved.

As more and more people flooded across the arid Great Basin into California, a more practical route following a system of rivers became more desirable. John C. Frémont (1813–90) led a series of expeditions that, among other duties, made an extensive survey of the Great Basin, hoping to discover a better route to California. On a number of wide-ranging explorations, Frémont discovered numerous areas previously unseen by Europeans. During the second expedition, on May 23, 1844, Frémont made the pronouncement that this vast area of the Southwest was an interior drainage, a "great basin." With the backing of the federal government and the technical support of trained cartographers, Frémont's discovery became the cornerstone for understanding the topography of the Great Basin.

Although hundreds of immigrants traveled across Nevada over the next fifteen years on their way to California, few of those souls decided to establish roots within the Great Basin. Nevada remained a sparsely populated area until 1859, when gold and silver were discovered in what became the Comstock Lode. Following this discovery, thousands of miners, entrepreneurs, and support personnel poured into the area. The hillsides of the neighboring Tahoe Basin were practically denuded of timber to support the infrastructure necessary to fuel the burgeoning mining mecca.

The immense wealth pouring out of the Comstock, coupled with the need for additional congressional votes to pass the Thirteenth Amendment to the Constitution abolishing slavery, pushed the Nevada Territory toward statehood. On October 31, 1864, Nevada became the thirty-sixth state to gain admission into the Union.

NATIONAL PARKS AND WILDERNESS   Over 86 percent of Nevada is owned and managed by the federal government. Despite this ownership, protection of Nevada's wildlands has had a rather checkered past. A tiny parcel of land in the extreme eastern part of the state was set aside in the 1920s to become Lehman Caves National Monument. Only one area of Nevada was offered protection in the original wilderness bill passed by Congress in 1964—the Jarbidge Wilderness containing almost 65,000 acres.

The concept of a national park centered on Wheeler Peak in the southern Snake Range surfaced as far back as the 1920s, when nearby Lehman Caves received national monument status. Over the years, the concept of a national park resurfaced a few times, always with the same result. Many different groups expressed strong opposition to the idea, fearing that a national park designation would prevent, or at least alter, their beloved activities. Ranchers, who had used the seasonal rangelands in the mountains for grazing cattle and sheep since the 1800s, vehemently opposed the possible removal of their grazing rights. Miners were equally as vocal about accessing their claims within the potential park, especially a beryllium strike on the west slope of Mt. Washington. Logging interests had obvious misgivings about a park that would likely end timber harvesting, despite the fact that very little wood was ever harvested in the Snake Range. Hunters understood that national park status would eliminate their sport within park boundaries, and even anglers expressed concern about how a potential change in management might affect fishing regulations within the new park. If all of this opposition wasn't enough, even the multiple-use-oriented U.S. Forest Service weighed in on the park proposal, expressing a lack of interest in turning over their jurisdiction of the area to the preservation-oriented National Park Service.

As time wore on, new developments emerged that would propel Great Basin National Park into existence. The discovery of a 5000-year-old bristlecone pine and the rediscovery of a bona fide glacier within the Great Basin inspired a group of scientists to join the expanding chorus of those already committed to the idea of a national park for scenic and recreational purposes. The Forest Service acquiesced to an intermediate step of creating the Wheeler Peak Scenic Area, which promoted the construction of a scenic highway. Management of the scenic area would be similar to that of a wilderness area, but with a continuing emphasis on multiple use. Oddly enough, economics would eventually cast the deciding vote for creation of Great Basin National Park.

Ely was a booming mining town of almost 10,000 residents forty air miles west of the Wheeler Peak area. When two major mining operations left the area in the 1970s and 1980s, the resulting decline in population and increase in unemployment inspired local officials to consider alternate sources of revenue. Increased tourism from the creation of a nearby national park was seen as a potential means to recoup some of the revenue lost from the closure of the mines. With this added support, the proposal for a park gained momentum and Great Basin National Park became a reality in October 1986, although only after numerous compromises were made with opponents. Miners altered the eventual boundary of the park to exclude some of their mining operations. Ranchers were allowed to continue their grazing privileges, although environmental groups planned to buy the grazing rights and in turn grant them back to the government. Anglers decried the policies of the Park Service, which canceled the stocking of streams practiced by the Forest Service in favor of returning the waterways to natural populations. Despite the minor backlash, the 77,180-acre park welcomes thousands of visitors each year, offering many opportunities for enjoying a fine piece of Nevada's exquisite scenery.

Three years after the creation of Great Basin National Park, President George H. W. Bush signed the Nevada Wilderness Protection Act on December 5, 1989. Following much debate and compromise, thirteen new wilderness areas were added and Jarbidge was expanded by 48,500 acres, increasing the total acreage of designated wilderness in Nevada to just under 800,000 acres. All fourteen of the wilderness areas are under the management of the Forest Service.

Another Nevada wilderness was added in 1994 with the passage of the California Desert Protection Act. The 44,000-acre Death Valley National Park Nevada Triangle is administered by the National Park Service.

Ten additional wilderness areas came into existence in 2000, when Congress passed the Black Rock Desert–High Rock Canyon Emigrant Trails National

Conservation Area Act. Administered entirely by the Bureau of Land Management, 757,500 acres were added to Nevada's wilderness system.

Through the Clark County Conservation of Public Land and Natural Resources Act of 2002, seventeen more wilderness areas were designated and the Mt. Charleston Wilderness was expanded. Under the jurisdiction of the National Park Service, Bureau of Land Management, and Forest Service, another 451,915 acres of wilderness brings the total acreage of protected wilderness in Nevada to over 2 million.

In addition to the one national park and forty-two wilderness areas, the federal government administers three National Conservation Areas through the Bureau of Land Management: Black Rock Desert–High Rock Canyon–Emigrant Trails, Red Rock Canyon, and Sloan Canyon. Nevada oversees several state parks sprinkled throughout the state, some of which offer hiking trails.

As mentioned above, the federal government owns Nevada—at least 86 percent. The Bureau of Land Management, Forest Service, National Park Service, the U.S. Air Force, Army, and Navy, and the Atomic Energy Commission oversee the bulk of this land. The acreage of lands designated as wilderness represents a small slice of that pie, but opposition to the setting aside of lands within Nevada as wilderness remains significant. The wild areas of Nevada are a precious resource, deserving of respect and protection.

MODERN-DAY ISSUES The discovery of gold and silver in the Comstock initiated a pursuit of minerals that continues to this day. Hardly a range in the state remained untouched by the various mining booms that have swept through the region. Both large-scale and small-scale mining continues in Nevada, although the activity fluctuates with the rise and fall of prices for the mineral being mined. A loophole in the original wilderness act of 1964 allows mining of existing claims to continue within wilderness areas. Although these claims tend to be small operations, you may see evidence of limited mining activity in some of the otherwise wild areas of the state.

If the mining bug didn't captivate the hearts of rural Nevadans, about the only other viable economic pursuit was ranching. Most of the early settlers favored the valleys at the base of the mountains for their homes, enduring the relatively milder winters of the lower elevations. However, the raising of cattle and sheep oftentimes necessitated the moving of herds into the mountains during the summers for grazing purposes. The introduction of domesticated animals into the montane ecosystems decimated a high percentage of the native vegetation during the late 1800s. Much of the area that we see today as covered in a sea of sagebrush was composed of 75–90 percent grasses prior to this period of cattle and sheep grazing.

As a compromise for passage of the 1989 Nevada wilderness bill, Congress allowed the existing grazing rights of ranchers to continue within wilderness area boundaries. To have disallowed this practice would have terminated or drastically reduced the cattle and sheep raising that ranching families had practiced for generations. Without the forage available in the mountains during the summer months, ranchers claimed there would be no economically feasible alternative.

Unfortunately, cattle and sheep grazing in montane and riparian areas of Nevada's mountains have had many deleterious effects. A backcountry traveler can easily see the harm that grazing does on streamside environments and meadows; hooves trample moist soil into a muddy quagmire, grassy areas are gnawed down to the ground, plant species are destroyed, and vibrantly alive streams become wide, shallow, and unhealthy through the subsequent erosion. Many a pleasing campsite becomes less than desirable amid a field of cow pies and a swarm of buzzing flies. Cow and sheep urine and feces can't have a positive effect on water quality. In addition to these obvious maladies, domestic sheep have decimated native sheep populations by passing disease.

The dilemma is substantial with no easy solutions acceptable to all parties. In the grand scope of ranching, grazing on all the millions of acres of Nevada's ranchland produces approximately the same amount of beef as the small state of Vermont. However, cattle and sheep raising has been historically synonymous with the West, a practice carried on by several generations of Nevada families. As administrations come and go with varying affections on either side of the spectrum, the debate over grazing on public lands will continue.

Perhaps a greater concern to the wild lands of Nevada than the practice of ranching in rural areas of the state is the unprecedented population growth in southern and western Nevada. Unchecked development in and around Las Vegas and Reno-Sparks has resulted in an urban sprawl few would have imagined possible a couple of decades ago. Nowadays, Las Vegas subdivisions on the border of Red Rock Canyon or Mt. Charleston Wilderness are not unthinkable. In the north, governments are dealing with a potential loss of public access to the Carson Range and environmental destruction of fragile lands on Peavine Peak. Substantial challenges remain for the future of Nevada's pristine backcountry.

Traveling in the backcountry of Nevada offers many wonderful rewards—unparalleled beauty, solitude and serenity, far-reaching vistas through clear skies, and dependable sunshine, to name a few. However, there are a few concerns specific to the area that are worth mentioning as well.

SEASONS

When to hike Nevada's trails is perhaps the most changeable aspect in this guidebook, as conditions may vary considerably from year to year. In drought years, traveling on snow-free trails just about anywhere in the state is possible at virtually any time of the year. In contrast, during years of abundant snowfall, hikers may have to wait until midsummer to experience their favorite mountain trail without snow. The canyons of southern Nevada have completely different considerations, as snowfall is rarely, if ever, a problem, but intense summer temperatures may suggest visitation in the months outside of summer as the optimum time to enjoy a hike. In general, hiking on mountain trails is best from June through mid-October. The prime time for a canyonland trek in southern Nevada is usually in October through November or March through May.

LIGHTNING

Thunderstorms that produce lightning may not be regular occurrences in the backcountry of Nevada, but neither are they uncommon events, particularly in mountainous regions. Hikers will want to avoid two aspects of lightning—the direct strike and ground currents. The best place to observe a lightning storm, other than near the warmth of a fire behind the plate-glass window of a mountain lodge, is a broad valley near the shorter trees in a dense stand of timber. However, since a great percentage of Nevada's backcountry is characteristically lacking in the dense forest department, little protection is afforded the potential lightning strike victim. The best rule of thumb is to be lower than the surrounding projections. If you find yourself on an open ridge during the development of a thunderstorm, retreat immediately to lower ground. Avoid hollows, depressions, overhangs, and small caves, as these areas increase the exposure to ground currents.

HYPOTHERMIA

Hypothermia is a condition where a person's temperature drops below normal in response to prolonged exposure to cold. Air temperature is not necessarily the determining factor in becoming hypothermic, as many cases occur when temperatures are above freezing. Wind chill, fatigue, and wetness from exposure to precipitation, submersion, or even excessive perspiration, may be more important factors than air temperature. The progressive symptoms of mild hypothermia include accelerated shivering, decline of motor skills, lack of mental acuity, and uncooperative or isolative behavior. In advanced hypothermia shivering ceases, but muscle and nervous system disorders become more obvious. Behavior is irrational or confused. Left untreated, hypothermia leads to unconsciousness and ultimately death.

The best way to deal with hypothermia is not to become hypothermic in the first place. Prevention is the best watchword; avoid becoming too cold or too tired while hiking. Always be prepared for changing weather conditions with the right equipment and clothing. Dress in layers and adjust those layers in response to changing conditions in order to avoid becoming either too cold or too hot. Adjusting clothing to prevent overheating will avoid the saturation of your apparel with perspiration, wetness that eventually turns cold and chills your body. Refrain from pushing on toward exhaustion, which puts your body more at risk for hypothermia. Keep yourself well hydrated by drinking plenty of fluids and consume an adequate supply of high-energy foods.

If you suspect someone in your party is becoming hypothermic, immediately treat the victim to stop the heat loss and begin rewarming. Remove the victim from windy and wet conditions and remove wet clothing. In mild cases of hypothermia, providing shelter, dry clothing, and liquids are usually sufficient steps to return the victim to normal. In severe cases of hypothermia, evacuation and gentle rewarming is necessary.

ALTITUDE

Mountain sickness is possible at the higher elevations of Nevada's backcountry, particularly for people residing near sea level who are not properly acclimatized. Symptoms may include headache, fatigue, loss of appetite, shortness of breath, nausea, vomiting, drowsiness, dizziness, memory loss, and slight loss of mental acuity. Although extremely rare at Nevada's altitudes, acute mountain sickness (AMS) is possible. This severe form of mountain sickness is much more serious and can ultimately lead to death.

Most Nevada residents already live at an elevation high enough that their bodies are adequately prepared for the higher elevations found in the state. The best way to avoid mountain sickness for those living at lower elevations beyond Nevada's borders is to allow enough time at moderate elevations for one's body to adjust to higher elevations. Other precautions may help ward off the symptoms of mountain sickness—drinking plenty of fluids and eating a high-carbohydrate diet prior to your trip.

The only way to deal with mountain sickness is a rapid descent to lower elevations.

SUN

Higher altitudes with less atmosphere to filter the sun's rays can turn one of Nevada's prime attractions into a potential detriment—too much sun. Unprotected exposure to the sun at high altitudes for as little as a half-hour may be enough for fair-skinned folk to develop a sunburn.

Use a high-rated sunblock on exposed areas of skin and reapply as necessary. Protect your eyes with a decent pair of sunglasses that filter at least 90 percent of UVA and UVB rays. Light-colored, loose fitting, and lightweight clothing worn along with a wide brimmed hat will provide additional protection.

During periods of high temperatures, avoid the potential for more serious sun-related maladies, such as heat stroke, heat exhaustion, dehydration, and cramps, by maintaining a proper intake of fluids and salts.

WATER

Water is a scarce commodity in much of Nevada's backcountry—completely unavailable in some areas. In drought years this situation can become even more of a problem. Many backcountry trails require a modicum of proper planning to ensure that rest stops and campsites have an adequate supply of water nearby.

Although most water concerns in Nevada have to do with its scarcity, too much water can be a hazard as well. Thunderstorms can produce heavy rains, which in turn can result in localized flooding. During such conditions, stay away from narrow and deep canyons and retreat to higher ground if necessary. Winters of heavy snowfall may produce heavy runoff in creeks during the spring and early summer, creating potentially hazardous stream crossings. Unfortunately, limited resources ensure that you won't find too many bridges at dangerous fords and crossings.

Always bring plenty of extra water for the start and finish of your trips, as many trailheads are dry. Carry extra water on the trail, replenishing your supply wherever possible. While water quality in the backcountry of Nevada hasn't gained widespread attention, the only way to ensure safe drinking water is to treat or filter all acquired water. Check with the appropriate agency about current trail conditions if flooding or stream crossings are legitimate concerns.

ANIMALS

Nevada is blessed with an abundant, diverse, and thriving wildlife population. Only a handful of animals are potentially dangerous to humans, and the chance of a negative encounter is very unlikely.

The only area of Nevada where bears exist is along the extreme western border with California, primarily within the Carson Range. Bears have yet to become a nuisance. If you plan to camp overnight in the Carson Range, properly hanging your food is about the only action to consider. Everywhere else you can lay your head on your pillow with the assurance that bears won't raid your food.

The next largest predatory animal in the backcountry of Nevada is the mountain lion, or cougar. A sighting of one of these large cats is a rare experience, as they tend to avoid all human contact. Mountain lions might see you, but you will almost never see them. If concerned about mountain lions, or their smaller cousin, the bobcat, avoid traveling alone in the backcountry—they avoid humans but will avoid groups of humans even more. Small children should never be left unattended in cougar country. If you encounter a cat, conventional wisdom suggests that you don't run or they may consider you to be prey. Make yourself appear as large as possible—don't crouch or hide. Either hold your ground or back away slowly while facing the animal. If the lion appears to be aggressive, wave your arms or throw rocks. If attacked, fight back!

Rattlesnakes are common residents of the desert and lower elevations of the mountains. However, the chance of a negative encounter is very low. A watchful eye is perhaps the best defense against surprising a rattler. Bear in mind that a rattlesnake wants to see you even less than you want to see it, so always provide a way of retreat for the snake. If you encounter a rattlesnake in the backcountry, back away slowly to a safe distance. Rattlesnake bites are uncommon and almost never fatal.

Ticks would be simply blood-sucking pests except for the rare possibility of infection from a handful of debilitating tick-borne maladies. Ticks seem to be most prevalent in spring, following periods of above-average precipitation. You can inhibit their bites by using a potent repellent and by wearing long-sleeved shirts and long pants with the cuffs tucked into your socks. Light-colored clothing makes sighting the tiny insects easier and daily inspection of your skin and clothing is a good practice. If bitten, use a pair of tweezers to apply gentle traction on the tick's body and back it out of your skin, making sure not to leave behind any parts. Wash the wound thoroughly with antibacterial soap, dry completely, and apply an antibiotic ointment. If flu-like symptoms or a rash develop, consult a physician.

Mosquitoes and black flies can be pesky pests, but their respective seasons are fairly short in Nevada.

TRAILS

The unfortunate reality of these times is that all governmental agencies charged with administration of the backcountry are understaffed and underfunded. Consequently, trails away from the major population centers of Reno-Sparks and Las Vegas may not be in the best of condition. Don't expect to find well-maintained trails marked with trail signs. Wherever you go, pack along a good topographic map and have the know-how to navigate your way through the backcountry.

Far from any major population centers, the backcountry of northwestern Nevada provides remoteness and serenity along with splendid scenery. Great Basin rarities like waterfalls and glacier-carved lakes can be found in this region, along with abundant wildlife, lush flora, and expansive vistas. Anglers should find the fishing to be excellent as well.

The first hike covered in this section travels to the remote Blue Lakes. Such remoteness is due not to the distance of the hike, which is a mere 0.75 mile, but to the long travel time necessary just to reach the trailhead. Although currently under study for wilderness protection, the Bureau of Land Management oversees the administration of 20,500 acres surrounding Blue Lakes.

Hikes 2–6 are within the Santa Rosa–Paradise Peak Wilderness, a 31,000-acre unit thirty miles north of Winnemucca overseen by the Humboldt-Toiyabe National Forest. Characterized by lofty granite peaks and deeply cut stream canyons, the Santa Rosas offer serenity and plenty of sweeping vistas. Diverse wildlife, extensive aspen groves, and an early summer wildflower display that rivals any in the state will please devotees of the natural world.

FYI ■ Although major highways suitable for all vehicles will get you close to the trails, the final approach over dirt roads is best handled with a high-clearance vehicle. The closest town with a complete range of services is Winnemucca; be sure you have an adequate supply of gasoline before leaving town.

Since the Blue Lakes are a long way from just about anywhere, most parties will plan on combining the hike with an overnight camping trip. Semi-developed sites can be found around Onion Valley Reservoir and several primitive sites are near the trailhead. Bring plenty of water, as none is available at either location except for the untreated water in the reservoir. Firewood is virtually nonexistent as well.

Hikes in the Santa Rosa Range begin at relatively low elevations. When hiking during the height of summer, an early start will pay big dividends by midday, when temperatures routinely soar into the nineties. Late spring to early summer, when the creeks are full and wildflowers are blooming, or autumn, when groves of aspen are ablaze, may be the best times for a visit. Lack of use and limited budgets for maintenance ensure that trails in the Santa Rosas will most likely be in a primitive state. Although the routes described in this section are straightforward, don't expect the best of conditions or any trail signs to assist you.

Although the chance of an encounter is low, keep your eyes peeled for rattlesnakes, especially in the lower parts of the canyons. Like most reptiles, rattlesnakes will avoid humans. They seek cool and shady hideouts during hot spells, and seek sunny locations when the air is chilly.

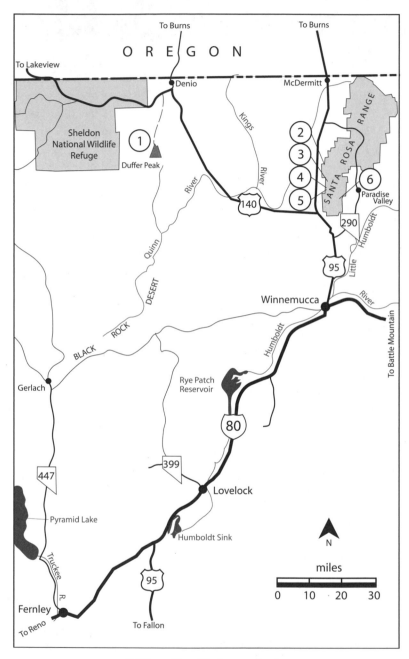

MAP 3 | Hikes of Northwestern Nevada

Spring hikers in the Santa Rosas should be on the alert for ticks, especially after particularly wet winters or during wet springs. As a precaution, wear light-colored, long-sleeved shirts and long pants, and stop every so often to check for ticks that may have jumped aboard. At the end of the trip, make a thorough check to make sure you're not transporting a pest back home, either on your body or your clothes. If a tick happens to take up residence in your flesh, use a pair of tweezers to get a firm grip near its head and while using gentle traction pull the pest out, being careful not to crush the body or leave any part behind. Thoroughly wash the wound after removal. If a rash around the wound or flu-like symptoms develop, consult a physician.

HIKE 1 | BLUE LAKES

The Blue Lakes Trail provides a short trip to a true Great Basin rarity— a string of glacier-sculpted lakes.

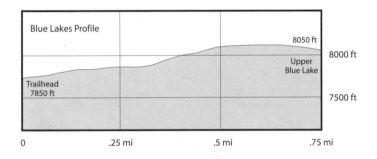

DISTANCE & ROUTE:	1.5 miles round trip
DIFFICULTY:	Easy
SEASON:	Summer
TRAILHEAD ACCESS:	High-clearance vehicle recommended
WATER:	Available at lakes
GUIDEBOOK MAP:	4
USGS MAP:	Duffer Peak

INTRODUCTION Between the California border and the Santa Rosa Range, Duffer Peak at 9397 feet is the highest summit in northwestern Nevada. At such a rarefied height for mountains in this part of the high desert, geologists theorize that this area of the Pine Forest Range was subjected to the sculpting forces of glaciation during the last Ice Age. Not only are lakes in general a scarce commodity in the Great Basin, but glacial lakes scoured out of granite basins are even more unusual, which makes the Blue Lakes particularly appealing.

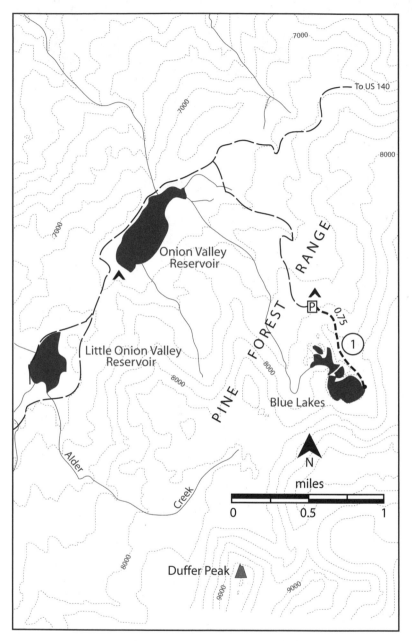

7000

To US 140

8000

7000

Onion Valley
Reservoir

P I N E   F O R E S T   R A N G E

P

0.75

1

Little Onion Valley
Reservoir

8000

8000

Blue Lakes

Alder

Creek

N

miles

0   0.5   1

8000

Duffer Peak

9000

9000

MAP 4 | Blue Lakes

Cradled into a cirque below Duffer Peak and dammed by a moraine, the Blue Lakes offer hikers some incredibly unique mountain scenery. Hikers can access the lakes via an easy 0.75-mile hike up an old road that the BLM wisely closed to vehicles some time ago. While the hike may be short and easy, the road to the trailhead is a long journey from just about anywhere, the last 18.5 miles of which are best negotiated with a high-clearance vehicle.

DIRECTIONS TO TRAILHEAD From the U.S. 95/S.R. 140 junction, approximately 31 miles north of Winnemucca, head west on S.R. 140. After 52 miles, just 0.5 mile southeast of the Quinn River Maintenance Station, turn northwest onto Road 2014, signed BLUE LAKE, ONION VALLEY RESERVOIR, KNOTT CREEK. Proceed on good dirt road across the floor of the valley and into the canyon of Alta Creek on a rising climb across the Pine Forest Range. At 6.5 miles from the junction is the Alta Creek Basin, where the road veers south and continues to climb across the mountains. About 10.5 miles from S.R. 140, you reach the crest and proceed on a mild descent into Theodore Basin. After a 0.75-mile climb from the basin, the road bends west and continues several miles to a junction between the road to the trailhead on the left and the road straight ahead to Onion Valley Reservoir, 17.25 miles from S.R. 140. Developed campsites with picnic tables and pit toilets can be found along the shoreline of the reservoir.

To reach the trailhead, turn left and make a 1.25-mile ascent up rougher dirt road to a small knoll, where you'll find a trailhead signboard and a modern pit toilet. A number of primitive campsites are scattered about, some with fire pits and picnic tables.

DESCRIPTION Continue up the hillside on the extension of the closed road, initially through areas of sagebrush before encountering an extensive aspen grove. After a sustained climb, you momentarily break out of the aspen near the crest of a sub-ridge, one-third mile from the trailhead. From the ridge, you follow gently graded trail to the lakes through aspen, mountain-mahogany, sagebrush, willow, and currant. Use trails branch away from the main trail to the shoreline of the first two lakes, while remaining on the main trail will take you to the last and largest of the Blue Lakes, 0.75 mile from the trailhead.

Cliffs above the lakes jutting out of the cirque walls testify to the granitic composition of the Pine Forest Range. With granite outcroppings, scattered whitebark pines, and patchy groves of aspen, the area seems more reminiscent of the Sierra Nevada than the typical Nevada high desert range. Combined with 9397-foot Duffer Peak looming over the basin less than 1.5 miles away to the south, the area has a decidedly subalpine ambiance.

One of the Blue Lakes, Pine Forest Range

The lakes are replenished each year primarily by meltwater from the previous winter's snowpack. Consequently, following winters of subnormal precipitation, a significant bathtub ring may develop around the lakeshores as the summer progresses. Numerous campsites rim the shorelines of each lake, luring backpackers into an overnight stay, an easy reward for the short hike. If not for the inordinate distances that recreationists must drive just to reach the trailhead, a large influx of opportunistic campers would certainly overrun the campsites spread around the lakes. A healthy population of fish will tempt anglers, mainly native brook trout with a small percentage of cutthroat hybrids.

WHITEBARK PINE Along with the Carson Range in the extreme west and a handful of mountain ranges within Elko County, the Pine Forest Range is one of a small number of areas in Nevada where hikers can see the high-elevation whitebark pine. Nutcrackers are attracted to the purple cones of the whitebark pine, which tend to remain on the tree rather than fall to the ground like other pines. The birds harvest the seeds, eating some and storing a portion in the ground for consumption at a later time. Seeds the nutcrackers fail to reclaim will eventually replenish the forest. Hikers should anticipate seeing a number of Clark's nutcrackers flitting between the branches of the whitebark pines in the Pine Forest Range.

A five-mile climb through a steep canyon leads to a picturesque, aspen-covered basin below the impressive granite wall of Santa Rosa Peak's towering north face.

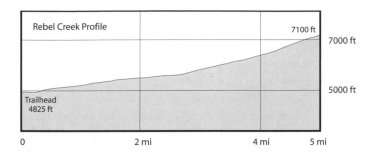

DISTANCE & ROUTE:	10 miles round trip
DIFFICULTY:	Moderate
SEASON:	Late spring to early summer, fall
TRAILHEAD ACCESS:	High-clearance vehicle recommended
WATER:	Available in Rebel Creek
GUIDEBOOK MAP:	5
USGS MAP:	Santa Rosa Peak
USFS MAP:	Santa Rosa–Paradise Peak Wilderness

INTRODUCTION The Rebel Creek section of the 29-mile-long Summit Trail begins in the narrow, V-shaped canyon of a tumultuous stream amid sagebrush-covered slopes accented by interesting metamorphic rock outcroppings. The climax of the almost 5-mile hike occurs near the crest of the range in an aspen-filled basin beneath the rugged, alpine-looking north face of 9701-foot granitic Santa Rosa Peak.

DIRECTIONS TO TRAILHEAD Follow U.S. 95 north of Winnemucca for 46.5 miles to F.R. (Forest Road) 533, signed N. REBEL CREEK ROAD. Follow the well-graded road to a slightly confusing intersection, 0.8 mile from the highway, where you proceed on a less traveled road headed toward the mountains (the more traveled road bends toward Rebel Creek Ranch). Follow a twin-tracked gravel road to a gate at 1.4 miles, and then descend toward Rebel Creek, which the road crosses four times before you arrive at the trailhead. Cottonwoods shade some primitive campsites nearby.

DESCRIPTION   Follow the trail along the north bank of cottonwood-lined Rebel Creek through the narrow, V-shaped canyon across slopes covered with sagebrush, cheat grass, and scattered wildflowers, where periodic outcroppings of phyllite add character to the surroundings. Just past a seasonal drainage, you cross into the Santa Rosa–Paradise Peak Wilderness.

Proceeding up the canyon, you can't help but notice the deeply eroded banks and debris deposits left behind by past flooding, as you follow the tumbling and winding stream through wild rose, elderberry, cottonwood, and aspen. Eventually, the trail angles into a large side canyon, where you hop across a diminutive stream before returning to the main gorge of Rebel Creek. Views toward the crest of the range improve as you progress up the canyon.

Skirt another side canyon and continue above the serpentine creek into a large meadow, where the tread becomes indistinct. The canyon narrows beyond the meadow, forcing the trail higher above the creek to avoid heavy brush and low cliffs. You step across a small side stream lined with dense foliage and then veer back down toward Rebel Creek. Pass through an opening in a fence near the confluence of two branches of the creek beneath a large hill, and head down to a crossing of the north branch, 3 miles from the trailhead.

Past the crossing, you climb high above the creek on a moderate ascent into a narrow and steep canyon, where quaking aspens carpet the far hillside. The trail seemingly ends in some thick brush, but reappears farther upstream amid a pocket of aspen. A pair of switchbacks takes you higher above the creek and then the trail bends around to the south up a steep, aspen-choked part of the upper canyon.

The climb continues, leading to crossing of the creek near a shady grove of aspen, where the canyon bends east again. You ascend out of the canyon to broader topography as the massive west face of Santa Rosa Peak springs into view. A rugged ridge of steep granite runs along the north side of the peak before culminating in the 9701-foot summit. Beneath the ridge lies a basin that rivals any in the state for alpine beauty. As snow clings to the shady clefts of the peak, a huge stand of aspen blankets the basin below, perhaps one of the largest stands in the Great Basin. Although the Summit Trail continues east toward the crest of the range, easy cross-country travel is available in the basin below Santa Rosa Peak for those with extra time and energy.

REBEL CREEK   This creek was supposedly named as the result of an encounter between a Union soldier and Confederate soldier; the two fought each other for the right to place their appellation upon the stream, with the Confederate combatant prevailing.

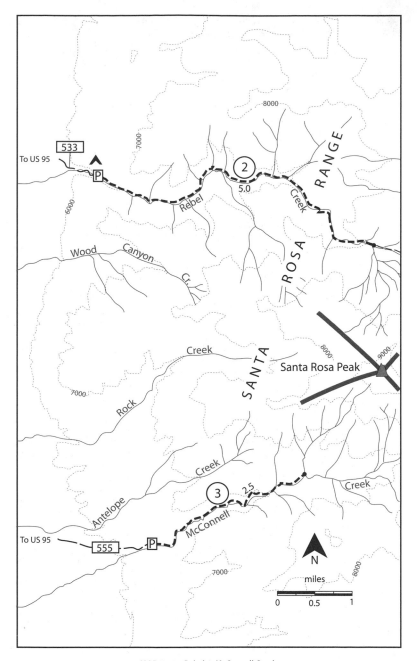

MAP 5 | Rebel & McConnell Creeks

A secluded hike along a tumbling stream leads to a scenic basin on the south side of Santa Rosa Peak.

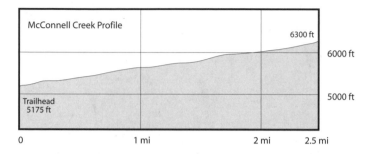

DISTANCE & ROUTE: 5 miles round trip

DIFFICULTY: Moderate

SEASON: Late spring to early summer, fall

TRAILHEAD ACCESS: High-clearance vehicle recommended

WATER: Available in McConnell Creek

GUIDEBOOK MAP: 5

USGS MAP: Santa Rosa Peak

USFS MAP: Santa Rosa–Paradise Peak Wilderness

INTRODUCTION McConnell Creek is a delightful stream with bountiful cascades and inviting pools hemmed into a winding, steep-walled canyon on the west side of the Santa Rosa Range. Anglers will find this stream an enticing challenge, plying the waters for the resident brook trout. Interesting geology adds flavor to the gorge, with dramatic phyllite outcroppings adorning the lower canyon, and the granite flanks of 9701-foot Santa Rosa Peak dominating the scenery of the upper basin.

DIRECTIONS TO TRAILHEAD Follow U.S. 95 north of Winnemucca for 41.5 miles to F.R. 555, which begins at a rest area just south of the town of Orovada. Follow the dirt road east toward the mountains, passing through a gate at 0.75 mile from the highway, and crossing over Antelope Creek at 1.6 miles. Pass through another gate at the National Forest boundary at 3 miles, and continue another 0.3 mile to the trailhead, where the road simply dead-ends at a narrow turnaround.

DESCRIPTION Mildly graded trail follows the north bank of McConnell Creek into a steep-walled, V-shaped canyon, where jagged phyllite formations periodically jut into the canyon above the willow-lined stream. You pass above a number of small punch bowls and swirling pools that are sure to entice even the most indifferent angler.

Proceeding up the trail, erosion of the stream banks and scattered debris provide evidence of a major flood that roared through the canyon in the spring of 1984. A heavy snowpack and soaring temperatures produced unstable conditions perfect for the development of a 100-year event, as mudslides and high water tore through the canyon, leaving visible reminders to this day of nature's potential fury.

Follow the trail alongside the winding creek to a grassy meadow on a bench above the stream, where the path becomes sketchy. Granite boulders scattered across the meadow look out of place below cliffs of metamorphic phyllite, but the flooding creek deposited the rocks here in 1984. Discernible tread resumes beyond the meadow, as the trail continues upstream following the serpentine nature of the canyon. Just past a seasonal side stream, you cross the wilderness boundary.

Continue to snake your way up the gorge. The canyon briefly widens at another grassy meadow bordered by wild rose, but soon narrows again as the trail draws closer to the cascading creek. Farther upstream, pockets of aspen begin to fill the main canyon and side drainages. A short and steep climb leads to the top of a rock rib, as you gain your first good views of the southwest face of Santa Rosa Peak.

Beyond the rib, the grade of ascent increases as the trail climbs high above the creek, passing a couple of seasonal rivulets along the way. Eventually, the path all but disappears close to where the creek divides into multiple channels that drain the slopes below the mountain. Although the trail falters, the upper part of the canyon is open for further exploration for those who don't mind straightforward cross-country travel.

PHYLLITE AND GRANITE While the upper part of the Santa Rosa Range is composed primarily of granitic rock, the western foothills are made up of phyllite, a gray, metamorphic rock containing small flecks of mica. Similar to other west-side streams, McConnell Creek follows the deep gash of a V-shaped canyon through the granite rocks near the headwaters and through the phyllite rocks in the lower reaches. With keen eyes you should be able to notice the transition of these two rock types on your journey up the canyon.

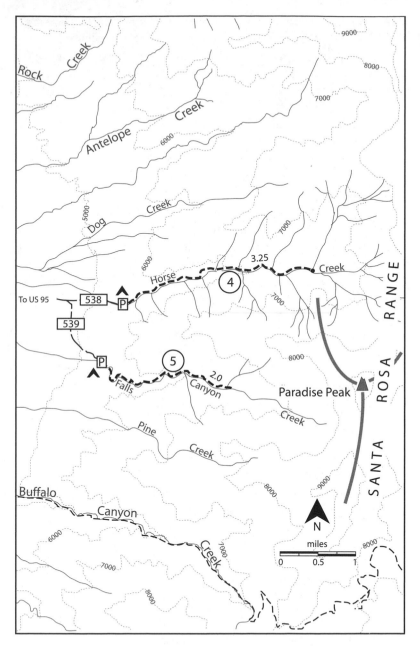

Rock Creek

Antelope Creek

Dog Creek

To US 95 538 539

Horse 3.25 Creek ④

Falls Canyon ⑤ 2.0

Pine Creek

Buffalo Canyon

Creek

Paradise Peak

SANTA ROSA RANGE

N

miles
0   0.5   1

MAP 6 | Horse & Falls Canyons

Follow the serpentine course of Horse Canyon from desert lowlands to mountain highlands.

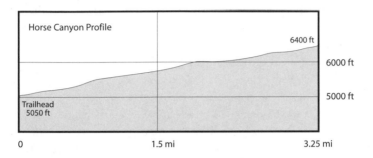

DISTANCE & ROUTE:	6.5 miles round trip
DIFFICULTY:	Moderate
SEASON:	Late spring to early summer, fall
TRAILHEAD ACCESS:	High-clearance vehicle recommended
WATER:	Available in Horse Creek
GUIDEBOOK MAP:	6
USGS MAP:	Santa Rosa Peak
USFS MAP:	Santa Rosa–Paradise Peak Wilderness

INTRODUCTION The Horse Canyon Trail is perhaps the best trail in the Santa Rosa–Paradise Peak Wilderness, at least as far as the actual condition of the tread is concerned. Well-graded and distinct, the path leads along the cascading stream farther into the mountains than other trails on the west side of the Santa Rosas, with the exception of the Rebel Creek section of the Summit Trail. The 3.25-mile trail leads well into the canyon to the upper basin, where steep walls of granite rise up to a serrated ridge at the crest of the range, providing hikers with some grand mountain scenery.

DIRECTIONS TO TRAILHEAD Follow U.S. 95 north of Winnemucca for 40 miles to F.R. 538, signed HORSE CANYON ROAD, and turn east. Cross over Horse Creek at 0.6 mile and again at 1.8 miles. You reach a signed intersection at 2.6 miles with F.R. 539 to the right, which leads to the Falls Canyon trailhead (see hike 5). Remain on F.R. 538 to the Horse Canyon trailhead at a wide grass-covered flat, 3.3 miles from the highway. A primitive campsite with fire ring is nearby.

DESCRIPTION   Avoid the temptation to follow a more defined track leading down to and across Horse Creek, as that path quickly disappears in thick brush a short distance upstream. Instead, follow an inconspicuous old road that heads south from the grassy meadow and climbs above the cascading creek across the south side of the canyon. After a short descent to the canyon floor, the route becomes a bona fide trail that follows alongside the meandering stream to a crossing, 0.3 mile from the trailhead.

Proceed up the twisting canyon above the cottonwood-lined creek, on a steady climb through sagebrush, grasses, and scattered thickets of wild rose. Enter the signed Santa Rosa–Paradise Peak Wilderness just past a dry side canyon. After quickly surmounting a minor ridge, the canyon momentarily widens before a series of ninety-degree bends lead to a small meadow, where impressive granite cliffs at the head of the canyon spring into view. Although the USGS Santa Rosa Peak map indicates the trail ends at the meadow, a well-defined path continues upstream.

Beyond the meadow, the trail closely follows Horse Creek through pockets of aspens and cottonwoods. Careful observation reveals a transition from the metamorphic phyllite of the lower canyon to the igneous granite of the upper elevations. On the far side of the creek, a dense stand of aspen runs almost to the ridgeline, interspersed with a smattering of limber pines. After hopping across a small side stream, you encounter a round, boggy meadow fed by springs and rimmed with aspen. Leaving the meadow, the trail becomes exceedingly steep for a short distance before mellowing. Fine views up the canyon reveal a serrated crest above vertical granite cliffs.

The grade of ascent increases again after stepping over a stream that drains a narrow side canyon choked with young aspens. Follow the course of the winding canyon past two more side streams into more open terrain with improving views. After surmounting a low rise, you continue alongside the main creek to the crossing of a narrow rivulet draining the upper slopes to the north. The trail ends a short distance beyond the crossing; a lone campsite is on the opposite bank in a small grassy clearing.

WILDLIFE   You may see a horse while hiking along the Horse Canyon Trail, but most likely the animal will be of the domesticated variety, not one of the wild horses that used to roam the area and for which the canyon was named. Wild creatures you might hope to see nowadays in the Santa Rosas include mule deer, marmots, or red-tailed hawks. Mountain lions, bobcats, and bighorn sheep inhabit the region but are seldom seen.

A short stroll past striking cliffs to a dramatic waterfall is sure to please both young and old alike. Solitude seekers will be lured farther up the trail.

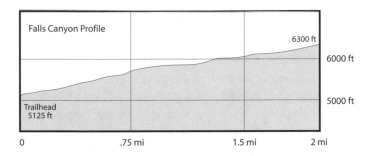

DISTANCE & ROUTE:	1 mile round trip to waterfall; 4 miles round trip to end of trail
DIFFICULTY:	Easy; moderate
SEASON:	Late spring to early summer, fall
TRAILHEAD ACCESS:	High-clearance vehicle recommended
WATER:	Available in Falls Creek
GUIDEBOOK MAP:	6
USGS MAP:	Santa Rosa Peak, Five Fingers
USFS MAP:	Santa Rosa–Paradise Peak Wilderness

INTRODUCTION   A relatively easy 0.5-mile hike leads to a rarity in the Great Basin—a significant waterfall. To appreciate the full grandeur of the falls, plan your hike for springtime, when the creek is at full force. However, be forewarned that the creek must be forded twice before reaching the falls and you'll most likely get your feet and legs wet in early season. Along with the falls, dramatic phyllite cliffs enhance the scenery in the lower canyon.

Even though the most spectacular features of this trip occur within the first half mile, the trail continues farther up the canyon to an upper basin, where you'll have excellent views of Paradise Peak. Past the falls, solitude is almost guaranteed.

DIRECTIONS TO TRAILHEAD   Follow U.S. 95 for 40 miles north of Winnemucca to F.R. 538, signed HORSE CANYON ROAD, and turn east. Cross over Horse Creek at 0.6 mile and again at 1.8 miles. You reach a signed intersection at 2.6 miles, where F.R. 538 continues to the Falls Canyon trailhead (see hike 4). Turn right onto F.R. 539, pass through a gate at 0.8 mile and cross Falls Canyon Creek a couple of times before reaching the trailhead, 1.1 miles from the junction. Several informal campsites are sheltered by mature cottonwoods next to the creek.

DESCRIPTION   The primitive Falls Canyon Trail, which doesn't even appear on the USGS maps, leads quickly up the narrow canyon to two tenuous stream crossings. Aside from these fords, the trail would be easy and short enough for smaller children. Beyond the creek crossings, the path heads up the densely vegetated creek bottom into what at first glance appears to be a box canyon. In actuality, the route follows the stream through a sharp S-bend beneath dramatically steep phyllite cliffs. You then reach an unsigned junction, between the main trail curving left, which climbs above cliffs, and the path continuing along the creek to the base of the falls.

To reach the falls, follow the creekside path through thick brush. After about 75 yards of brush beating, you stand near the base of the waterfall, which plunges dramatically below jagged phyllite cliffs and over a rock wall into a churning pool below. The wind-driven mist is especially refreshing on a typically hot summer day.

To travel farther up the canyon, return to the junction, ascend around the rock pinnacles above the falls, and then come back alongside the creek farther upstream. A switchback leads down to a crossing of the creek and then you continue along the south bank on a sweeping curve into a narrow and rocky section of the canyon. A steep climb above the creek leads to fine views of Paradise Peak from the top of a ridge and the wilderness boundary a short distance farther along the path. Following a stretch of gently graded trail, you encounter a grass-covered meadow lined with quaking aspen.

This scenic meadow has the potential to be an excellent spot for a rest stop, or a fine overnight destination for backpackers. Unfortunately, cattle have been allowed to graze here in the past, and if the meadows have been trampled by hooves and littered with cow pies, you probably won't want to linger here too long. Cows aren't the only ones to receive blame for the possibly undesirable condition of the area, as careless hunters have left behind bones from deer carcasses and random piles of garbage as well.

The trail continues upstream to the upper basin, where hillsides are carpeted with sagebrush, the drainages are filled with swaths of aspen, and views of Paradise Peak abound. Just past a branch of the creek draining slopes on the north side of the basin, the trail ends below a large grove of aspens.

Falls Canyon Falls, Santa Rosa Range

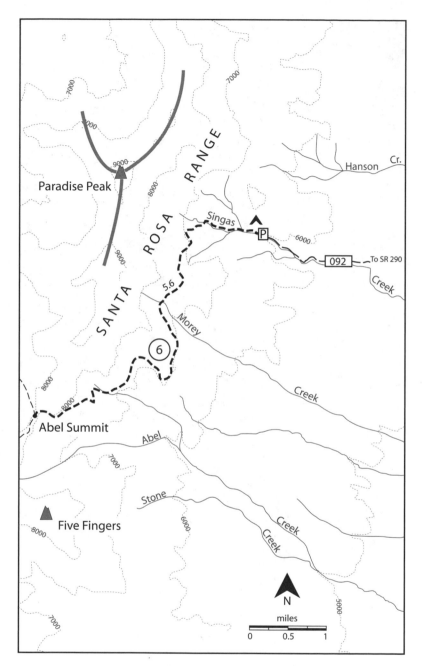

Paradise Peak

SANTA ROSA RANGE

Hanson Cr.

Singas

P

092 To SR 290

Creek

5.6

Morey

6

Creek

Abel Summit

Abel

Stone

Five Fingers

Creek

Creek

N

miles

0   0.5   1

MAP 7 | Singas Creek

QUAKING ASPEN Although the quaking aspen is one of the most familiar trees in North America, many people are not aware of its reproductive habits. In the western United States, aspens are rarely propagated by seed germination, but rather are dependent upon root sprouts for the reproduction of new trees. Therefore, aspens do not grow as individual trees in a forest matrix; they are genetically identical replicas in a collective grove or clone connected together by an extensive network of roots.

HIKE 6 | SINGAS CREEK

Lush foliage, vibrant wildflowers, and dense aspen stands create a virtual desert oasis on this journey along the east side of the Santa Rosa Range. If those attributes aren't tempting enough, throw in some great views as well.

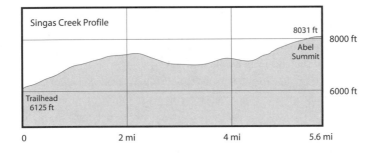

DISTANCE & ROUTE:	11.2 miles round trip
DIFFICULTY:	Moderate
SEASON:	Late spring to early summer, fall
TRAILHEAD ACCESS:	High-clearance vehicle recommended
WATER:	Available in Singas, Morrey, and Abel Creeks
GUIDEBOOK MAP:	7
USGS MAP:	Five Fingers
USFS MAP:	Santa Rosa–Paradise Peak Wilderness

INTRODUCTION The 0.75-mile Singas Creek Trail leads to a junction with the 29-mile-long Summit Trail, which this description follows southbound to Abel Summit. Along the way, hikers pass through some of the most luxuriant vegetation imaginable for a Great Basin range. In particular, the Singas Creek basin is home to a wide variety of wildflowers, plants, and shrubs, as well as dense stands of quaking aspen. Farther along the trail, expansive views abound in the basins of Morey and Abel Creeks below the steep slopes of 9415-foot Singas Peak, and at Abel Summit.

DIRECTIONS TO TRAILHEAD   Follow U.S. 95 for 22 miles north of Winnemucca to S.R. 290, signed PARADISE VALLEY. Travel on S.R. 290 for 16.8 miles and turn left onto Singas Creek Road.

Proceed on the well-graded, graveled Singas Creek Road toward the east front of the Santa Rosa Range, reaching an intersection at 1.5 miles. Continue straight ahead on a narrow, twin-tracked dirt road, as the gravel road bends left toward a ranch. Ignore a lesser road at 3.2 miles and follow the main road into the narrow and deep canyon of Singas Creek. You reach the trailhead at a wide turnaround, 5.6 miles from the highway. Primitive campsites are near the trailhead and a short distance up the trail.

DESCRIPTION   From the trailhead, follow the remnants of an old and overgrown roadbed on a moderate climb across fields of sagebrush and through thick groves of aspen. After hopping over a pair of spring-fed tributaries, enter the Santa Rosa–Paradise Peak Wilderness and continue the ascent to a crossing of the main channel of Singas Creek. At 0.75 mile from the trailhead, your climb brings you to the junction with the Summit Trail, where a pair of round poles is all that remains from an old trail sign.

From the junction, turn left (south) and follow more distinct tread on a gently ascending traverse across the upper slopes of the Singas Creek basin; the mild grade is a welcome change from the steep climb up Singas Creek. Travel beneath tall aspens and beside dense vegetation, including a nice variety of wildflowers, to a pair of small, seasonal rivulets that trickle past moss-covered rocks and lush riparian foliage. As you continue across the basin, the vegetation parts occasionally, allowing fine views of the valley below, but when you reach the top of a sagebrush-covered ridge, you will have an expansive view of Singas Creek basin, Paradise Valley, and distant mountain ranges to the east.

From the ridge crest, continue the traverse across slopes covered with sagebrush, scattered snowberry, and sporadic tufts of lupine, to a short descent into the Morey Creek drainage. You cross seasonal streams flanked by aspen groves to the willow-lined main channel, 2 miles from the trailhead, where wildflowers such as paintbrush and bluebell abound. A swift climb leads out of the drainage to a protracted descent around the protruding southeast ridge of Singas Peak, alternating between hillsides carpeted with lush foliage and open slopes of sagebrush. As you round the nose of the ridge and enter the Abel Creek basin, commanding views of Paradise Valley and the distant ranges continue.

The Summit Trail makes a horseshoe bend in the Abel Creek basin across the sagebrush-covered slopes on the south side of Singas Peak, and then

Lone mountain-mahogany in Singas Basin, on Summit Trail, Santa Rosa Range

traverses past seasonal streams, where aspens and willows thrive in the moist soil. Eventually, a short descent leads into an area of dense vegetation on the approach to a tributary of Abel Creek, the trail becoming overgrown and hard to follow. At the stream, the route follows the top of a rock-and-wire dam, built for who knows what purpose. Beyond this structure, a short climb leads to the top of a ridge, covered with scattered boulders and mountain-mahoganies. From the crest, the trail becomes indistinct as you descend toward the main branch of Abel Creek, the track easily lost in a tangle of brush and small trees. At 4.5 miles you hop over the creek and then begin a steep ascent.

After a 0.25-mile climb, gain a ridge and continue a winding ascent toward the crest of the Santa Rosa Range. Approximately 30 yards before the actual crest, you reach a junction with a path heading south along the top of the ridge that eventually descends into Andorno Creek canyon. An old wooden sign greets you at the crest: SINGAS CREEK 5, BUFFALO CREEK 4, ANDORNO CREEK 6, ABEL SUMMIT. Views both near and far from Abel Summit are quite impressive, a grand reward for the effort.

PARADISE   In 1863 a band of miners crossed the Santa Rosas to a lush valley near the eastern base of the range. Impressed with the verdant surroundings, one of the prospectors, a man named W. B. Huff exclaimed, "What a paradise!" and the glen has been known as Paradise Valley ever since. Apart from a few Indian uprisings, the valley lived up to the name, becoming a quite productive agricultural region.

The three ranges mentioned in this chapter contain some of the state's most picturesque mountain scenery. Blessed with more moisture from Pacific storms than the typically more arid Nevada range, the Jarbidge and Ruby Mountains and the East Humboldt Range offer a bounty of lakes, wildflower-carpeted meadows, and rushing streams.

Following David Bourne's discovery of gold in 1908, the town of Jarbidge sprung into existence as fifteen hundred miners flooded the area. Ore valued at over $10 million was produced in just two decades, but the gold eventually ran out in the 1930s and after the mines were closed the population diminished to less than two hundred souls. The fact that the tiny mining town of Jarbidge lives on into the present is somewhat curious, as reaching the tiny burg requires a very long drive on a gravel road, part of the route careening through a narrow canyon some twenty miles from the nearest paved road. Several structures remain from the bygone days, rebuilt after a 1919 fire swept through town. Jarbidge has at least one historical claim to fame: the last known stagecoach robbery took place just outside of town in 1916. At my last visit, this middle-of-nowhere community offered two saloons, a gas station, motel, bed and breakfast, and trading post. Travelers searching for an authentic Wild West town without the excessive commercialism plaguing most other old settlements will find Jarbidge quite appealing.

The Jarbidge Mountains were the centerpiece of Nevada's only designated wilderness area when the original wilderness bill was passed in 1964. Comprising 64,667 acres, this remote landscape was characterized by tall peaks, deep canyons, expansive vistas, teeming wildlife, and abundant wildflowers. Another 48,500 acres were added to the wilderness in 1989 with passage of the Nevada Wilderness Protection Act.

Mostly volcanic in origin, the Jarbidge Mountains seem to share few of the attributes of the typical Nevada range. While most other ranges within the state are linear spines with a north-south trending crest, the Jarbidge Mountains appear to have been dropped in a clump by the Creator, with multiple crests and radiating canyons. Dense stands of subalpine fir and whitebark pine add legitimacy to the national forest designation, sometimes a bit of a misnomer in other Great Basin ranges.

The Ruby Mountains are considered by many to be the premier mountain range in Nevada. Revealing signs of extensive glaciation, the Rubies harbor

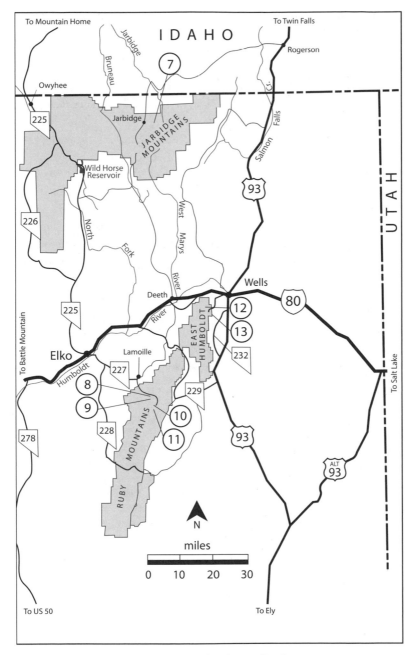

MAP 8 | Hikes of Northeastern Nevada

deep U-shaped canyons, cirques holding serene lakes, hanging valleys, polished rock walls, and glacier-carved summits, presenting an alpine appearance that oftentimes leaves first time visitors awestruck. Named by U.S. Army soldiers who mistakenly identified their discovery of garnets as rubies, the Ruby Mountain chain is the gem of Nevada, perhaps the state's most heralded range. However, despite this renown, the remote location far away from major metropolitan areas ensures that visitation remains light.

The Rubies have something for everyone. Auto-bound visitors can enjoy the magnificent scenery along the Lamoille Canyon Road National Scenic Byway, which leads through a picturesque canyon dubbed "the Yosemite of Nevada." In addition to a number of hiking, backpacking, and equestrian trails, Lamoille Canyon offers picnic areas, campgrounds, interpretive displays, and nature trails. Hikers will experience wildflower-covered slopes that rise to precipitous, snow-clad, craggy peaks, as well as rushing streams propelled by the icy runoff from countless creeks and springs, and picturesque lakes with backdrops of rugged cliffs.

The neighboring East Humboldt mountains are a compact version of the Rubies, offering many of the same features on a smaller scale. Away from the range's center of activity at Angel Lake, where recreationists fish, camp and picnic, hikers will find ample doses of solitude on the two trails described in this section, both leading to scenic lakes with outstanding mountain views.

FYI ■ Reaching the famed wildflowers and deep canyons of the Jarbidge Wilderness, which was Nevada's only designated wilderness when the original wilderness bill was signed in 1964, requires a significant amount of time behind the wheel. The nearest paved highways, U.S. 93 to the east and S.R. 225 to the west, lie many miles away from any Jarbidge trailhead, forcing motorists to extended drives on secondary dirt roads just in order to reach the trails. A high-clearance vehicle is recommended for the one trip into the Jarbidge Mountains described in this section, as well as getting to most of the other trails in the area. Whether your journey takes you through the Nevada towns of Wells, Elko, or Jackpot, or Twin Falls, Idaho, motorists should plan on filling their tanks in one of these towns, as gas stations are few and far between around the Jarbidge Mountains, and what gas is available will be very expensive.

Hikers in the Rubies should be prepared for changing weather conditions, as summer thunderstorms are not uncommon. Those bound for Liberty Pass (10,400 feet) should adjust to the altitude and check with the Forest Service about current conditions, as snowfields often cover the trail through midsummer. As with the Ruby Mountains, summer thunderstorms are a possibility in the Jarbidge and East Humboldt mountains as well.

Spectacular vistas through the rarefied air above the Jarbidge Mountains are nearly a constant companion on this short hike.

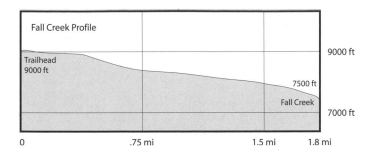

Fall Creek Profile

Trailhead
9000 ft

9000 ft

7500 ft

Fall Creek

7000 ft

0   .75 mi   1.5 mi   1.8 mi

DISTANCE & ROUTE:	3.6 miles round trip
DIFFICULTY:	Moderate
SEASON:	Summer, fall
TRAILHEAD ACCESS:	High-clearance vehicle recommended
WATER:	Available in Fall Creek and tributaries
GUIDEBOOK MAP:	9
USGS MAP:	Robinson Creek, Gods Pocket Peak
USGS MAP:	Jarbidge Wilderness

INTRODUCTION Just reaching the Jarbidge Mountains requires a long drive from just about anywhere, and once you do get there, most of the trails are better suited for multi-day backpacking rather than short day hikes. However, the Fall Creek Trail provides a nice exception to that rule, as the views from the upper part of the short trail are some of the most spectacular in the region. Strolling through mostly open terrain allows for nearly continuous vistas of the Jarbidge crest, the deep canyons of the East Fork Jarbidge River and its tributaries, and the distant terrain of southern Idaho. Beginning at 9000 feet on top of Sawmill Ridge, stunning views begin almost immediately and continue as the trail drops steeply, before a long descending traverse leads to the banks of Fall Creek.

Enjoying such grand scenery does come at a price. The road to the trailhead is fairly rough, particularly over the last couple of miles, where a high-clearance vehicle will be an absolute necessity. The unmaintained trail is in reasonable condition for only the first couple of miles, but the tread virtually disappears once you reach Fall Creek and then parallels the stream to a union with the East Fork Jarbidge River Trail. If you plan on hiking all the way to the river, be

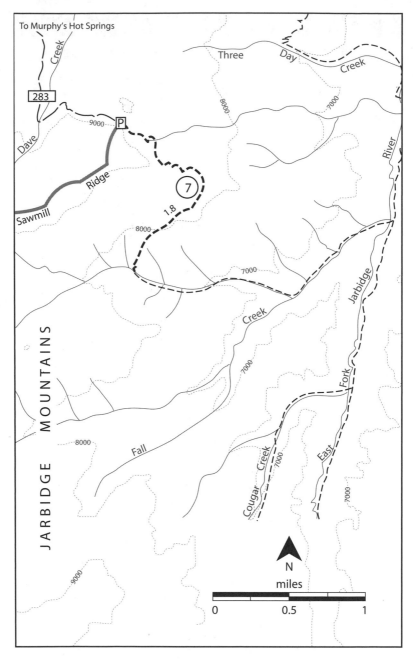

MAP 9 | Fall Creek

prepared to bushwhack over numerous deadfalls and through thick brush. However far down the canyon you decide to travel, bear in mind that the return hike is uphill all the way.

DIRECTIONS TO TRAILHEAD   From U.S. 93, about 86 miles north of Wells, or 30 miles south of Twin Falls, Idaho, in the tiny burg of Rogerson, Idaho, turn west onto the Rogerson–Three Creek Road. Proceed for 49 miles to Murphy Hot Springs and turn left near the Desert Hot Springs Store onto F.R. 073, signed DAVE CREEK WILDERNESS.

Follow F.R. 073 across the East Fork Jarbidge River and then on a 2-mile climb to the top of Wilkins Island. Once on the broad plateau, the dirt road continues south toward the mountains, eventually passing underneath and then following a power line through grasslands. At 8.3 miles from the highway, continue straight ahead at a signed junction, marked JARBIDGE WILDERNESS. After another 0.5 mile, you enter National Forest lands and proceed, ignoring lesser roads branching to the left and right. Just beyond a patch of thick forest you encounter a clearing, at 11.7 miles, where an unsigned road to the left proceeds to the Three Day Creek trailhead.

Continue straight ahead on F.R. 283 into thick forest, where the road becomes rough, impassable to anything other than a high-clearance vehicle. At 12.6 miles is a Y-junction, where you veer left, cross Dave Creek 0.2 mile farther, and then proceed another 0.5 mile to the end of the road atop Sawmill Ridge.

Outfitters have used the trailhead as a staging area, so be sure to park your vehicle away from their facilities. An old road branches to the left of the trailhead area, heading northeast from the ridge and eventually connecting with the Three Day Creek Trail just before the wilderness boundary.

DESCRIPTION   From the trailhead, the route of the trail continues along the old roadbed through a pole gate with a wilderness boundary sign attached, amid a forest of subalpine firs and limber pines. As the road bends to the right, follow a single-track footpath to a large, grassy clearing, where the trail momentarily disappears, only to appear again on the far side. Just beyond the clearing, you encounter a trickle of spring-fed water. Soon the forest parts, providing you with a spectacular view of the East Fork Jarbidge River canyon stretching toward the distant plains of southern Idaho.

A series of switchbacks lead sharply downhill through sparsely distributed pines and firs to a long, sweeping, gradually descending traverse across the upper slopes of the Fall Creek basin. Across the grass-and-sagebrush-covered slopes, expansive views abound of the canyons below and the Jarbidge crest above. After stepping across a couple of seasonal drainages, the long traverse brings you to the northern tributary of Fall Creek.

A discernible path heads downstream for a while through thick subalpine fir forest to a crossing of the creek, where the unmaintained trail disappears in a tangle of deadfalls and thick brush on the opposite side. Although an actual path is hard to follow, the general direction of the route is straightforward, following Fall Creek to a union with the East Fork Jarbidge River.

> **JARBIDGE** The namesake term is a corrupted form of a Shoshone name, either a word meaning "devil" or a another word based upon a colorful legend about a crater-dwelling giant who wandered Jarbidge Canyon capturing Native Americans. This giant would carry his prey to his crater in a basket strapped to his back (perhaps the first backpacker in Nevada) and then devour the tasty morsels.

HIKE 8 | RIGHT FORK LAMOILLE CREEK

Those who consider Nevada to be nothing other than arid desert will be amazed at the sight of this verdant hanging valley beneath lofty alpine peaks.

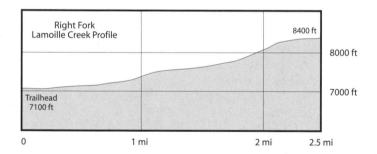

DISTANCE & ROUTE:	5 miles round trip
DIFFICULTY:	Moderate
SEASON:	Summer, fall
TRAILHEAD ACCESS:	All vehicles
WATER:	Available in Right Fork Lamoille Creek
GUIDEBOOK MAP:	10
USGS MAP:	Lamoille
USFS MAP:	Ruby Mountains and East Humboldt Wildernesses

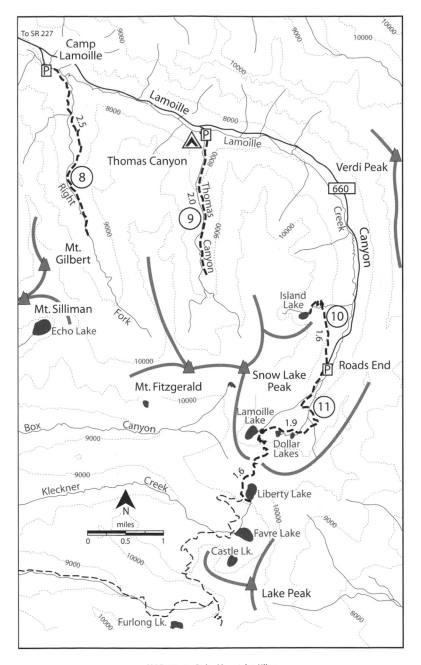

MAP 10 | Ruby Mountains Hikes

INTRODUCTION The Ruby Mountains are so named for good reason, and the Right Fork Lamoille Creek canyon is a relatively undiscovered jewel of a basin. Only 2 miles from a bustling summer camp is a seldom-visited, flourishing, verdant valley rimmed by alpine-looking peaks and steep canyon walls. The trail passes through some of the most luxuriant vegetation in the Great Basin, alongside one of the most rambunctious streams, and into a dramatic glacier-carved, hanging valley that will rival any in the state for mountain beauty. Boundless alpine scenery and extended opportunities for exploration await the hiker willing to invest the effort required to reach this truly spectacular hanging valley. Although outside wilderness protection, a concession to a local heli-ski operation, the upper part of the canyon is as pristine and magnificent as any spot in the Ruby Mountains Wilderness.

DIRECTIONS TO TRAILHEAD Leave I-80 at the ELKO DOWNTOWN exit and head south for 0.8 mile to a left-hand turn onto Business 80. Proceed another 0.8 mile and turn right at 5th Street onto S.R. 228, observing signs for SPRING CREEK, LAMOILLE, JIGGS. Follow S.R. 228 out of downtown and across an overpass spanning the railroad tracks and the Humboldt River. Pass the Last Chance Road intersection on your left, which leads to the Ruby Mountains Ranger District office, and continue southeast to the intersection of S.R. 227 and S.R. 228, 7.3 miles from I-80.

Following a sign for LAMOILLE, SR227E, proceed straight ahead at the intersection, now on S.R. 227. At 7.5 miles from the junction, 0.5 mile before the small community of Lamoille, turn right onto F.R. 660, also referred to as the Lamoille Canyon Road National Scenic Byway.

Follow paved road across the National Forest boundary and into glacier-carved Lamoille Canyon. At 5 miles from S.R. 227, turn right at the signed turnoff for Camp Lamoille, operated by the Elko Lions Club. Drive on gravel road to the gate at the camp entrance and park off the road in a wide parking area beside a grove of mountain-mahogany trees.

DESCRIPTION Leave the parking area and follow the road into Camp Lamoille, proceeding courteously to the edge of camp beyond some A-framed cabins. Follow a twin-tracked jeep road, which eventually becomes a single-track trail, past small aspens over to the west bank of Right Fork Lamoille Creek. Head upstream, where you quickly come to a fork in the trail; the left-hand branch leads across a pair of bridges to the camp's archery area. You continue up the right side of the creek for a short distance to another informal junction, where the main trail curves down to a ford of the creek. The path straight ahead follows the creek on a primitive trail through dense foliage to a series of cascades that tumble dramatically down rock cliffs.

If logs are in place, you can use them to make the crossing; otherwise you'll be forced to ford the creek, which can be a challenge during peak runoff. Once across the stream, follow the trail up the east bank through grasses, shrubs, and wildflowers, including monkey flower, columbine, and lupine. Soon the trail forsakes the creek bottom on a steep, switchbacking climb up the hillside through dense stands of aspen and lush trailside vegetation. After the stiff climb, the grade abates for a while as you pass into the Ruby Mountains Wilderness, 1.1 miles from the parking area.

The stiff ascent resumes and the vegetation diminishes enough to reveal a series of small ponds on a bench below the trail. Soon the dense foliage returns, providing shaded passage across a couple of narrow tributary streams. Eventually, the thick vegetation is left behind for a spell as the route ascends a succession of granite slabs, benches, and clearings accented by a brilliant display of seasonal wildflowers. The trail becomes faint where aspens and brush return and the path seems to reach a dead end at a massive rock wall that nearly pinches off the canyon. However, a path tenuously clings to a narrow gap between the base of the rock and the churning creek. Beyond this obstacle, tread becomes distinct again, as you climb over more rock slabs away from the cascading creek. Where the route is hard to discern, ducks should successfully guide you through this rocky stretch and into the widening upper basin.

Heading into the magnificent hanging valley of the upper canyon, the tread diminishes for good in verdant vegetation encircling a beaver pond. Many hikers will be satisfied with the rewarding scenery from here following the 2.5-mile journey. However, the basin is wide open and ripe for easy off-trail exploration up the verdant, glacier-carved gorge, where the clear stream courses below serrated ridges and picturesque peaks.

ALPINE FLORA One gaze upon the verdant slopes of Lamoille Canyon is enough verification of the fact that the Ruby Mountains are blessed with the largest number of alpine plants in the state, consisting of 189 species classified as alpine tundra. Early July generally is the beginning of a stunning wildflower display that usually extends into August.

A short hike leads from Lamoille Canyon into a picturesque side canyon with excellent views of rugged Mt. Fitzgerald, an alpine summit rivaling any western peak for mountain scenery.

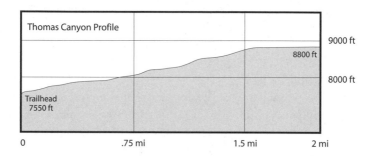

DISTANCE & ROUTE:	4 miles round trip
DIFFICULTY:	Moderate
SEASON:	Summer, fall
TRAILHEAD ACCESS:	All vehicles
WATER:	Available in Thomas Creek
GUIDEBOOK MAP:	10
USGS MAP:	Lamoille, Ruby Dome
USFS MAP:	Ruby Mountains and East Humboldt Wildernesses

INTRODUCTION   The Thomas Canyon Trail offers one of the best views of a "mountaineers' mountain" anywhere in the Ruby Mountains. Alpine-looking, 11,215-foot Mt. Fitzgerald looms high above the glacier-carved canyon like a sentinel guarding the valley. The trail follows alongside a delightful stream into the picturesque upper canyon past numerous cascades. Despite the shortness of the trail, you may have the area to yourself, which is a bit of a mystery considering the outstanding scenery.

DIRECTIONS TO TRAILHEAD   Leave I-80 at the ELKO DOWNTOWN exit and head south for 0.8 mile to a left-hand turn onto Business 80. Proceed another 0.8 mile and turn right at 5th Street onto S.R. 228, observing signs for SPRING CREEK, LAMOILLE, JIGGS. Follow S.R. 228 out of downtown and across an overpass spanning the railroad tracks and the Humboldt River. Pass the Last Chance Road intersection on your left, which leads to the Ruby Mountains Ranger District office, and continue southeast to the intersection of S.R. 227 and S.R. 228, 7.3 miles from I-80.

Rivulet in Upper Thomas Canyon, Ruby Mountains

Following a sign for LAMOILLE, SR227E, proceed straight ahead at the intersection, now on S.R. 227. At 7.5 miles from the junction, 0.5 mile before the small community of Lamoille, turn right onto F.R. 660, also referred to as the Lamoille Canyon Road National Scenic Byway.

Follow paved road across the National Forest boundary and into glacier-carved Lamoille Canyon. At 5 miles from S.R. 227, drive past the Camp Lamoille entrance and continue up Lamoille Canyon Road another 2.4 miles to the entrance into the Thomas Creek Campground. Follow the campground access road to the trailhead.

DESCRIPTION Follow a narrow path on a steep climb up the hillside through tall grasses to an overlook beneath some mountain-mahoganies, offering a glimpse of a short, cascading waterfall. You continue the steep climb to a flat, where the grade moderates for a while. Thomas Creek delightfully swirls, eddies, and glides over rock shelves and into small pools below this section of the trail. As the climb resumes, Mt. Fitzgerald, a classic-looking alpine peak with a pyramidal summit and lingering snowfields, springs into view, dominating the surroundings at the head of the canyon.

The canyon widens and the grade eases momentarily as the creek adopts a more gentle demeanor. Wildflowers and shrubs blanket the slopes and the views of Mt. Fitzgerald and the upper canyon improve as you progress up the trail. The grade increases again, where the canyon becomes steeper and the glistening creek cascades over rock outcroppings.

Continuing to climb alongside the stream, the trail course becomes hard to discern. The USGS map depicts the trail remaining on the east side of the creek for another 0.5 mile, but signs on the ground suggest that the trail perhaps crosses the stream and proceeds up the west bank. Travel farther up the valley is possible whichever side of the creek is chosen, although you will have to contend with some brush on either side. Travel on the east side of the creek may be easier initially. If you select the west bank, some boggy areas near a spring will have to be negotiated, but you may find the trail again farther up the canyon. Even though the trail falters, the upper canyon is well worth the minor hassle of having to beat some brush. By following the west branch of Thomas Creek, a little scrambling takes you to a lush meadow directly below the stunning north face of Mt. Fitzgerald. By following the east branch, you enter a picturesque basin of rock below scenic Snow Lake Peak.

THOMAS CANYON The canyon received its name as the result of a tragic accident, when Raymond Thomas, an Elko schoolteacher, died in 1916 while rescuing students from a surprise October blizzard. Mt. Fitzgerald was named for the thirty-fifth president of the United States, John Fitzgerald Kennedy.

Sweeping vistas of Lamoille Canyon cheer you on the way to subalpine Island Lake, nestled into a beautiful cirque basin carpeted with seasonal wildflowers.

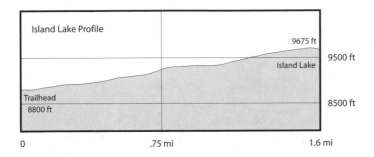

DISTANCE & ROUTE:	3.2 miles round trip
DIFFICULTY:	Moderate
SEASON:	Summer, fall
TRAILHEAD ACCESS:	All vehicles
WATER:	Available in Island Creek
GUIDEBOOK MAP:	10
USGS MAP:	Ruby Valley School, Ruby Dome
USFS MAP:	Ruby Mountains and East Humboldt Wildernesses

INTRODUCTION The trail to Island Lake offers a condensed sample of some of the best aspects of the Ruby Mountains: a scenic mountain lake set in a craggy cirque basin, a spectacular display of wildflowers amid lush foliage, and a vigorously cascading stream. However, don't expect a great deal of solitude, as the trailhead location at the end of the Lamoille Canyon Road, coupled with the short hike, make this trail one of the most popular in the area for hikers, anglers, and sightseers alike.

DIRECTIONS TO TRAILHEAD Leave I-80 at the ELKO DOWNTOWN exit and head south for 0.8 mile to a left-hand turn onto Business 80. Proceed another 0.8 mile and turn right at 5th Street onto S.R. 228, observing signs for SPRING CREEK, LAMOILLE, JIGGS. Follow S.R. 228 out of downtown and across an overpass spanning the railroad tracks and the Humboldt River. Pass the Last Chance Road intersection on your left, which leads to the Ruby Mountains Ranger

Island Lake, Ruby Mountains

District office, and continue southeast to the intersection of S.R. 227 and S.R. 228, 7.3 miles from I-80.

Following a sign for LAMOILLE, SR227E, proceed straight ahead at the intersection, now on S.R. 227. At 7.5 miles from the junction, 0.5 mile before the small community of Lamoille, turn right onto F.R. 660, also referred to as the Lamoille Canyon Road National Scenic Byway.

Follow paved road across the National Forest boundary and into glacier-carved Lamoille Canyon. At 5 miles from S.R. 227, drive past the Camp Lamoille entrance and continue up Lamoille Canyon Road another 7.2 miles to the parking area at Roads End, where you'll find pit toilets, water, horse-loading facilities, and a picnic area. The Island Lake trailhead is at the north end of the loop.

DESCRIPTION   The sign at the trailhead lists the distance to Island Lake as 2 miles, but the actual distance is closer to 1.6 miles. However, after the climb up the west wall of Lamoille Canyon to the lake, you may be convinced of the higher mileage. From the parking area, follow well-graded trail amid lush foliage and wildflowers, including paintbrush, lupine, phlox, potentilla, and larkspur. A steady climb with occasional switchbacks offers increasingly grand views of Lamoille Canyon, as you progress across the hillside. Through scattered limber pine, the route enters the canyon of the outlet stream, where a rock-and-timber bridge spans the picturesque creek, 1 mile from the trailhead.

The bridge offers a splendid opportunity to relax as you watch the creek spill out of a notch above and then pour down rock slabs on the way to a union with Lamoille Creek in the valley below.

Away from the bridge, you ascend sagebrush-carpeted slopes via a series of switchbacks to the lip of the lake basin. At the top of the switchbacks, cross the creek once more on an easy boulder-hop and follow the trail on a short climb to the lakeshore.

Island Lake sits in a wildflower-filled basin, where verdant slopes of green and stone-gray talus fields rise up toward steep cliffs of dark gray and reddish brown. Pockets of snow cling to the north-facing cirque wall well into summer, lending a decidedly alpine feel to the surroundings. The lakeshore harbors thick brush and a few limber pines shelter some campsites near the east end. The namesake island is a small, irregularly shaped, grassy patch of ground in the middle of the lake. A host of anglers, lured by the short hike, seem to enjoy fishing for the resident brook trout.

LIMBER PINE (*PINUS FLEXILIS*)   Limber pines are the most widely distributed high-elevation pine in Nevada, residing within fifty-one of the state's mountain ranges. The swaying branches of this five-needled pine are well suited to the windswept conditions found along the ridge tops of Nevada's mountains.

HIKE 11 | DOLLAR, LAMOILLE, AND LIBERTY LAKES

This journey to a few of the Ruby Lakes is possibly the most renowned hike in Nevada's backcountry, boasting incredible mountain scenery, picturesque lakes, interesting geology, beautiful vistas, and stunning wildflower displays.

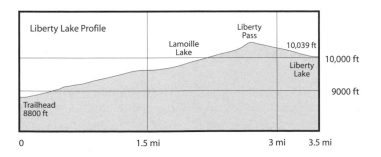

DISTANCE & ROUTE:	7 miles round trip
DIFFICULTY:	Difficult
SEASON:	Summer, fall
TRAILHEAD ACCESS:	All vehicles
WATER:	Available in creeks and lakes
GUIDEBOOK MAP:	10
USGS MAP:	Ruby Dome
USFS MAP:	Ruby Mountains and East Humboldt Wildernesses

INTRODUCTION While lakes are in short supply in most of Nevada's backcountry, the Ruby Lakes area boasts a whole handful of picturesque specimens. Within the first 2 miles, hikers can enjoy the symmetrical Dollar Lakes, encircled by spongy and lush meadows, and Lamoille Lake, a much larger and more austere body of water with a backdrop of rugged cliffs. Along the way, additional delights include the refreshing waters of tumbling Lamoille Creek, and a spectacular display of wildflowers. Hikers in search of a relatively easy morning or afternoon hike will find the trip to Lamoille Lake an ideal choice.

Hikers with plenty of extra stamina can accept the challenge of a steep climb on rocky trail over 10,400-foot Liberty Pass to Liberty Lake, deemed by many to be perhaps the most scenic backcountry lake in the entire state. Although the 7-mile round-trip distance doesn't appear to be that imposing for many hikers, a nearly 2100-foot climb at elevations over 10,000 feet make any trip to Liberty Lake and back a significant endeavor. Most visitors to the lake make the journey as an overnight backpack. Snow may cover portions of the trail in early season and thunderstorms are not uncommon at any time during the summer, two factors which may further compound the usual difficulties of reaching the lake.

DIRECTIONS TO TRAILHEAD Leave I-80 at the ELKO DOWNTOWN exit and head south for 0.8 mile to a left-hand turn onto Business 80. Proceed another 0.8 mile and turn right at 5th Street onto S.R. 228, observing signs for SPRING CREEK, LAMOILLE, JIGGS. Follow S.R. 228 out of downtown and across an overpass spanning the railroad tracks and the Humboldt River. Pass the Last Chance Road intersection on your left, which leads to the Ruby Mountains Ranger District office, and continue southeast to the intersection of S.R. 227 and S.R. 228, 7.3 miles from I-80.

Following a sign for LAMOILLE, SR227E, proceed straight ahead at the intersection, now on S.R. 227. At 7.5 miles from the junction, 0.5 mile before the small community of Lamoille, turn right onto F.R. 660, also referred to as the Lamoille Canyon Road National Scenic Byway.

Follow paved road across the National Forest boundary and into glacier-carved Lamoille Canyon. At 5 miles from S.R. 227, drive past the Camp Lamoille entrance and continue up Lamoille Canyon Road another 7.2 miles to the parking area at Roads End, where you'll find pit toilets, water, horse-loading facilities, and a picnic area. The Island Lake trailhead is at the north end of the loop.

DESCRIPTION Begin a moderate climb near the rushing waters of Lamoille Creek through open terrain carpeted with a bevy of wildflowers, including corn lily, cinquefoil, fireweed, larkspur, lupine, paintbrush, and yarrow. As you climb, don't forget to turn around and take in the stunning view down Lamoille Canyon, which seems to grow more and more impressive with each step. Just after crossing the creek on a wood bridge, a few limber pines begin to appear, continuing as your companions along the trail until the harsh conditions below Liberty Pass inhibit their survival.

About 0.33 mile from the first crossing of Lamoille Creek, the trail bends and crosses the east branch of the creek that drains the Dollar Lakes. You make two more stream crossings before a steeper climb leads to gentler terrain around Dollar Lakes. A ridge above the far shore forms a rugged backdrop to the meadow-rimmed and willow-lined lakes. Anglers will need to push on to Lamoille Lake, as there are no fish in the Dollar Lakes.

A gentle ascent leads away from Dollar Lakes 0.33 mile to the much larger Lamoille Lake, 1.9 miles from the trailhead. The lake is cradled in a deep gouge in the west edge of the upper part of Lamoille Canyon, where steep cirque walls give the lake basin a rugged and foreboding ambiance. The majority of hikers will more than likely be satisfied with Lamoille Lake as their destination, enjoying a picnic lunch, an afternoon nap, or simply appreciating the surroundings. The chilly waters provide brisk swimming for those robust souls willing to take the plunge, while anglers can ply the waters in search of brook trout.

Once past Lamoille Lake, the trail grows mercilessly steep for the duration of the 700-foot climb to Liberty Pass, following a winding ascent through acres and acres of boulders and rocks covering the slopes beneath towering and brooding cliffs. The lush vegetation of below is not to be found at these elevations; even the stunted limber pines eventually disappear amid the harsh and forbidding environs below the pass. Ice and snow cling to the crevices of the north-facing walls throughout the summer. Early-season hikers may have to deal with extensive snow patches covering the trail, which at times may require the use of an ice ax to successfully negotiate—make sure to check with the Forest Service regarding current conditions before your hike.

Upon reaching 10,400-foot Liberty Pass, you can rest in the knowledge that the remainder of your journey to Liberty Lake will be all downhill. The view

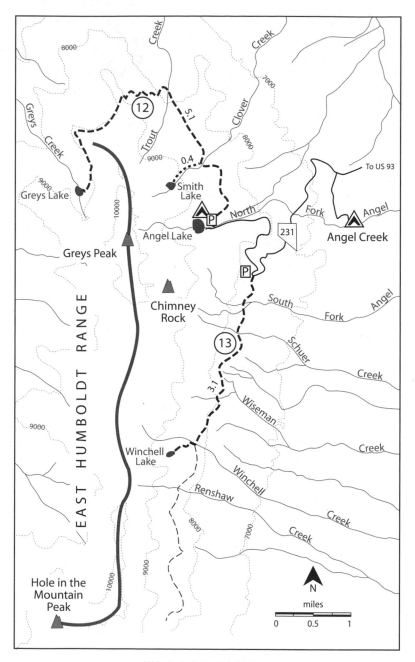

MAP 11 | East Humboldt Range

from the top is awesome, however, so don't rush off toward the lake before spending enough time to soak in the vista and catch your breath after the steep climb. Gazing south along the crest of the range, Lake and Wines Peaks (10,922 ft and 10,893 ft, respectively) will certainly grab your eye.

Cross the well-marked Ruby Mountains Wilderness near the pass and begin a stiff descent. Liberty Lake remains out of sight initially, tucked well back into a deep cirque near the head of the canyon. As you descend, the lake dramatically springs into view, reflecting vertical rock cliffs in the deep-blue waters. You arc high around the west edge of the cirque before dropping to a junction with a lateral trail, 0.6 mile from the pass. A short hike along the lateral leads to the southwest shore near the outlet.

Liberty is considered by many to be the quintessential mountain lake, a deep body of water cradled in an imposing glacier-carved cirque, perched high above the canyon of Kleckner Creek. For those hardy souls willing to expend the necessary energy to get here, the picturesque lake will satisfy even the most critical hiker. Extremely strong hikers and backpackers can extend the journey to Favre and Castle Lakes.

> **RUBY CREST TRAIL** The hike as described above follows the northernmost segment of the Ruby Crest National Recreation Trail, a 32-mile-long route spanning the heart of the range. Most backpackers take a minimum of four days to complete the journey from Harrison Pass to Lamoille Canyon, but the extraordinary scenery tempts travelers to spend even more time enjoying the Ruby Mountains Wilderness en route.

HIKE 12 | GREYS AND SMITH LAKES

Three picturesque lakes, one accessible by car, one accessible by trail, and one accessible by a short cross-country route lure travelers to the Greys Lake Trail and the East Humboldt Wilderness.

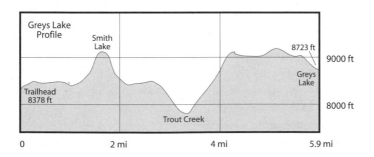

DISTANCE & ROUTE:	11 miles round trip
DIFFICULTY:	Moderate
SEASON:	Summer, fall
TRAILHEAD ACCESS:	All vehicles
WATER:	Available in creeks and lakes
GUIDEBOOK MAP:	11
USGS MAP:	Welcome
USFS MAP:	Ruby Mountains and East Humboldt Wildernesses

INTRODUCTION The Greys Lake Trail will take you from one scenic subalpine lake to another. The trip begins at Angel Lake, normally a hubbub of activity during the summer season, and ends at secluded Greys Lake. In between, hikers willing to make the 0.8-mile round-trip, off-trail journey have the opportunity to visit equally scenic Smith Lake as well. The mostly open terrain offers hikers plenty of expansive vistas of the rugged East Humboldt Range and the surrounding valleys. Bountiful displays of a wide variety of seasonal wildflowers grace both the trail and the lake basin.

DIRECTIONS TO TRAILHEAD From I-80, take the WEST WELLS exit and proceed briefly south on U.S. 93 to the junction with S.R. 231, signed ANGEL LAKE, immediately past the freeway. Follow paved road across Clover Valley and into the East Humboldt Range, entering Forest Service land at 7 miles, and passing the entrance to Angel Creek Campground 0.3 mile farther. At 9.7 miles from U.S. 93, in the middle of a hairpin turn, you pass by the Winchell Lake trailhead (see hike 13).

Continue on S.R. 231 toward Angel Lake. At 11.5 miles, turn right at a sign reading HUMBOLDT NATIONAL FOREST CAMPGROUND, ANGEL LAKE. Another set of signs direct you immediately to the right to the trailhead. If you continue up the highway to park in the Angel Lake Day Use Area, you will be subject to a fee.

DESCRIPTION Begin climbing up a hillside covered with shrubs, young aspens, and wildflowers to a switchback, where a use trail from the Angel Lake Campground intersects the main trail. Continue the ascent to the top of a low rise and pass through a steel gate. A fine view behind you reveals Angel Lake glistening below lofty Greys Peak and rugged Chimney Rock. A sea of sagebrush eventually replaces the verdant flora from below as you climb to the top of a ridge and enter the East Humboldt Wilderness.

From the ridge, begin a moderate descent, initially passing through dry and rocky terrain, where the tallest object is the occasional clump of blue lupine. Lush foliage returns as you drop farther into the canyon. At 1.25 miles, you reach the aspen-and-brush-choked banks of Clover Creek and easily cross the broad, shallow stream.

Clover Creek drains Smith Lake, which sits in a basin less than 0.5 mile off the trail. To reach the lake, follow the continuation of the Greys Lake Trail to a switchback, approximately 75 yards from the creek, which places you above the thick tangle of brush choking the brook. Leave the trail and head upstream, searching for the least brushy route across the steep slope above the north bank of the creek, which is not always an easy task. Head toward the top of the boulder-covered hillside at the lip of the lake basin, and then follow gentler terrain to the northeast shore of scenic Smith Lake.

Smith is a picturesque mountain lake tucked into a glacier-carved cirque basin, where talus slopes sprinkled with occasional limber pines rise up to a backdrop of rugged cliffs. Near the outlet, dense stands of limber pine shade a pair of infrequently used campsites. Anglers may enjoy fishing for cutthroat, golden, and American grayling trout, although much of the lakeshore harbors thick brush, making access a tad difficult in places.

Back on the main trail, a lengthy, moderate climb from Clover Creek takes you to the top of the ridge dividing the drainages of Clover and Trout Creeks. From there, a short traverse through lonely limber pines and scattered wildflowers leads to good views up the valley toward the East Humboldt crest above green-carpeted slopes. Reaching the edge of a broad, sweeping canyon, begin a moderately steep, 700-foot descent to aspen-lined Trout Creek, where an old sign nailed to an aspen reads POLE CANYON, ANGEL LAKE TRAIL, TROUT CREEK, ANGEL LAKE 3 MILES. Contrary to the given mileage, you are now 2.5 miles from Angel Lake.

After crossing Trout Creek with the aid of some downed aspens, follow a 1-mile-long, steep, switchbacking ascent past a large aspen grove to a windswept notch in a ridge, beneath the shadow of an unnamed peak sparsely forested with limber pines.

A mild descent leads to a small meadow, where the trail momentarily falters in the lush grasses. A well-placed sign, marked simply TRAIL, keeps hikers on track until distinct tread returns beyond the meadow. A short climb through limber pines, leads to the top of a ridge just below point 9210 on the USGS map.

Entering the deep canyon of Greys Creek, a 1-mile descent across the east wall is all that stands between you and the lakeshore. After a couple of switchbacks, you have an unobstructed view of Greys Lake, rimmed by steep cliffs on the south and west and by sweeping terrain to the east rising up toward the jagged summit of 10,674-foot Greys Peak. The creek tumbles down the canyon below, periodically cascading over low rock walls. After some more switchbacks, you arrive at the lakeshore, 5.1 miles from the trailhead.

Smith Lake, East Humboldt Range

Greys Lake is tucked into the head of a basin surrounded by high, rocky peaks, and green, sloping hillsides carpeted with wildflowers. Patches of snow cling to the cracks and crevices of the north-facing wall well into summer, lending an alpine feel to the basin. Greys Peak stands guard over the lake, nearly 2000 feet above the surface. Scattered limber pines dot the gentler slopes around the shoreline. Sparkling-clear water rushes down the inlet from a meadow-filled basin above the south shore. Greys Creek gently flows from the lake before cascading out of the cirque down a series of short steps and into the deep canyon. Anglers with the extra time might enjoy fishing for brook and cutthroat trout.

LUPINE (*LUPINUS*) One of the most common wildflowers seen along the trails in the East Humboldt Range is the lupine. A member of the pea family, lupines play an important part in the range's ecology, fixing nitrogen in the typically nitrogen-deficient sandy soils common to the drier slopes away from lakes and streams. Blue or purple blooms are most common, but some varieties of lupines may sport yellow or white flowers.

A mild hike along the eastern front of the East Humboldt Range delivers travelers to a picturesque mountain lake.

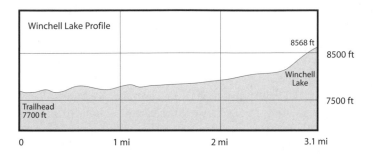

DISTANCE & ROUTE:	6.2 miles round trip
DIFFICULTY:	Moderate
SEASON:	Summer, fall
TRAILHEAD ACCESS:	All vehicles
WATER:	Available in creeks and Winchell Lake
GUIDEBOOK MAP:	11
USGS MAP:	Welcome, Humboldt Peak
USFS MAP:	Ruby Mountains and East Humboldt Wildernesses

INTRODUCTION   A short 3.1-mile hike with a modest elevation gain of slightly less than 1000 feet leads to a picturesque lake in the heart of the East Humboldt Wilderness. Several sparkling streams cross the trail en route to Winchell Lake, watering dense groves of aspen, lush pockets of foliage, and a nice variety of wildflowers. Excellent views of the eastern front of the East Humboldt Range occur from various points along the trail. Along with the basin holding Winchell Lake, the Wiseman Creek basin provides excellent scenery as well.

DIRECTIONS TO TRAILHEAD   From I-80, take the WEST WELLS exit and proceed briefly south on U.S. 93 to the junction with S.R. 231, signed ANGEL LAKE, immediately past the freeway. Follow paved road across Clover Valley and into the East Humboldt Range, entering Forest Service land at 7 miles, and passing the entrance to Angel Creek Campground 0.3 mile farther. At 9.7 miles from U.S. 93, in the middle of a hairpin turn, you pass by the Winchell Lake trailhead. Limited parking is available on the shoulder of the highway a short distance uphill from the trailhead.

DESCRIPTION The Winchell Lake Trail, not appearing on the USGS map, drops from the shoulder of the highway into a pocket of lush vegetation containing aspens and wildflowers. After hopping across a small, seasonal stream, the foliage parts enough to allow an expansive view of rugged Chimney Rock reigning over the verdant slopes of the East Humboldt Range and the distant ranchlands in the valley below. Continuing south, you follow the mildly undulating trail through lush vegetation alternating with sagebrush scrub. After entering the signed East Humboldt Wilderness, you proceed to a pair of crossings of South Fork Angel Creek. From the second crossing, almost the entire eastern flank of the East Humboldt Range is visible, from Chimney Rock in the north to Humboldt Peak in the south. Skirt a grove of aspens, pass through a gate in a barbed-wire fence to a grassy clearing, and continue to a crossing of Schoer Creek, 1.1 miles from the trailhead.

After crossing the brush-choked creek, wind around a hillside and descend to a seasonal stream. Beyond this swale, the grade of the trail moderates, as you traverse through pockets of aspens and clumps of tobacco brush past some beaver ponds well below the trail. The traverse lasts for about 0.75 mile, before a moderately steep descent takes you directly alongside one of the beaver ponds, where you get a first-hand glimpse into the activity of these busy rodents. Good tread leads away from the beaver pond to a somewhat confusing junction, where a path continues ahead, but the track bending uphill to the right marked by a cairn is the branch to follow.

Winchell Lake, East Humboldt Range

From the informal junction, head uphill to the west for about 75 yards before the trail bends south again on a traverse through more aspens and wildflowers. A short climb brings you into the scenic basin of Wiseman Creek, a horseshoe-shaped amphitheater of rock cliffs with a cascading ribbon of water spilling down the sheer face. As the path wanders across the floor of the picturesque basin, you expect to cross Wiseman Creek, but the stream adopts a subterranean course beneath marshland before reemerging in the canyon below.

Leaving Wiseman Creek basin, you ascend across a sagebrush-covered hillside and then follow the trail on an up-and-down course across slopes blanketed with tobacco brush. Finally, a short climb via a pair of switchbacks leads to a brief, gentle stroll to the shoreline of Winchell Lake.

Winchell Lake reposes in another dramatically scenic basin, where green, sloping hillsides rise up to steep and jagged peaks, 2000 feet above the lake. A trio of triangular-shaped spires above the inlet forms a dramatic backdrop to the dark waters of the lake. Lush meadows at the far end give way to dense foliage around the remainder of the shoreline. A smattering of limber pines dot the southwest slope in an otherwise open basin that hosts a diverse range of vegetation. Anglers should find the fishing to be good for cutthroat trout.

TOBACCO BRUSH (*CEANOTHUS VELUTINUS*) Also known as snowbrush for its clusters of white flowers, tobacco brush is one of the hardiest and most prolific shrubs in the Great Basin. Apparently named for its use by Native Americans as an alternative for tobacco, albeit a very poor one, tobacco brush does emit a characteristic odor that is more reminiscent of walnut, balsam, or cinnamon than of tobacco.

Assuredly, Lake Tahoe is northern Nevada's most scenic and popular natural feature. Not only is the Tahoe Sierra a backyard playground for Bay Area, Sacramento Valley, and northern Nevada residents, but the acclaimed region draws visitors from around the world as well. With plenty of state park and national forest lands surrounding the lake in both Nevada and California (including four designated wilderness areas), hikers, backpackers, mountain bikers, equestrians, and climbers alike have much backcountry to choose from for potential adventures. Some of the least visited of that backcountry is found on the Nevada side of Lake Tahoe within the Carson Range, a subrange of the Sierra Nevada.

Principally volcanic in composition, the Carson Range offers few of the granite peaks, rock-bound lakes, and dense forests that characterize the more popular California side of the Tahoe Sierra. However, hikers will find steep V-shaped canyons with tumbling streams, supreme views from summits and ridges, and a diverse sampling of plants within this vegetative transition zone between the flora of the Great Basin and the Sierra Nevada. In addition, the area boasts several trails offering a reasonable expectation of solitude, not exactly a common commodity on the California side of the lake.

Many of this section's trails are protected within the Mt. Rose Wilderness and Lake Tahoe Nevada State Park. The centerpiece of the Mt. Rose Wilderness is the namesake peak, at 10,776 feet Tahoe Basin's third highest summit. An extremely popular 5-mile trail leads "peakbaggers" to the top of the mountain and a superb 360-degree view. Lake Tahoe Nevada State Park offers picturesque lakes and exceptional Lake Tahoe views. With the exception of hike 14, paved highways provide easy access to all the trailheads.

FYI ■ Due to the generally porous volcanic soils found within the Carson Range, available water sources may be at a premium, especially on some sections of the Tahoe Rim Trail, which tend to follow dry ridges high above stream canyons. Packing extra water is a good idea for these sections of the TRT, especially as the hiking season progresses beyond midsummer.

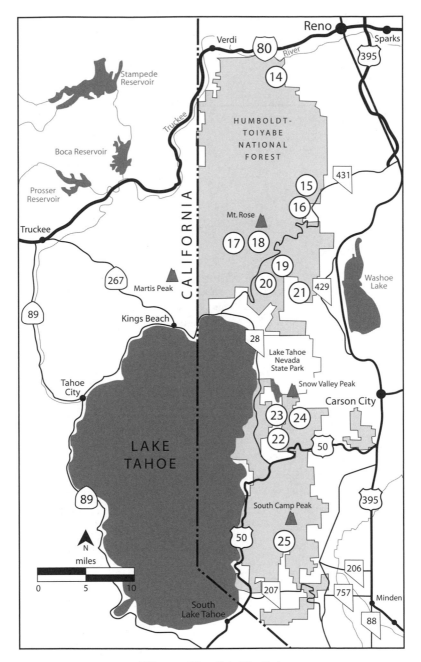

MAP 12 | Hikes of Lake Tahoe Region

Leave the suburbs to find an enchanting woodland and a delightful waterfall.

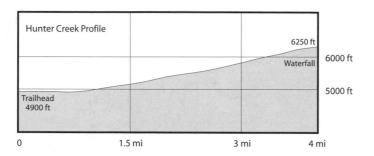

DISTANCE & ROUTE:	8 miles round trip
DIFFICULTY:	Moderate
SEASON:	Spring, summer, fall
TRAILHEAD ACCESS:	All vehicles (see below)
WATER:	Available in creek
GUIDEBOOK MAP:	13
USGS MAP:	Mt. Rose NW

INTRODUCTION   A relatively undiscovered hike on the very edge of Reno leads to some surprises, including a significant waterfall, lush meadows, and a forest grotto more reminiscent of a coastal hike than a foray into the eastern Sierra. Although access to the trail is uncertain, the first couple of miles are without shade, the tread is rough in parts, and rumors of rattlesnakes persist, numerous treasures await for those who persevere beyond the initial stretch of trail.

Access to the trail has been a looming concern ever since the 1980s, when rapid growth pushed the tentacles of development ever closer to the trailhead, restricting hikers from gaining entry to publicly owned national forest land. Ongoing negotiations between governmental agencies and private property owners may ultimately provide access to the Hunter Creek Trail and the nearby Steamboat Ditch Trail. One can hope that by the time this book is printed, a reasonable settlement will be negotiated and recreationists will have a permanent solution to this dilemma. A new trailhead has been proposed with approval of The Ridges at Hunter Creek subdivision, with the owner dedicating the land and Washoe County footing the bill for construction, which could

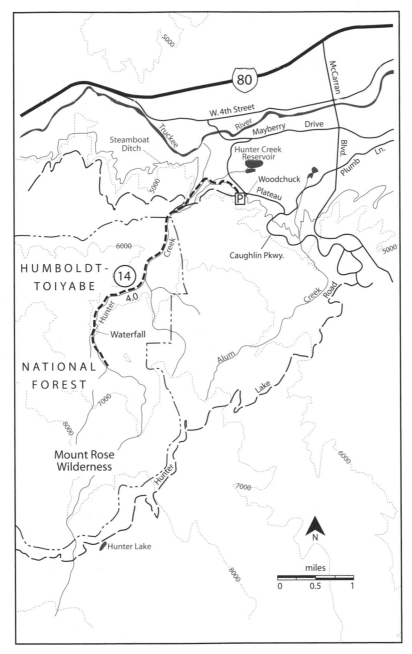

MAP 13 | Hunter Creek

possibly be completed in 2006. Check with the Carson Ranger District for an update on the current access to the trailhead.

Thanks to the low elevation, the trail is usually snow-free for six months out of the year, providing a rare early-season opportunity for hikers to shake off the cobwebs and stretch out the legs, as they wait for the Sierra snowpack to melt in the higher elevations. Spring is the best time to view the waterfall and witness the tumbling creek, while autumn can be equally enjoyable when brilliant colors adorn the canyon. Summers tend to be quite hot, so plan on an early start to help beat the heat.

Hardly the best example of trail-building and maintenance in the Mt. Rose Wilderness, the Hunter Creek Trail is rough, indistinct for stretches, poorly graded in spots, rocky in parts and severely eroded in others. Families with small children may find that keeping track of their progeny is a bit nerve wracking on the more precarious sections of trail, including a potentially dangerous crossing of the Steamboat Ditch a mile into the hike. Despite these drawbacks, the trip is well worth the effort for larger folk, rewarding diligent hikers with some unexpected delights.

DIRECTIONS TO TRAILHEAD   Until a permanent solution for access to the trailhead is in place, you may be able to reach the Hunter Lake Trail by following these directions: From the West McCarran Boulevard–West Plumb Lane–Caughlin Parkway intersection, turn west onto Caughlin Parkway and proceed for 1.2 miles to a right-hand turn onto Plateau Road. Continue another 0.6 mile on Plateau and then turn left at Woodchuck, immediately encountering an informal parking area on the right just past the Steamboat Ditch crossing. Since this access is far from certain, please respect the surrounding property owners and exercise the utmost care at the trailhead by reducing noise to a minimum, keeping pets under strict control, and removing every speck of trash or debris.

If the Woodchuck access is closed, you can reach the Steamboat Ditch and Hunter Lake Trails from the west via the Tom Cooke Trail, although the hike will be 1.25 miles longer. From West McCarran Boulevard, head west on West Fourth Street for 1.9 miles and turn left onto Woodland. After 0.1 mile turn right on White Fir, curve around toward a bridge over the Truckee River, and park on the shoulder near the bridge as space allows. The Tom Cooke Trail begins on the far side of the river. From the trailhead, a 0.5-mile climb takes you to a T-junction with the Steamboat Ditch Trail, where you should turn left and continue another 1.75 miles to join the description below at the bridge over Hunter Creek.

To access the proposed new trailhead, motorists will continue on Woodchuck (despite current signs falsely indicating the road as private property) to

The Ridges at Hunter Creek subdivision entrance and then make a right-hand turn into the parking area.

DESCRIPTION   Head west on the Steamboat Ditch Trail, which is tightly sand-wiched between the ditch immediately to your left and the fenced backyards of the upscale homes of Caughlin Ranch to your right. The ditch is lined with willows, while the hillside above is carpeted with typical sagebrush scrub and dotted with junipers. Proceed along the winding course of the ditch trail beneath power lines and past a fenced diversion structure. After 0.6 mile, you leave the subdivision homes behind and bend sharply southwest into the canyon of Hunter Creek. Walk upstream along the ditch trail to where the trail and ditch make bridged crossings over Hunter Creek, 1 mile from the parking area.

The crux of the route involves getting across the Steamboat Ditch to the in-formal paths on either side of Hunter Creek. On the left is a relatively wide but springy steel grate that spans the ditch, while on the right is a pair of slender rails. Although the grate appears to be the safest choice, you'll have to take at least one step on the narrow concrete wall directly above the ditch and the creek before reaching terra firma on the east bank of the creek. Although not partic-ularly difficult, the crossing of the ditch is not for the faint of heart either, at least when the ditch is flowing.

Once across the ditch, follow one of the boot-beaten paths upstream along either side of the creek. Although neither path provides particularly straight-forward travel, the path on the east bank seems slightly less difficult to negoti-ate than its western counterpart. After 0.3 mile, the trails merge with a jeep road at a ford of the creek. The new trailhead will ultimately provide direct access to this road well below the ford. If you followed the east bank of the creek, find the wood plank over the creek immediately upstream of the ford and make the crossing over to the west side.

Continue upstream on the jeep road for 0.2 mile to a sharp bend opposite a diversion structure on the far side of Hunter Creek. Proceed straight ahead, past a short path to a gauging station on the far side of the creek, to the start of single-track trail, where a brown vinyl marker heralds your passage into the Mt. Rose Wilderness.

Follow the primitive trail up the narrowing canyon on an undulating course across the steep, sagebrush-covered hillside, well above the level of the stream. Precipitous cliffs and periodic washouts plague the initial section. As you progress up the canyon, mountain-mahogany and scattered ponderosa pines appear, lending a subtle hint that a light forest awaits farther up the canyon. Along the creek, typical eastern Sierra riparian vegetation chokes the banks, in-cluding aspen, willow, cottonwood, and elderberry.

At 2 miles from the trailhead, you enter a forested grove that seems totally out of place this far east of the Sierra crest. A canopy of mixed conifers, including ponderosa pines, white firs, and incense-cedars, shades a lush understory of ferns and other shade-loving plants. Following the trail through the grove, you hop across a trio of tiny rivulets along the way. The path may be a bit hard to follow in this section, but more distinct trail appears as you leave the woodland and emerge into a small clearing.

Beyond the clearing, the trail descends to a crossing of the main branch of Hunter Creek, where a large tree has conveniently fallen across the stream, providing a relatively easy way over the tumbling creek. Nearby is a waterfall, which puts on quite a display during peak flow. At one time, a more distinct trail climbed the hillside above the waterfall to a large meadow. Unfortunately, this path fell into disuse after a recent forest fire and is now hard to follow. For those willing to make the short climb without aid of a decent trail, the meadow is quite picturesque. Past the meadow, the trail disappears completely and progress farther up the narrowing, brush-choked canyon is extremely difficult.

HUNTER CREEK The creek and nearby lake of the same name were named for John M. Hunter, who built and operated a toll bridge across the Truckee River at Hunters Crossing. Tracks of the Central Pacific Railroad reached Hunters Crossing in 1868. From there, regularly scheduled stagecoaches would transport passengers to Virginia City.

HIKE 15 | THOMAS CREEK

Enjoy tumbling streams, cool woodlands, and a picturesque meadow in Reno's backyard.

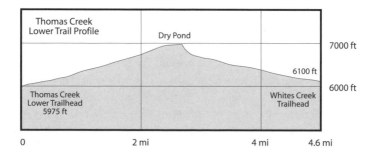

DISTANCE & ROUTE:	6.1 miles round trip (Lower Trail), 9.2 miles round trip (Upper Trail)
DIFFICULTY:	Moderate
SEASON:	Late spring, summer, fall
TRAILHEAD ACCESS:	All vehicles (Lower Trail), high-clearance vehicle recommended (Upper Trail)
WATER:	Available in creek
GUIDEBOOK MAP:	14
USGS MAP:	Mt. Rose NE, Mt. Rose NW

INTRODUCTION   A delightful and lonely canyon, minutes away from Reno, beckons the hiker to come and explore the pleasures of Thomas Creek canyon. With recent trail construction in the lower canyon and over the south ridge to a new trailhead in Whites Creek, travelers now have a pair of hiking options in this area.

With improved access from the newly built Thomas Creek trailhead parking area near the lower end of the canyon, hikers can stroll along the banks of Thomas Creek and then climb the Dry Pond Trail over the forested ridge separating the canyons of Thomas and Whites Creeks. Near the top of the ridge, a verdant meadow holding a seasonal pond (hence the name "Dry Pond") provides an excellent rest or lunch spot with a nice view of the volcanic summits of Mt. Rose and Slide Mountain. After a view-packed descent to the Whites Creek Trail, hiking downstream leads to the new Whites Creek trailhead. Without a second vehicle, a 1.5-mile walk along roads provides a return to the new Thomas Creek trailhead. Be aware that the Whites Creek trailhead is day-use only and fires are not permitted at either the Whites Creek or Thomas Creek trailheads. Lying wholly outside the Mt. Rose Wilderness, the lower trail is open to mountain bikes.

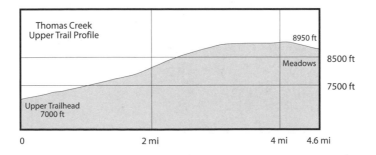

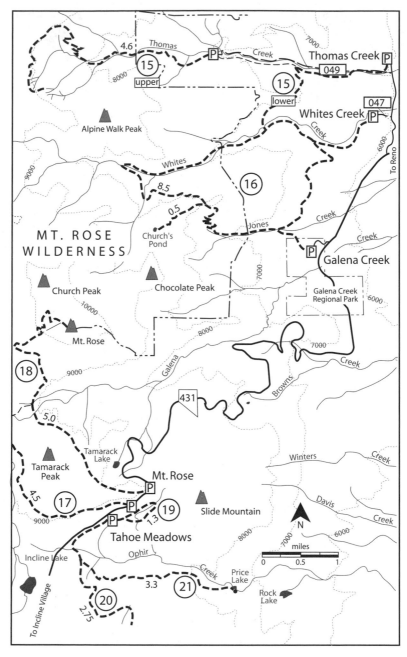

MAP 14 | Carson Range Northeast

A high-clearance vehicle is recommended for access to the upper trailhead. From there the trail follows a roaring stream into the Mt. Rose Wilderness (no bikes permitted) and up a broad ravine to a large verdant meadow encircled by a dense stand of pines. A dramatic rock formation below the meadow juts out of the head of the canyon to enhance the scenery. Springtime brings a plethora of mule ears and smaller wildflowers in the meadow, and the aspen filled canyon below is ablaze with color during autumn. While hundreds of hikers on a typical summer weekend may be struggling to reach the summit of nearby Mt. Rose, you may be alone or only one of the few on the upper part of the Thomas Creek Trail.

DIRECTIONS TO TRAILHEAD

LOWER TRAIL   From the Mt. Rose Highway, 2 miles west of U.S. 395, turn onto Timberline Drive and proceed north past newly built homes. At 0.5 mile from the highway is the signed turnoff on the left for the day-use Whites Creek trailhead (pit toilet, picnic tables, no fires). Shuttle parties should leave a vehicle at the Whites Creek trailhead. Proceed on Timberline Drive across bridges over Whites and then Thomas Creek. Immediately after the second bridge, continue past Thomas Creek Road and reach the paved Thomas Creek trailhead parking area on the left, 1.2 miles from the highway (pit toilet, picnic tables, no fires).

UPPER TRAIL   Follow the directions above to Thomas Creek Road. Turn left onto the rough dirt road (F.R. 049) and continue past a junction with private roads near the crest of a hill at 2.2 miles from Timberline Drive. Drop to a crossing of Thomas Creek at 2.3 miles, and then proceed to a closed gate at 2.6 miles. Park near the gate as space allows.

DESCRIPTION

LOWER TRAIL   From the Thomas Creek trailhead, head south on single-track trail for a short distance to Thomas Creek Road. Following trail signs, cross the road and walk upstream through an informal parking area between the road and Thomas Creek, and find the resumption of single-track trail on the west end. Proceed along the creek through mixed forest of Jeffrey pines, aspens, and cottonwoods. About 0.33 mile from the road, the trail leads to a trio of stream crossings over a braided section of Thomas Creek. Once you reach the south bank, continue on an upstream course through mixed forest. Dense riparian vegetation lines the creek, while the forested slopes farther away from the creek harbor tobacco brush, sagebrush, bitterbrush, and grasses. At 1.5 miles, you reach a three-way junction of the Dry Pond Trail on the left and the continuation of the Thomas Creek Trail straight ahead.

Turning left on the Dry Pond Trail, head away from Thomas Creek on a moderate climb through a forest of Jeffrey pine and mountain-mahogany, soon reaching the first in a series of switchbacks. An open area midway up the slope offers fine views of the upper canyon and, to the east, the Truckee Meadows and the Virginia Range beyond. Head back into the trees and continue the ascent. At the top of the ridge, you emerge out of the forest into an extensive, grass-covered meadow rimmed by sagebrush, 2.3 miles from the trailhead. Across the meadow is a fine view of Slide Mountain and Mt. Rose. Early in the season there may be water in Dry Pond near the far end of the meadow.

After the trail skirts the east side of the meadow, begin a switchbacking descent toward the floor of Whites Creek canyon. Along the way are good views of the canyon below, Slide Mountain and Mt. Rose to the south, and Washoe Valley to the southeast. At 3.3 miles you reach a boulder hop over Whites Creek and then immediately intersect the old roadbed that constitutes the route of the Whites Creek Trail.

Follow the road on a shady descent through Whites Creek canyon. After 0.8 mile, pass the three-way junction of the connector to Jones Creek on the right and continue downstream. Another 0.5 mile along the road brings you to the Whites Creek trailhead. Without shuttle arrangements you'll have to walk the Whites Creek Road for 0.8 mile, turn left (north) onto Timberline Drive, and walk another 0.7 mile to the Thomas Creek trailhead.

UPPER TRAIL   If you are without a high-clearance vehicle, or you prefer a longer hike, starting from the new Thomas Creek trailhead near the mouth of the canyon is possible. By doing so you will add an extra 2.7 miles onto the following distances. Follow the previous description to the junction with the Dry Pond Trail. Proceed straight ahead, heading upstream along Thomas Creek for another 1.2 miles to the upper trailhead near a closed gate.

From the gate, follow the closed road through aspen and pine past the edge of some privately owned meadows. Beyond the meadows, you eventually draw near to the creek and soon spy the wilderness signboard, which heralds your arrival at the old Forest Service trailhead, 1.25 miles from the gate.

From the trailhead, quickly ford or boulder-hop Thomas Creek and continue up the old road alongside the stream. Away from the lush riparian vegetation lining the creek, the trail cuts a path through alternating sections of sagebrush-covered hillsides and mixed forest composed of Jeffrey pines, white firs, and quaking aspens. After stepping across a pair of tributaries, single-track trail proceeds through tall grasses to a final crossing of Thomas Creek.

Beyond the crossing, you ascend a manzanita-covered hillside to a series of switchbacks that lead to the top of a subsidiary ridge across open slopes harboring rabbitbrush, sagebrush, mountain-mahogany, and an occasional Jeffrey pine. From there a long traverse curves across the head of the canyon to a large, green, sloping meadow bordered by dense forest behind an angular rock outcrop that stands guard over the upper canyon. Gazing south over the broad canyon below, you spy the meadow that is your ultimate destination, a mere mile away. Mt. Rose, third highest peak in the Tahoe Basin, is visible in the background, its dark grey slopes contrasting vividly with the green hillsides rimming Thomas Creek canyon.

Beyond the sloping meadow, the trail follows an ascending traverse that continues the route across the head of the canyon. Soon the open terrain is replaced by pine forest. At 4 miles from the trailhead, you intersect the unsigned, inconspicuous junction with an old, unmaintained trail that switchbacks over the crest of the Carson Range and descends to Davis Meadow. (If you choose to hike this route be aware that the path from the crest to the meadow has disappeared altogether and that the section of Mt. Rose Trail shown on the MT. ROSE NW map is extremely sketchy.) From the junction, head south to a small, spring-fed, wildflower-laden meadow. Continue for another 0.25 mile through aspens and pines to the fringe of the larger meadow you saw earlier across the canyon. Step across a narrow stream and proceed to the end of discernible trail near a copse of pines.

The upper meadow is a sea of green broken only in early season by thousands of blooming yellow mule ears. Along with the verdant meadow, the sweeping view down Thomas Creek canyon is ample reward for the 4.6-mile hike.

HIKE 16 | JONES CREEK–WHITES CREEK LOOP

A fine loop trip in the Carson Range visits a pair of canyons with tumbling streams and a serene pond with a backdrop of the eastern slopes of Mt. Rose.

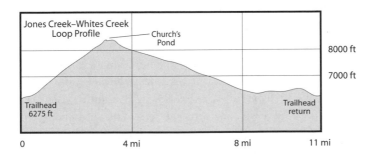

DISTANCE & ROUTE:	11 miles one way (including side trip to Church's Pond) in loop
DIFFICULTY:	Moderate
SEASON:	Summer, fall
TRAILHEAD ACCESS:	All vehicles
WATER:	Available in creeks
GUIDEBOOK MAP:	14
USGS MAP:	Washoe City, Mount Rose, Mt. Rose NW, Mt. Rose NE

INTRODUCTION This fine loop trip leads from lowland forest up to a sweeping panorama of the east flank of the Sierra, which includes the summits of Mt. Rose and Slide Mountain; views eastward of Washoe Valley, the Virginia Range, and the south Truckee Meadows are quite nice as well. Along with the vistas, the loop takes hikers alongside a pair of tumbling creeks that slice through steep canyons filled with quaking aspen, providing an outstanding display of fall color. Near the high point, a 0.5-mile lateral leads to Church's Pond, a diminutive pool nestled into a shallow basin below the looming hulk of Mt. Rose. Despite the close proximity to Reno, the trail sees less use than one might imagine.

DIRECTIONS TO TRAILHEAD Follow the Mt. Rose Highway (S.R. 431) to the north entrance into Galena Creek Regional Park. Proceed on the gravel road through the park, looping around to the trailhead parking area, 0.5 mile from the highway.

DESCRIPTION From the trailhead in Galena Creek Regional Park, walk along gravel and dirt roads through manzanita, sagebrush, and a light forest of Jeffrey pines to the Humboldt-Toiyabe National Forest boundary, heeding signs along the way for the Jones Creek Trail and Jones Creek–Whites Creek Loop. Continue to a crossing of Jones Creek, 0.75 mile from the trailhead, soon followed by the signed junction between the initial section of trail ascending Jones Creek to the left and your return route from Whites Creek on the right.

Veer to the left and follow the moderately steep path up the canyon of Jones Creek past the signed Mt. Rose Wilderness boundary, 1 mile from the trailhead. Jeffrey pine, manzanita and wildflowers are the dominant members of the plant community, as you continue the ascent to a series of long-legged switchbacks, which ultimately lead to the crest of the ridge separating the two canyons. The top of the ridge is blessed with unobstructed views of the surrounding terrain, including Mt. Rose and Slide Mountain to the west, and Little Washoe Lake and the Virginia Range to the east. At 2.7 miles from the trailhead, you encounter a three-way junction between the continuation of the loop trail towards Whites Creek on the right and the half-mile lateral to Church's Pond straight ahead.

To visit Church's Pond, continue the mild climb southwest along the ridge for 0.4 mile and then drop another 0.1 mile to the northeast shore. The shallow pond has no inlet or outlet, dependent solely on snowmelt for its existence. Gently sloping, sagebrush covered slopes that sweep up nearly 2500 feet toward the gray volcanic hulk of Mt. Rose flank the pond. Although an assortment of widely scattered pines and clumps of aspens line the far shore, most of the basin remains open.

Return to the three-way junction and begin a descent from the ridge crest toward Whites Creek, quickly noticing the change in vegetation from the southern exposure in Jones Creek canyon to the northern exposure of Whites Creek canyon. In contrast to the drier terrain found previously, aspens, grasses, and an assortment of wildflowers carpet the upper slopes, while dense stands of white firs dominate the hillsides near the bottom of the canyon. The path winds down the hillside to a bridged crossing of a tributary stream, 1 mile from the junction. After a very brief climb away from the creek, you resume the descent and, after 0.5 mile, reach the floor of the canyon and an unbridged crossing of the main channel of Whites Creek.

Once across Whites Creek, you follow sandy trail on a moderate descent through the canyon. The lush vegetation of the opposite side is now replaced by ceanothus, sagebrush, and Jeffrey pine. You follow the gurgling creek for 1.5 miles to the final crossing of Whites Creek, a potentially difficult task during high water.

Across the stream, the trail merges into an old road that follows Whites Creek downstream to the new Whites Creek trailhead. A short distance beyond the creek, you exit the Mt. Rose Wilderness at the signed boundary. Another mile of easy descent along the old road leads to a junction with a single-track trail to your right, 6.8 miles from the trailhead. The junction is marked by a 4 × 4 post but can be easily missed if you're not paying attention.

Leave the old roadbed and follow the trail away from the junction on a moderate climb through a dense stand of Jeffrey pines to a saddle, where the pines thin and sagebrush, grasses, and wildflowers thrive. Once again, Mt. Rose, Slide Mountain, and a part of Washoe Valley spring into view. From the saddle, make an angling, sidehill traverse through open sagebrush down into the next canyon, where Jeffrey pines reappear. Climb out of the canyon and wander along a minor ridge for a while, before beginning the long gradual descent towards Jones Creek. Following the descent, a short, mildly rising climb closes the loop at the junction with the Jones Creek Trail. From there, turn left and retrace your steps 0.75 mile to the parking lot.

JEFFREY PINE (*PINUS JEFFREYI*) The Jeffrey pine is the most abundant conifer on the east side of the Carson Range between 5000 and 8000 feet. Preferring dry and open slopes, this three-needled pine has reddish-brown bark that emits a vanilla-like aroma when scratched. Jeffrey pines are often confused with ponderosa pines, a similar pine with three needles, but which can be distinguished from Jeffrey pine by their smaller cones.

HIKE 17 | RELAY PEAK

A nearly 5-mile hike to the highest point along the Tahoe Rim Trail reveals stunning views of Lake Tahoe and the surrounding terrain.

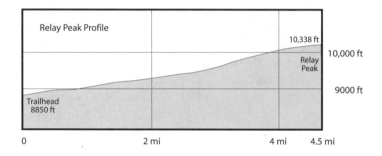

DISTANCE & ROUTE:	9 miles round trip	
DIFFICULTY:	Moderate	
SEASON:	Summer, fall	
TRAILHEAD ACCESS:	All vehicles	
WATER:	Available in Third Creek	
GUIDEBOOK MAP:	15	
USGS MAP:	Mount Rose	

INTRODUCTION Excellent views of the greater Lake Tahoe region are common along this section of the Tahoe Rim Trail, providing more than adequate rewards for hikers who may not want to travel the slightly longer route to the summit of nearby Mt. Rose for similar views. For most of the journey, this trip shares the path with the old route of the extremely popular Mt. Rose Trail, following the course of a gravel service road to a junction near the base of Relay Ridge. Beyond the old Mt. Rose junction, near a pleasant, meadow-rimmed pond, the road continues a short distance to the top of the ridge, where a newly

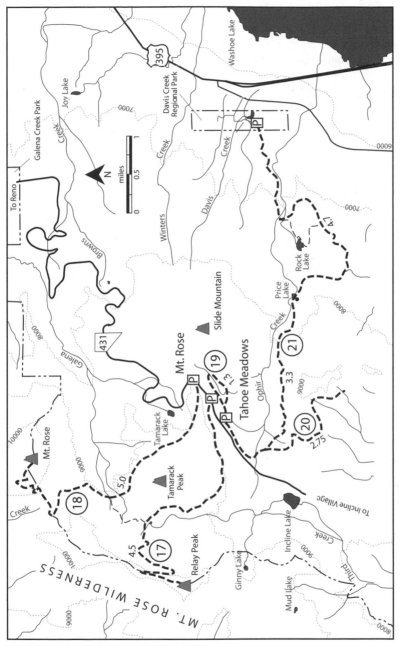

MAP 15 | Carson Range, Hikes 17–21

constructed single-track section of the Tahoe Rim Trail takes over. From there a 0.6-mile climb leads to fine views atop the summit of Relay Peak of the Lake Tahoe basin and the surrounding terrain. Keep a watchful eye for mountain bikers while hiking along the road.

FUTURE ROUTE   Additional plans for the Tahoe Rim Trail may one day provide an alternate route to Relay Peak. As described in hike 18, a section of the TRT was recently rerouted to follow the new Mt. Rose Trail 3.6 miles to a 9731-foot saddle, 0.8 mile southwest of Mt. Rose's summit. From there a new section of the TRT would be constructed over Mt. Houghton and then along Relay Ridge to a connection with existing single-track trail south of the communication towers. Contact the Tahoe Rim Trail Association at (775) 298-0012 for updates or volunteer opportunities.

DIRECTIONS TO TRAILHEAD   Drive on S.R. 431, also known as the Mt. Rose Highway, to the old Mt. Rose trailhead, 0.3 mile southwest of the Mt. Rose Highway summit, near a concrete-block telephone building and a closed gate across a gravel access road. Park along the north shoulder of S.R. 431 as space allows.

DESCRIPTION   Make a steady ascent along the closed road, through stands of lodgepole pine alternating with sagebrush-covered slopes adorned with mule ears, lupine, pennyroyal, paintbrush, penstemon, and balsamroot. The open slopes allow increasingly fine views southwest of Lake Tahoe and the snow-clad peaks of Desolation Wilderness above the southwest shore. Below is the verdant swath of subalpine Tahoe Meadows, where Ophir Creek sinuously courses through the lush, deep-green meadowlands before tumbling steeply down a canyon toward a union with Washoe Lake. As you continue farther on the roadbed, Incline Lake pops into view just west of the highway.

Bending northwest around the shoulder of Tamarack Peak and above Third Creek canyon, you enter a thicker lodgepole pine forest and say farewell to the lake views, at least for the moment. You continue the climb up the road nearing the head of Third Creek to a small pond encircled by meadow, known locally as "Snow Pond," for the usual lingering snow bank, or "Frog Pond," for the resident Pacific tree frogs. The damp environment around the pond harbors a fine variety of wildflowers, including shooting star, elephantshead, buttercup, and arnica. Just past the pond, 2.5 miles from the highway, you reach a junction, where the old Mt. Rose Trail splits off to the right (north).

From the junction, remain on the access road. Soon the road passes over a culvert carrying the nascent waters of spring-fed Third Creek. Ahead is Relay Ridge with an array of communication towers and antennas lining the crest. The grade of the road increases as you zigzag toward the top, passing the base of an old tramway used for the construction and service of the equipment on the ridge. After a final switchback, an additional 0.5-mile climb takes you to the top of Relay Ridge, where a 360-degree view awaits. As you crest the ridge, several features spring into sight that were previously hidden from view. The California community of Truckee, along with Donner Lake and peaks around Donner Summit lie to the west. To the northwest, in the near distance, are Boca, Stampede, and Prosser Reservoirs. Farther afield, the dark ramparts of Sierra Buttes and the volcanic slopes of distant Lassen Peak tower over the surrounding terrain. On crystal-clear days, you may even be able to make out the profile of snow-capped Mt. Shasta, nearly 200 miles away.

Once at the ridge, turn south and follow a newly constructed, single-track section of the Tahoe Rim Trail into the Mt. Rose Wilderness (no bikes). Climb along the crest toward Relay Peak past wind-sculpted whitebark pines for 0.6 mile to the 10,338-foot summit, 4.5 miles from the Mt. Rose Summit trailhead. This lofty aerie is the highest point along the 164-mile Tahoe Rim Trail. The view of Lake Tahoe and the surrounding terrain is quite stunning and geographical landmarks are nearly too numerous to count. Unfortunately, the scenic panorama includes charred acreage to the northwest from the extensive 2001 Martis Peak Fire.

GRAY LAKE Strong hikers can continue another 3 miles from Relay Peak to serene Gray Lake by descending from Relay Peak on the TRT to switchbacks on the west side of the ridge. Approaching Slab Cliffs, cross over to the east side of the ridge, with good views of Ginny Lake, Tahoe Meadows, and Slide Mountain. A mild traverse around Slab Cliffs leads past excellent views of Lake Tahoe, Incline Village, and Diamond Peak Ski Area. After more switchbacks, proceed above aptly named Mud Lake to a junction near a saddle. Leave the TRT, following a section of the old Western States Trail on a stiff descent past small pockets of flower-filled meadow alternating with stands of lodgepole pine toward meadow-rimmed Gray Lake.

A popular climb to the summit of the Tahoe Basin's third highest peak— the highest summit accessible by maintained trail—rewards those who reach the top with grand views in all directions.

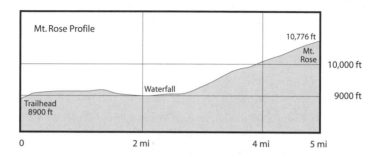

DISTANCE & ROUTE:	10 miles round trip
DIFFICULTY:	Strenuous
SEASON:	Summer, fall
TRAILHEAD ACCESS:	All vehicles
WATER:	Available in Galena Creek
GUIDEBOOK MAP:	15
USGS MAP:	Mount Rose

INTRODUCTION   The path to the summit of Mt. Rose, the Tahoe Basin's third highest peak, is certainly the most popular trail in northern Nevada. On a typical weekend day during the summer, you're likely to see a parking lot full of cars and a corresponding number of hikers strung out along the trail. The attractions of this trip are many despite the potential for crowds, including a grand view of the Lake Tahoe basin and Reno-Sparks from the summit, along with a delightful display of wildflowers near Galena Creek. Leisurely hikers or families with small children may find the trip to Galena Creek a more reasonable goal than a full-fledged assault on the summit.

DIRECTIONS TO TRAILHEAD   The new Mt. Rose trailhead was completed during the summer of 2005. Hikers can now park their vehicles in a parking lot adjacent to Mt. Rose Highway Summit (8900 ft.) on S.R. 431.

DESCRIPTION   From the parking lot at Mt. Rose Highway Summit, follow new trail on an ascending traverse above the Mt. Rose Highway across a sagebrush-and-grass-covered hillside dotted with boulders and sprinkled with lodgepole and whitebark pines. Mule ears and lupines add dashes of purple and yellow to the slopes in early to midsummer. As you continue the climb, the pines become even more widely scattered, allowing fine views of Lake Tahoe, rimmed on the far shore by towering peaks, and of the upper end of verdant Tahoe Meadows. Eventually the trail veers away from the highway and enters light forest on the way toward a saddle between Tamarack Peak on your left and Peak 9201 on your right.

Beyond the saddle the gently rising trail slices across the eastern flank of Tamarack Peak, where mountain hemlocks begin to intermix with the pines. Gaps in the trees permit periodic glimpses of meadow-rimmed Tamarack Lake 400 feet below, and the reddish-gray, volcanic summit of Mt. Rose looming above the treetops.

Near the 1.5-mile mark the climbing ends and you begin a mild descent across steep slopes on the northeast side of Tamarack Peak. After crossing a seasonal creek, proceed across a forested bench before continuing the descent across another steep section of hillside, where the pleasant sound of running water propels you onward. Reach the floor of Galena Creek canyon at 2.3 miles from the trailhead and stand below a scenic waterfall, where multiple ribbons of water spill picturesquely down dark rock walls. Downstream from the fall, an expansive meadow provides a fine foreground view for the massive hulk of Mt. Rose.

Away from the fall you cross the creek and skirt the base of a rock-strewn hill opposite the willow- and flower-lined creek and lush meadows to the right. A moderate climb leads away from the creek and meadows and winds uphill to the crossing of a small tributary stream. A short walk from the stream brings you to a junction with the old section of the Mt. Rose Trail, 2.5 miles from the trailhead. Turn right at the junction and descend to a crossing of Galena Creek, where an uninterrupted climb to the summit on single-track trail begins.

A stunning display of brilliant wildflowers lines the next section of trail, including monkey flower, lupine, paintbrush, angelica, larkspur, and mule ears. Leaving the luxuriant vegetation behind, you follow a moderate ascent across a sagebrush-covered hillside interspersed with more flowers into the narrow and steep gorge of a seasonal stream. Heading moderately steeply up this cleft, you cross and then recross the usually dry streambed, pass the wilderness boundary, and reach a junction with the trail to Bronco Creek at a saddle in the ridge crest, 3.6 miles from the trailhead.

Turn right at the junction and follow the southeast ridge of Mt. Rose through scattered whitebark pines, heading toward the reddish-gray, volcanic rock summit. Where the ridge meets the bulk of the mountain, the trail becomes steeper and follows a series of switchbacks to ascend the west slope of the peak. Beyond the switchbacks you make an ascending traverse around the northwest side of the mountain, leaving the stunted pines behind. From here to the summit, only compact, low-growing alpine plants survive on the rocky, windswept slopes. Another series of switchbacks leads you over rocky terrain to the summit ridge, where one last stretch of climbing takes you to the top.

A number of man-made improvements are found near the summit, including a climbing register and an assortment of rock walls built for protection from the prevailing winds that gust over the mountaintop. If you happen to arrive during calm conditions, count your blessings, as the blustery Mt. Rose winds are both frequent and notorious. The views are quite impressive in every direction. On extremely clear days, you may be able to see all the way past Lassen Peak to snow-capped Mt. Shasta in the distant northwest. On normal days, the pinnacled Sierra Buttes are visible in the same general direction above and beyond the Truckee River reservoirs of Prosser, Boca, and Stampede. Lake Tahoe is the preeminent gem, surrounded on all sides by the peaks and ridges that form the Tahoe Basin. Some of the more prominent peaks include Pyramid Peak and Mt. Tallac in Desolation Wilderness above the southwest shore, and Jobs Peak, Jobs Sister, and Freel Peak in the Carson Range above the southeast shore. The more developed Truckee Meadows, harboring Reno and Sparks, are clearly visible from the summit as well.

GALENA CREEK   Many years ago the Galena Creek area downstream from the Mt. Rose Trail was in jeopardy of being developed as a destination resort. The beautiful meadows and stately lodgepole pines would have been replaced with condominiums, golf courses, a ski area, and a casino. Thankfully, a land exchange orchestrated by members of Nevada's congressional delegation kept the area in a pristine state.

HIKE 19 | TAHOE MEADOWS NATURE TRAIL

A short wheelchair-accessible trail puts the highlights of Tahoe Meadows within easy reach of all who appreciate the outdoors.

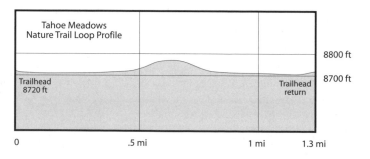

DISTANCE & ROUTE:	1.3 miles one way in loop
DIFFICULTY:	Easy
SEASON:	Summer, fall
TRAILHEAD ACCESS:	All vehicles
WATER:	Available at trailhead
GUIDEBOOK MAP:	15
USGS MAP:	Mount Rose

INTRODUCTION The Tahoe Meadows Whole Access Trail is a wheelchair-accessible trail providing a fine opportunity to experience a part of subalpine Tahoe Meadows. Not only will the wheelchair-bound enjoy this loop, but families with small children will appreciate the wide, gently graded, 1.3-mile-long path as well. The trail loops around the northeast finger of 8700-foot Tahoe Meadows, exposing hikers to a lush meadowland environment full of plants, flowers, and trickling streams, bordered by a light forest of lodgepole pines. Slide Mountain and Mt. Rose provide a fine backdrop to the scenery-rich meadows.

DIRECTIONS TO TRAILHEAD Drive on the Mt. Rose Highway (S.R. 431) to the Tahoe Meadows trailhead parking area, 0.8 mile southwest of Mt. Rose Summit. From Incline Village, the trailhead is 7.7 miles from the junction between S.R. 431 and S.R. 28.

DESCRIPTION From the parking lot, follow a wide, rock-lined path for 0.1 mile to a junction. Pedestrians are encouraged to turn right at the junction, following a counter-clockwise circuit on a loop around the northeast finger of Tahoe Meadows. Proceed across a long wooden bridge over a marshy stretch of ground to the far edge of the meadow and then veer northeast along the fringe, passing in and out of shady stands of lodgepole pine. Around the east edge of the meadow, a series of short wooden bridges take you across marshy areas and gurgling tributaries of Ophir Creek. As the loop bends around toward the trailhead, a short lateral leads onto a hummock of granite, where you have a fine view of the meadow from a slightly elevated vantage. Back on the main trail, follow the course of an abandoned road along the north fringe of the meadow to the junction. From here, make the easy climb back up to the parking lot.

Grand vistas of Lake Tahoe and Washoe Valley seem endless while hiking along this section of the Tahoe Rim Trail.

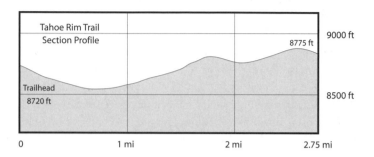

DISTANCE & ROUTE:	5.5 miles round trip to Incline Creek	
DIFFICULTY:	Moderate	
SEASON:	Summer, fall	
TRAILHEAD ACCESS:	All vehicles	
WATER:	Trailhead, Ophir and Incline Creeks	
GUIDEBOOK MAP:	15	
USGS MAP:	Mount Rose	

INTRODUCTION   The section of the Tahoe Rim Trail southbound from Tahoe Meadows is of fairly recent origin. Once you've taken in some of the excellent views from the trail, you can't help but be surprised that this trail didn't exist until recently. Many of the finest vistas of Lake Tahoe along the 164-mile trail are found on the Nevada side, some of which occur within the first few miles of this trip. Except for a short climb from Tahoe Meadows necessary to gain the north-south trending ridge that forms the northeastern rim of the Tahoe Basin, the gently graded trail provides pleasant hiking. Once you gain the ridge, impressive views of Lake Tahoe are a nearly constant companion—be sure to pack your camera. Farther on, where the Tahoe Rim Trail crosses over to the east side of the ridge, the vistas expand toward Washoe Lake and Washoe Valley and the desert peaks of the Virginia Range beyond.

Although this trip follows a multiple-use section of the Tahoe Rim Trail, mountain bikes are only allowed to use the trail on even days of the month, making the odd days more desirable for hikers.

DIRECTIONS TO TRAILHEAD   Drive on the Mt. Rose Highway (S.R. 431) to the Tahoe Meadows trailhead parking area, 0.8 mile southwest of Mt. Rose Summit. From Incline Village, the trailhead is 7.7 miles from the junction between S.R. 431 and S.R. 28.

DESCRIPTION   Leave the parking area and follow the Tahoe Rim Trail along the edge of subalpine Tahoe Meadows. Along the way, a couple of tiny seeps trickle across the path as you stroll past thickets of willow, bordered with rich meadow grass and an assortment of wildflowers, including lupine, paintbrush, senecio, and corn lily. After 0.5 mile of paralleling the Mt. Rose Highway, the TRT veers south at an informal junction with a use trail heading toward the shoulder of the highway. From the junction, the trail angles across damp meadowlands to a crossing of the main branch of Ophir Creek. The verdant landscape of Tahoe Meadows, bisected by the sinuous course of the creek, will certainly entice further exploration, especially at the height of wildflower season when bountiful numbers of buttercup, shooting star, penstemon, elephantshead, marsh marigold, paintbrush, and large-leaved avens carpet the ground. Hop over the meandering brook and continue across the meadows briefly before entering lodgepole pine forest. Soon, at 0.8 mile from the trailhead, you encounter a well-signed junction between the Ophir Creek Trail (see hike 21) and the continuation of your route along the TRT.

Continue on the mildly graded TRT through lodgepole and western white pines, which part just enough on occasion to grant glimpses of the hulks of Mt. Rose to the north and Slide Mountain to the northeast. Soon, a moderate climb leads you up a lightly forested hillside to periodic partial lake views. Near the top, you cross an old twin-tracked jeep road and begin a traverse of the west side of a north-south trending ridge, with even better views of Lake Tahoe and the mountains above the west shore. You continue the pleasant traverse through widely scattered conifers, mostly lodgepole and western white pines, with a smattering of mountain hemlock and an occasional white fir. The Lake Tahoe vista seems to improve with every step along this section of the TRT.

Eventually the Tahoe Rim Trail bends east and you arc around the head of a canyon to a thin ribbon of water trickling across the trail, a tributary of Incline Creek, lined with willows, young aspens, and wildflowers. The trail veers south again and, at 2.75 miles from the trailhead, you reach a second branch of Incline Creek. These two streams provide the last reliable water along the TRT for several miles, making them a good turnaround point for many hikers.

For those who wish to hike farther, the mildly graded TRT continues a southbound course along the eastern rim of the Tahoe Basin for several more miles.

From the west side of the ridge there are excellent views of the lake and the surrounding mountains. Where the trail travels on the east side of the ridge, Washoe Lake, Washoe Valley, and the Virginia Range are in view. The most difficult decision hikers may face on this trip is deciding when and where to turn around.

BIRDS You're sure to see several species of birds along this section of the Tahoe Rim Trail. Watch for Clark's nutcrackers searching for seeds from the whitebark pines and chickadees darting from the branches of the lodgepole pines. If you're very fortunate, you just might happen to spy a brightly colored mountain bluebird, Nevada's state bird.

HIKE 21 | OPHIR CREEK TRAIL

The Ophir Creek Trail provides hikers the opportunity to experience a subalpine meadow, a tumbling creek, a picturesque lake, and a glimpse of a significant natural catastrophe.

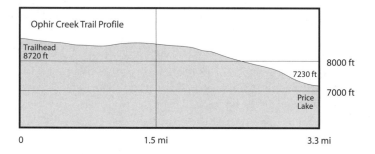

Ophir Creek Trail Profile
Trailhead 8720 ft
8000 ft
7230 ft
7000 ft
Price Lake

0   1.5 mi   3.3 mi

DISTANCE & ROUTE:	6.6 miles round trip to Price Lake
DIFFICULTY:	Moderate
SEASON:	Summer, fall
TRAILHEAD ACCESS:	All vehicles
WATER:	Trailhead, Ophir Creek
GUIDEBOOK MAP:	15
USGS MAP:	Mount Rose, Washoe

INTRODUCTION The Ophir Creek Trail exposes hikers to a diversity of landscapes, from the verdant, flower-filled, subalpine environment of Tahoe Meadows to the shoreline of Price Lake, reposing serenely beneath the ominous face of appropriately named Slide Mountain. In between, there are stands of mixed forest, pockets of lush meadows, and stretches of riparian communities alongside tumbling Ophir Creek. At Price Lake, hikers can witness the effects of a tremendous 1983 landslide, when a part of Slide Mountain broke loose and slid down Ophir Creek canyon, completely destroying what was known as Lower Price Lake, and substantially reducing the size of Upper Price Lake.

Although most hikers starting in Tahoe Meadows are quite content to go no farther than Price Lake, the Ophir Creek Trail does continue another 4.7 miles to a trailhead in Davis Creek Regional Park, located on the western edge of Washoe Valley and accessed from S.R. 429. With shuttle arrangements between the Tahoe Meadows and Davis Creek Park trailheads, this extension permits additional glimpses into the course of the slide's destruction on the way down Ophir Creek canyon.

DIRECTIONS TO TRAILHEAD Drive on the Mt. Rose Highway (S.R. 431) to the Tahoe Meadows trailhead parking area, 0.8 mile southwest of Mt. Rose Summit. From Incline Village, the trailhead is 7.7 miles from the junction between S.R. 431 and S.R. 28.

DESCRIPTION Leave the parking area and follow the Tahoe Rim Trail along the edge of subalpine Tahoe Meadows. Along the way, a couple of tiny seeps trickle across the path, as you stroll past thickets of willow, bordered with rich meadow grass and an assortment of wildflowers, including lupine, paintbrush, senecio, and corn lily. After 0.5 mile of paralleling the Mt. Rose Highway, the TRT veers south at an informal junction with a use trail heading toward the shoulder of the highway. From the junction, angle across damp meadowlands to a crossing of the main branch of Ophir Creek. The verdant landscape of Tahoe Meadows, bisected by the sinuous course of the creek, will certainly entice further exploration, especially at the height of wildflower season when bountiful numbers of buttercup, shooting star, penstemon, elephantshead, marsh marigold, paintbrush, and large-leaved avens carpet the ground. Hop over the meandering brook and continue across the meadows briefly before entering lodgepole pine forest. Soon, at 0.8 mile from the trailhead, you encounter a well-signed junction between the Tahoe Rim Trail (see hike 20) and the continuation of your route along the Ophir Creek Trail.

Veer left (southeast) at the junction, leaving the TRT to follow the gently descending Ophir Creek Trail through a forest of lodgepole pines. Proceed past a twin-tracked jeep road, skirt a flower-lined meadow, and then begin a steep decline, as Ophir Creek begins a steeper tumble toward Washoe Valley below. Farther down the canyon, stands of mixed forest, composed of mountain hemlock, lodgepole pine, and western white pine, alternate with pockets of

Upper Price Lake with Slide Mountain, Carson Range

flower-bedecked meadow. Corresponding to a further drop in elevation, Jeffrey pines and red and white firs join the mix farther down the canyon. Willows, alders, and quaking aspens line Ophir Creek, as well as several of the tributaries that the trail crosses en route to a signed junction with a steep lateral to Price Lake, 2.8 miles from the trailhead.

Veer left at the junction and follow the 0.5-mile lateral to Price Lake on a steep decline through mixed forest. At 3.3 miles, you reach the shore of what is now known as Price Lake, overshadowed by the looming, grayish hulk of Slide Mountain.

After enjoying the surroundings of Price Lake, round-trip hikers must make the 3.3-mile, 1600-foot climb back to the Tahoe Meadows trailhead. With arrangements for pickup at Davis Creek Park on the western fringe of Washoe Valley, continuing on the Ophir Creek Trail provides an alternative to retracing your steps and climbing back to the Tahoe Meadows trailhead. From Price Lake, head downstream following a faint path adjacent to the diversion ditch south of the outlet to the dirt track of Little Valley Road. Turn right and climb on the road a short distance to a signed junction with the single-track Ophir Creek Trail headed west. Continue on the road, traversing south for 0.5 mile to a second signed junction, where single-track trail veers left. From here, follow the trail over a sandy ridge and down a steep, winding descent through mixed forest that takes you past a junction with a lateral to Rock Lake and then arcs around a hillside to a crossing of Ophir Creek. From the creek, continue the stiff descent 1.6 miles to the trailhead in Davis Creek Park.

THE LANDSLIDE OF 1983 In late spring of 1983 a very sizeable chunk of appropriately named Slide Mountain, composed of meltwater-saturated soils, broke loose and slid into Lower Price Lake. The displaced water created a semi-fluid mass of debris that hurtled down Ophir Creek canyon in a matter of seconds, wreaking all sorts of havoc and destruction along the way. Tons of debris spilled across the plain of Washoe Valley, killing one person, destroying homes and property, and temporarily closing U.S. 395. As a result of the slide, Lower Price Lake completely disappeared and Upper Price Lake was reduced in size. After three decades of recovery, the area immediately around Price Lake reveals few hints of the prior destruction. However, a glance toward the bare southeast slopes of Slide Mountain hints that perhaps more slides are possible at some unknown time in the future.

HIKE 22 | SPOONER LAKE

An easy stroll around a scenic lake offers a surprisingly wide range of habitats.

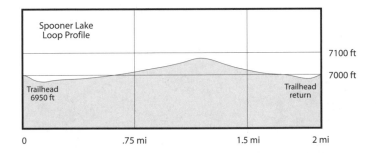

DISTANCE & ROUTE:	2 miles one way in loop
DIFFICULTY:	Easy
SEASON:	Summer, fall
TRAILHEAD ACCESS:	All vehicles
WATER:	Available at trailhead
GUIDEBOOK MAP:	16
USGS MAP:	Glenbrook

INTRODUCTION A gently graded 1.6-mile path encircles Spooner Lake, providing hikers of all ages a fine opportunity to enjoy the picturesque surroundings. Interpretive displays with information on the natural and human history of the area and park benches scattered around the lakeshore enhance the

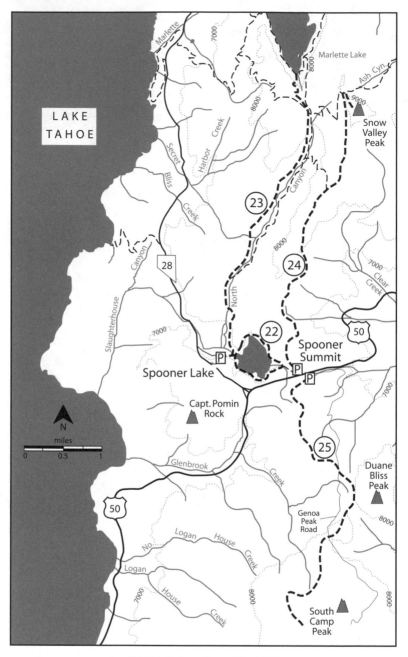

MAP 16 | Carson Range, Hikes 22–25

experience. Naturalists will appreciate the diversity found along the trail, including Jeffrey pine forest, aspen groves, flower-filled meadows, and sagebrush scrub. A wide range of wildlife may be seen as well, particularly a number of bird species, including hawks, warblers, thrushes, chickadees, and nuthatches. The area boasts many fine locations for a picnic lunch, and hot summer days will entice swimmers into the cool waters of the lake.

The loop trail around Spooner Lake is open to pedestrians only (equestrians may use the north side of the Spooner Lake Trail between North Canyon Road and the lateral to the Tahoe Rim Trail). Pets must be leashed. Catch-and-release fishing is allowed with use of barbless artificial lures only. A $6 fee (in 2005) is charged for entry into the park.

DIRECTIONS TO TRAILHEAD   Drive on S.R. 28 to the entrance into the Spooner Lake section of Lake Tahoe Nevada State Park, 1 mile northwest of the junction with U.S. 50. Follow the access road to the picnic area parking lot.

DESCRIPTION   A short walk from the parking lot leads to a signed, four-way junction. Following directions to Spooner Lake, you stroll past a signboard and begin a clockwise loop around the lake by passing over the low dam. Circling around the lake, you encounter a variety of vegetation: large sagebrush-filled clearings sprinkled with bitterbrush and mule ears, pockets of willow, and stands of Jeffrey pine forest. On the east side of the lake, dense aspen groves shimmer with a splash of grayish green in summer and a blaze of yellow-gold in fall.

You reach a junction with a lateral on the left that climbs up to the Tahoe Rim trailhead at Spooner Summit. Veer right at this junction and proceed across a wood bridge over diminutive Spooner Creek. After the bridge, you near the lakeshore again and pass through a flower-filled meadow, which provides a fine habitat for several species of birds, including osprey, bald eagle, and killdeer. Continue around the lake to the four-way junction at the close of the loop and then retrace your steps to the parking lot.

SPOONER LAKE   The lake was created as a millpond when a dam across Spooner Creek was built in the 1850s. Water from the lake was used for irrigation after the dam was rebuilt in 1929. The lake and the nearby highway summit on U.S. 50 were named for M. Spooner, owner of Spooners Station, a wood camp not far from the present site of the lake.

Hikers and equestrians will appreciate the new single-track trail up North Canyon to lovely Marlette Lake.

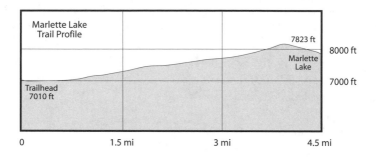

DISTANCE & ROUTE:	9 miles round trip
DIFFICULTY:	Moderate
SEASON:	Summer, fall
TRAILHEAD ACCESS:	All vehicles
WATER:	Available at trailhead, Secret Harbor Creek, and Marlette Lake
GUIDEBOOK MAP:	16
USGS MAP:	Glenbrook, Marlette Lake
LTNSP MAP:	Marlette-Hobart Backcountry

INTRODUCTION For years the route to Marlette Lake along the North Canyon Road has been extremely popular with hikers, mountain bikers, and equestrians alike, which has resulted in potential conflicts and safety issues. Upon completion of the single-track Marlette Lake Trail in 2005, these user groups will each have their own trail to use; hikers and equestrians will follow the new trail to Marlette Lake, while mountain bikers will exclusively use the slightly longer, older route via the North Canyon Road. All recreationists will continue to share the track for the first 0.75 mile, from the parking area to the start of the new trail.

The route begins in sagebrush meadow near Spooner Lake and proceeds into the mixed forest of North Canyon. Sprinkled throughout the canyon are a number of picturesque aspen stands that are particularly attractive at the peak of autumn's colorful display. Once at Marlette Lake, hikers can inspect the fish spawning station at the south end of the reservoir, enjoy a picnic lunch along the lakeshore, or take a cool dip in the refreshing waters.

A fine trip extension from Marlette Lake leads to a beautiful Lake Tahoe vista from the Marlette Overlook at a knoll above the east shore. Strong hikers can consider other options, including a climb of Snow Valley Peak, or an alternate return to the trailhead along a section of the Tahoe Rim Trail.

DIRECTIONS TO TRAILHEAD   Drive on S.R. 28 to the entrance into the Spooner Lake section of Lake Tahoe Nevada State Park, 1 mile northwest of the junction with U.S. 50. Follow the access road to the parking lot near the picnic area. There is a $6 fee (in 2005) for entrance to the park.

DESCRIPTION   Check with park officials before your trip to see if the Marlette Lake Trail has been completed—if not, you'll have to follow the 5-mile-long road to Marlette Lake.

Leave the parking lot and head toward Spooner Lake, soon reaching a four-way junction of the North Canyon Road and the trail around Spooner Lake. Veer left at the junction and follow the road northbound over the outlet from the lake and across an open sea of sagebrush scrub. Eventually the sagebrush meadow is left behind, as you venture into a mixed forest of Jeffrey pines, lodgepole pines, and white firs.

Pass by a marked lateral on the right that leads to Spooner Lake Cabin (see next page). A short distance from the junction, you pass rustic Spencer's Cabin on the left. Soon after this cabin, just before a steel gate bars vehicle access to the road, you reach a signed junction between the North Canyon Road and the new Marlette Lake Trail.

For the next 3.25 miles of single-track trail, you make a steady climb up North Canyon through mixed forest. Near the 2-mile mark from the parking area, the trail crosses a tributary of Secret Harbor Creek, which diverts the majority of North Canyon Creek's stream flow away from Spooner Creek on a shortcut west to Lake Tahoe. Approximately 0.5 mile beyond the creek crossing is an old cabin site, where a woodcutter took up residence in the early 1900s. Protected by a split-rail fence and marked by an interpretive sign, all that remains of the old cabin is a pile of fireplace stones and a single row of logs.

At 4 miles from the Spooner trailhead, you reach the apex of the climb at a saddle separating North Canyon from Marlette Lake's basin. An old road on the left provides a steep westbound route down to Chimney Beach on the east shore of Lake Tahoe. A right turn onto the road provides a connection to the North Canyon Road just north of a junction with the Snow Valley Road.

From the high point, a 0.5-mile descent leads to the Marlette Lake Road along the south shore of picturesque Marlette Lake. Nearby is a trout spawning

Marlette Lake and Lake Tahoe from Tahoe Rim Trail near
Snow Valley Peak, Carson Range

station built in 1987 and operated by the Nevada Division of Wildlife (fishing is not allowed in Marlette Lake). Turning left (northwest) on the road leads to the dam and the beginning of the Flume Trail, a classic mountain bike route. A walk along the road to the right (northeast) will take you to a restroom and a junction with the road to the Marlette Overlook. By following this road on a mile-long climb to the northeast, you'll reach a wonderful view of Lake Tahoe from the overlook. A short walk from the junction south on the North Canyon Road is well worth the little effort for the lush wildflowers and dense grove of aspens alone.

SPOONER LAKE CABINS Spooner Lake and Wild Cat cabins are a pair of hand hewn, Scandinavian style, log structures within Lake Tahoe Nevada State Park operated by a concessionaire and available for year-round rental. The cabins sleep two to six adults and are equipped with heating and cooking stoves, kitchen utensils, photovoltaic and propane lights, and drinking water. Odor-free composting toilets are nearby. For more information check out the Web site at www.spoonerlake.com or call (775) 749-5349.

After 4 miles of forested hiking, breathtaking views of Lake Tahoe abound from the slopes and summit of Snow Valley Peak.

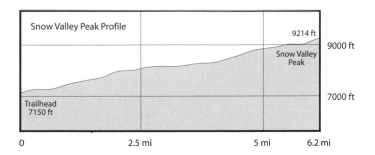

DISTANCE & ROUTE:	12.4 miles round trip
DIFFICULTY:	Strenuous
SEASON:	Summer, fall
TRAILHEAD ACCESS:	All vehicles
WATER:	None
GUIDEBOOK MAP:	16
USGS MAP:	Glenbrook, Marlette Lake
LTNSP MAP:	Marlette-Hobart Backcountry

INTRODUCTION If you're looking for impressive views of Lake Tahoe, then this trip to the summit of Snow Valley Peak will be right up your alley. However, you'll first have to endure nearly 4 miles of densely forested hiking before breaking out of the trees to some of the grandest views in the Lake Tahoe basin. Following a section of the Tahoe Rim Trail that is closed to mountain bikes, hikers make a steady climb from the Spooner Summit trailhead all the way to Snow Valley Peak. For hikers daunted by the 6.2-mile distance necessary to reach the summit, a trio of vista points easily accessible off the main trail provides less impressive views at 1.3, 1.9, and 2.25 miles.

DIRECTIONS TO TRAILHEAD Follow U.S. 50 to Spooner Summit, 0.75 mile east of the junction with S.R. 28 and park on the north side of the highway in the well-signed Tahoe Rim Trail parking lot.

DESCRIPTION From the parking lot a short, mild climb leads into light forest of Jeffrey pine and red fir to a signed junction with a descending lateral trail that connects with the loop trail around Spooner Lake. Beyond this junction, a moderate ascent proceeds through increasingly dense forest. Gaps in the trees allow brief glimpses of Spooner Lake below, but the overwhelming majority of the first 4 miles of trail is through viewless forest. At 1.3 miles from the trailhead, a 4 × 4 post marks a short lateral to the first of three vista points, offering a view to the east of U.S. 50 winding down Clear Creek canyon.

Continue the steady ascent through the trees, winding around minor hills and ridges along the way. Reach a second marked junction with a viewpoint lateral at 1.9 miles, where a short path leads to a boulder-covered knoll with views of Carson Valley to the southeast and Desolation Wilderness peaks to the southwest above a sliver of Lake Tahoe.

Proceed on a northbound course through moderate forest cover, as the path veers west and climbs to a ridge crest, where you reach a junction with a third lateral to a viewpoint at 2.25 miles. Follow this lateral for a few hundred feet and then scramble over boulders to a hilltop offering a passable, partial view of Lake Tahoe.

From the junction, the trail generally follows the Carson Range crest for the next 1.75 miles on a more gently graded ascent. At 4 miles from the trailhead is a junction with a 1.2-mile-long connector to North Canyon Road, 700 vertical feet below. As an alternative to continuing toward Snow Valley Peak, you could descend this path to the road, head south to Spooner Lake, follow the trail around Spooner Lake to a junction near the southeast shore, and then ascend a lateral 0.75 mile back to the trailhead at Spooner Summit. (See hikes 22 and 23.)

A mild climb leads away from the junction, passing through open terrain on the east side of the ridge that allows views of Carson Valley and the Pine Nut Mountains. Following a switchback, the trail moves to the west side of the ridge, where Lake Tahoe suddenly springs into view, a fine reward for the previous miles of forested hiking. A few groves of conifers interrupt these views temporarily, but soon you break out into the open for good to follow an angling ascent across a hillside carpeted with tobacco brush, sagebrush, and bitterbrush. The views of the Lake Tahoe basin are quite impressive. Rather than head directly toward the summit, the TRT climbs steadily toward a saddle northwest of the peak, where you encounter a junction with the old Snow Valley Peak jeep road, 5.8 miles from the trailhead.

Turn right, briefly follow the old road, and then turn right again onto an old track heading toward the summit of Snow Valley Peak. After a winding 0.4-mile climb, you reach the 9214-foot summit. Despite the communication towers and accompanying equipment, the views from the summit are stunning, although the broad topography requires that you move about to get the best views in all directions. Lake Tahoe is the preeminent gem, with Marlette Lake shimmering in the foreground below you. To the east are Carson City and Carson Valley, and to the northeast, Washoe Lake, Washoe Valley, and the Truckee Meadows.

> **RED FIR (*ABIES MAGNIFICA*)**   Red firs, one of only two firs found in the Carson Range, tend to grow in monocultural stands between 7000 and 9000 feet. Quite similar in appearance to white firs, red firs are distinguished by the red furrows of their bark and by cones that are nearly twice as long as those of the white fir. The crowns of a mature red fir are prone to lightning strikes, which tend to clear openings in the forest, thereby promoting secondary succession.

HIKE 25 | SOUTH CAMP PEAK

A superb view of Lake Tahoe can be reached via a little-used section of the Tahoe Rim Trail.

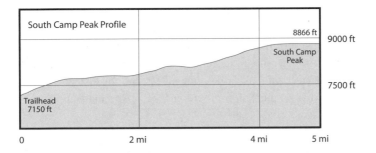

DISTANCE & ROUTE:	10 miles round trip
DIFFICULTY:	Strenuous
SEASON:	Summer, fall
TRAILHEAD ACCESS:	All vehicles
WATER:	None
GUIDEBOOK MAP:	16
USGS MAP:	Glenbrook

INTRODUCTION   As one of the West's most highly prized landscapes, Lake Tahoe has been admired by sightseers and photographers alike. However, it is likely that only a small percentage of those devotees have had the privilege of seeing the incredible vista from the open, 1-mile-long summit plateau of South Camp Peak. After a 4-mile climb from Spooner Summit, gazing across the

Lake Tahoe from Tahoe Rim Trail, Carson Range

sparkling waters of the lake to the towering peaks above the southwest shore creates a visual impression that's not soon forgotten.

Although this hike is nearly ideal, a couple of cautions are worth mentioning. There is no water along the entire route of the trail—make sure you're carrying a sufficient amount for both the hike in and the hike out. Maintain a cautious eye while on the trail, as mountain bikes are permitted on this section of the TRT.

DIRECTIONS TO TRAILHEAD   Follow U.S. 50 to Spooner Summit, 0.75 mile east of the junction of S.R. 28 and park on the south side of the highway in the Tahoe Rim Trail parking lot. A picnic area with pit toilets is nearby.

DESCRIPTION   A switchbacking climb on sandy trail leads up the hillside and away from the din of traffic on U.S. 50, as you ascend shrub-covered slopes of sagebrush, tobacco brush, currant, chinquapin, and manzanita. A smattering of Jeffrey pines and quaking aspens dot the hillside. Eventually, you gain a ridge and begin a more tolerable climb along its crest, where an open forest of Jeffrey pines and red firs allows occasional glimpses of Carson Valley to the southeast and Lake Tahoe to the west. Early season wildflowers include mule ears, lupine, and paintbrush. Eventually the ascent leads to a knoll, 1.5 miles from the trailhead, where a very short use trail leads to impressive views.

Undulating trail leads across a dirt road at 2.5 miles, followed by a mildly rising traverse below Duane Bliss Peak. At 0.25 mile beyond the first road, you step across an abandoned road and then return to the crest. A moderate climb along the ridge takes you just below a rocky knob, where a short use trail leads to a fine vista of the Carson Valley and the Pine Nut Mountains. Leaving the views behind, make a gentle descent through a mixed forest of western white pines, Jeffrey pines, and red firs. At 3 miles is a signed crossing of the Genoa Peak Road (F.R. 14N32), a major backcountry route of four-wheel-drive enthusiasts and mountain bikers.

Climb away from the road and as you gain elevation mountain hemlocks and lodgepole pines join the dense forest. Nearing the crest at the north end of South Camp Peak, approximately 1.3 miles from Genoa Peak Road, you suddenly break out of the forest into a sublime Tahoe vista. A very brief climb leads to a rocky knoll with an even better view of Tahoe. A detailed map of the Tahoe basin will aid in your identification of the numerous Tahoe landmarks visible from this dramatic vista point.

The essentially flat-topped plateau of South Camp Peak stretches south for another mile, providing nearly continuous views of the lake and surrounding peaks and ridges. A log bench positioned near the south end of the plateau is a curious article, but it does offer an excellent perch from which to enjoy the incredible view.

WESTERN WHITE PINE (*PINUS MONTICOLA*)   The western white is a pine found in the higher elevations of the Tahoe basin, generally not below 8000 feet. Perhaps the easiest way to identify this five-needled pine is by the slight curve of the cones, about five to ten inches in length. Bark tends to be gray and scaly.

Trails in the mountain ranges of central Nevada offer remoteness, exceptional vistas, and the occasional streamside romp.

Boundary Peak at the north end of the White Mountains rises sharply above the surrounding terrain, casting a long shadow on the neighboring valleys. The 13,140-foot mountain lures "peakbaggers" with a siren call to stand atop Nevada's highest point in one of the state's smallest designated wilderness areas at 10,000 acres. Despite the absence of a maintained trail all the way to the summit, a fairly well defined use trail can be followed almost the entire distance, and although considered to be a physically strenuous trip, the climb itself is technically easy. Successful summiteers will be treated to sweeping vistas, including a parade of mountain ranges across the Great Basin to the east and the mighty barrier of the Sierra Nevada to the west.

Comprising the southern third of the Toiyabe Range, the Arc Dome Wilderness is Nevada's largest wilderness area at approximately 115,000 acres, holding a convoluted assemblage of canyons and ridges dissimilar to the linear nature of the typical Great Basin mountain range. The namesake peak and centerpiece of the wilderness is the tenth highest summit in the state at 11,773 feet. A fine network of trails takes hikers to summits with extensive vistas, through deep canyons, and alongside vibrant streams.

Thanks to the range's lofty heights, the Toiyabes capture a relative abundance of moisture left over from the Pacific storms that slam into the Sierra Nevada and sporadically cross the Great Basin. Consequently, myriad waterways course through the mountains, including three named rivers: the Reese, South Twin, and North Twin. By most standards the term "river" is misapplied to these streams, which was aptly stated by Mark Twain's description of Nevada rivers in *Roughing It:* "People accustomed to the monster mile-wide Mississippi grow accustomed to associating the term 'river' with a high degree of watery grandeur. Consequently, such people feel rather disappointed when they stand on the shores of the Humboldt or the Carson and find that a 'river' in Nevada is a sickly rivulet which is just the counterpart of the Erie Canal in all respects save that the canal is twice as long and four times as deep. One of the pleasantest and most invigorating exercises one can contrive is to run and jump across

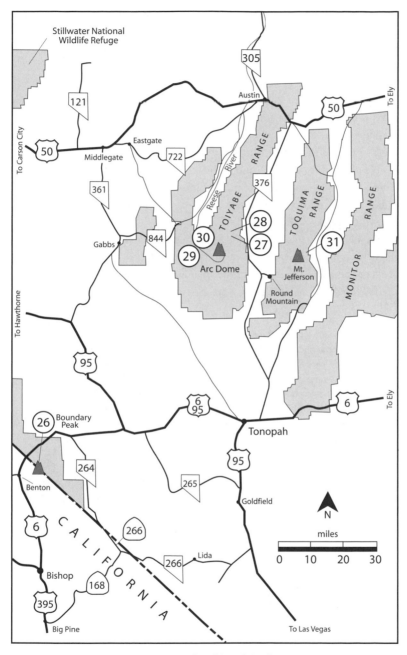

MAP 17 | Hikes of Central Nevada

the Humboldt River till he is overheated, and then drink it dry." Despite Mr. Twain's disdain for the misuse of the term "river" in Nevada, the streams within the Arc Dome Wilderness are a welcome delight, supporting a diverse ecosystem of flora and fauna.

Located near the geographical center of the state and directly east of the Toiyabes, the Toquima Range contains several unique features that beckon the adventurous hiker. The focal point of the range and the surrounding Alta Toquima Wilderness is Mt. Jefferson (11,941 feet at South Summit). Wild, remote, and seldom visited, the area boasts dramatic, glacier-carved canyons filled with tumbling streams and high alpine tablelands with a unique desert-alpine flora and vistas that span from California to Utah. Along with the interesting natural history, the Toquimas lay claim to some archaeological and historical significance as well.

Although none of the trails in the neighboring Table Mountain Wilderness in the Monitor Range were chosen for this guide, hikers looking for additional challenges may find the trails in this area to be quite appealing. The highlight of the Monitor Range is the aspen-covered plateau atop Table Mountain.

FYI ■ Access to all the trailheads described in this section will involve long drives from both major cities and sizeable towns, requiring several miles of travel on dirt roads.

The high altitude and the chance of thunderstorms are both potential hazards that should be considered when contemplating a trip to Boundary Peak.

Almost all of the trails in central Nevada have suffered from budget cuts to the Humboldt-Toiyabe National Forest. Low use and lack of maintenance have not been a good combination for ensuring that trails are well defined and in good condition, or that trailheads and junctions are signed. Before setting out on any trip in the region, checking with the nearest ranger station about current trail conditions is a wise idea. Despite Forest Service and USGS maps of the area indicating a 50-mile network of trails, most of the designated trails in the Toquima Range have deteriorated into little more than cross-country routes. If you plan on venturing away from the Pine Creek Trail described in this section, be prepared for extensive route-finding challenges.

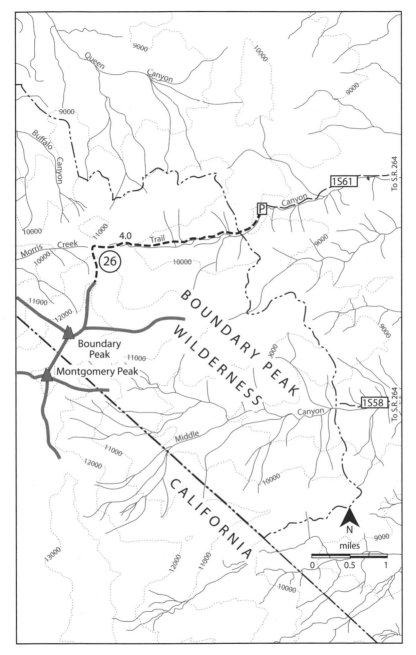

MAP 18 | Boundary Peak

A strenuous trip on an unmaintained path leads to the summit of Nevada's tallest mountain and an expansive view of the Sierra Nevada and Great Basin ranges.

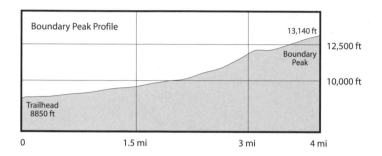

DISTANCE & ROUTE:	8 miles round trip
DIFFICULTY:	Strenuous
SEASON:	Summer
TRAILHEAD ACCESS:	High-clearance vehicle recommended
WATER:	Available in Trail Canyon Creek
GUIDEBOOK MAP:	18
USGS MAP:	Boundary Peak

INTRODUCTION Boundary Peak strikes a dramatic mountain profile visible for many miles in virtually any direction. Situated at the north end of the White Mountains, within one of the smallest wilderness areas in Nevada, the peak's lofty, pinnacled summit stands a mere 0.25 mile from the California border. Most of the White Mountains chain lies within California, and some would argue that Boundary Peak, the highest peak in Nevada at 13,140 feet, is not a bona fide mountain at all, but a subsidiary point on the north ridge of its taller neighbor, Montgomery Peak (13,440 feet). If the Von Schmidt Line of 1873 was still recognized as the official boundary between California and Nevada, the issue of Boundary Peak's legitimacy would be moot, as the mountain would reside wholly within California. However, the accepted boundary places Boundary Peak squarely within Nevada (the origin of the name is certainly no mystery). Whether you view Boundary Peak as a mountain unto itself, or simply as a point on a ridge, it's still the highest piece of terra firma in Nevada, and well worth the effort to conquer.

Who could pass up the opportunity to stand atop the highest point in the most mountainous state in the lower 48? Impressive vistas of distant ranges, coupled with dramatic views of neighboring peaks, reward diligent hikers who persevere all the way to the summit. Nearly 10,000 feet of elevation in a mere 7 miles separate the roof of the White Mountains from the floor of Owens Valley, providing an unimpeded vista of the majestic Sierra Nevada range to the west. To the east, additional mountain ranges march in succession across the high desert of Nevada, interrupting the Great Basin with generally north-to-south linear rows of mountain spines.

While 90 miles to the south, hikers are vying for a limited number of permits to climb California's highest peak, Mt. Whitney (at 14,495 feet also the highest in the lower 48), wilderness permits are not even required for an ascent of Boundary Peak. The remoteness of west-central Nevada insures that you won't have to share the mountain with too many fellow hikers and climbers—perhaps you'll have the area all to yourself.

During certain summer weather patterns, thunderstorms are a concern to hikers and climbers on Boundary Peak. When thunderstorms are possible, the best plan is to start early and be off the mountain by mid-afternoon. The customary afternoon winds can also create a wind chill factor on the summit that can be markedly different than temperatures in Trail Canyon, so be sure to carry appropriate clothing in your pack. Altitude can also be a potential hazard, so be sure to give your body plenty of time to acclimatize for an ascent to 13,140 feet. Also, drink plenty of fluids during the climb, remembering to carry extra water in your pack, as none is available beyond the creek in Trail Canyon.

DIRECTIONS TO TRAILHEAD   Boundary Peak is a prominent landmark across much of west-central Nevada, luring auto-bound hikers and climbers like a beacon. The first step is to reach S.R. 264, either from the north via U.S. 95, from the east via U.S. 6 (both passing through Coaldale), or from the west via U.S. 395 and then S.R. 120 through Benton or U.S. 6 through Bishop. If traveling from the south or southwest, you can reach S.R. 264 from S.R. 266; coming from the northwest S.R. 264 is accessible directly from U.S. 6; and from the northeast via S.R. 773.

From S.R. 264 in Fish Lake Valley, turn west onto a dirt road (F.R. 2N07), 5.8 miles south of the junction of S.R. 773, or about 10.5 miles north of the small community of Dyer. This junction is approximately 200 yards north of a ranch house adjacent to Chiatovich Creek. Follow the dirt road through typical sagebrush terrain for 7.1 miles to a prominent intersection, where a sign reads MIDDLE CANYON straight ahead and TRAIL CANYON to the right.

Turn right and follow the main road (F.R. 1S61) heading north and then northwest into Trail Canyon. Pass an artificial pond on the left and proceed to a lush meadow alongside the creek in Trail Canyon, approximately 12.25 miles from the highway, where you'll find a number of adequate campsites. Continue up Trail Canyon for another mile to a grassy parking area on the right, suitable for a half-dozen vehicles.

DESCRIPTION Proceed upstream on the continuation of the road past a trail register and into a meadow, where campsites are available not too far from the creek. Pass through lush riparian vegetation of willows and wildflowers, as the road soon narrows to a single-track trail. At 0.4 mile from the trailhead, you cross over to the south bank of the creek and follow a distinct path up the canyon through dense foliage. As you continue upstream, the trail becomes hard to follow in places. However, with a little luck, you may be able to stay on a bona fide trail all the way to Trail Canyon Saddle, the obvious low point at the head of the canyon. Although the easiest route is not always obvious, remain on the south bank, avoiding the dense brush adjacent to the creek. Try not to stray too far from the creek either, or you may end up battling thickets of sagebrush and snowberry. In early season, you may have to dodge boggy patches near a few springs as well.

Near the head of the canyon, beyond the last of the springs, the creek dries up after snowmelt. Farther on, a stand of limber pine breaks up the sagebrush-covered terrain. As you surmount the last hill below the saddle, the route crosses to the north side of the canyon and ascends to Trail Canyon Saddle, 2.25 miles from the trailhead. Scattered pockets of grasses and ground-hugging plants are the only vegetation that survives in the harsh, wind-swept environment in the saddle. A portion of the High Sierra appears to the west, a mere precursor of the spectacular vista awaiting you at the summit.

A number of use trails lead away from the saddle, heading up the steep, rock-filled slopes to the south. The key is to select a trail the keeps you directly on, or close to, the top of the ridge. A well chosen path should take you almost all the way to the summit, except for a couple of places where you will have to make short scrambles over some rocks. After a steep, 1200-foot, 0.5-mile climb, you reach the top of a pass, where the rugged north face of Boundary Peak springs into view. The terrain from Trail Canyon Saddle to here would suggest that Boundary Peak would be nothing more than a huge talus pile. However, the unfolding view reveals dramatic scenery, with jagged spires and slanting rock faces composed of gray granite. Patches of snow cling to clefts and gullies in the north face well into summer, adding to the alpine character.

Beyond the pass, the trail makes a short traverse below an outcrop and then continues climbing south along the ridge. The terrain eases briefly, where the north and east ridges intersect, 0.25 mile east of the summit, affording an interesting view to the northeast into Trail Canyon. Resist the temptation to take this "shortcut" to Trail Canyon following your trip to the summit, unless you prefer

• Author in foreground at Boundary Peak, White Mountains

a tedious descent of a seemingly endless talus slope. Stay on the trail closest to the apex of the ridge as the route bends west toward the summit. Pass the last pinnacle on the right and scramble over large talus blocks to the summit.

From the top of Boundary Peak you have a commanding view toward distant horizons in nearly all directions. Vistas to the south are blocked by Boundary Peak's nearest neighbor, Montgomery Peak, and farther on by the rest of the White Mountains, including Mt. Dubois, the immense plateau of Pellisier Flats, and White Mountain Peak, highest summit in the range at 14,245 feet. The man-made boundary between California and Nevada runs directly through the bottom of the deep cleft separating the massive hulks of Boundary Peak and Montgomery Peak. The spectacular and popular eastern front of the Sierra Nevada looms large in the west. To the northwest, a piece of distant Mono Lake is visible. Distant, remote, and certainly less well known ranges to the east parade in seemingly endless succession across the Great Basin. Perhaps the most impressive picture is on the west side of Boundary and Montgomery Peaks, where rugged slopes drop dramatically 6500 feet to the floor of Queen and Benton Valleys.

Strong climbers can traverse the ridge from Boundary Peak for a climb of neighboring Montgomery Peak. Plan on a couple of extra hours for the round trip from Boundary Peak. The ascent of Montgomery Peak is not technically difficult, but a rope may be helpful for less experienced parties.

WHITE MOUNTAINS   Statistically, the White Mountains make up the fourth highest mountain range in the contiguous forty-eight states. Lying to the east of the massive barrier of the Sierra Nevada, the White Mountains receive a fraction of the precipitation that falls on its western neighbor, totaling a mere fifteen inches per year. With the relative lack of moisture, a much more arid plant community has developed than the typical vegetation found in wetter ranges. While the Ruby Mountains in northeast Nevada are home to almost two hundred species of alpine plants, only forty-eight have been identified in the White Mountains. Perhaps the most notable plant species is the bristlecone pine, preserved in the Ancient Bristlecone Pine Forest Natural Area. Designated in 1958, the area lies to the south of Boundary Peak and is accessible from S.R. 168, via the Ancient Bristlecone Pine National Scenic Byway.

HIKE 27 | SOUTH TWIN RIVER

Dramatic rock formations and lush riparian foliage are the highlights of this journey along one of central Nevada's most picturesque streams.

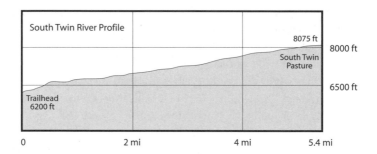

DISTANCE & ROUTE:	10.8 miles round trip
DIFFICULTY:	Moderate
SEASON:	Summer, fall
TRAILHEAD ACCESS:	All vehicles
WATER:	Available in South Twin River
GUIDEBOOK MAP:	19
USGS MAP:	Carvers NW, South Toiyabe Peak, Arc Dome

INTRODUCTION   Following the initial segment of the 66-mile-long Toiyabe Crest Trail, this trip takes you up to an excellent vista point of the South Twin River canyon, a deep gorge lined with steep rock walls topped with jagged

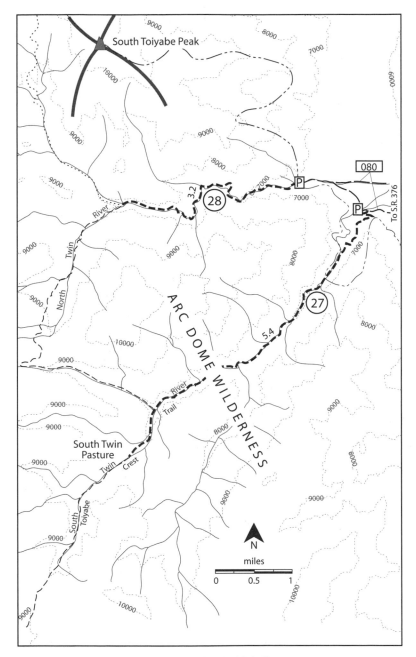

South Toiyabe Peak

9000
8000
7000
9000
10000
6000
080
P
7000
To S.R. 376
3.2
28
7000
8000
9000
A R C   D O M E   W I L D E R N E S S
27
5.4
8000
9000
10000
River
Trail
9000
8000
9000
Twin
North
Twin
South Twin
Pasture
Twin   Crest
9000
9000
9000
South
Toiyabe
9000
10000
10000

N
miles
0   0.5   1

MAP 19 | South & North Twin Rivers

spires. Past the viewpoint, you stroll alongside the river upstream to where the canyon eventually broadens at a picturesque meadow. The trail fords the river numerous times on the way—wearing short pants and an old pair of tennis shoes is an excellent game plan that you will quickly learn to appreciate.

DIRECTIONS TO TRAILHEAD　Drive along the west side of Big Smoky Valley on S.R. 376 to a signed turnoff for the South Twin River trailhead, approximately 40 miles south of a junction with U.S. 50 and 61 miles north of a junction with U.S. 6. Head northwest on F.R. 080, a single-track gravel road passable to the average sedan, for 3 miles to the trailhead, where parking is available in a wide turnout on the south side of the road.

DESCRIPTION　Avoid what at first glance appears to be the most logical route, following the continuation of the road upstream into the South Twin River canyon. Built in 1980, the road services a small mining claim near the South Fork (of the South Twin River), making a seemingly endless number of fords of South Twin River within the first 0.75 mile. The actual hiking trail begins in the opposite direction from the road, striking a diagonal course across the steep hillside to the south. Following a switchback, you climb steeply through pinyon pine, sagebrush, and ephedra toward a cluster of sharp cliffs. After cresting the cliffs, make a gentle descent to join the mining road from below, beyond which you ascend sharply to a knoll, 0.9 mile from the trailhead. A remarkable vista unfolds as you gaze down into the deep cleft of a canyon, framed dramatically by steep, jagged cliffs. While taking in the majestic view, you can't help but wonder how the South Twin River managed to cut such a circuitous course through the maze of cliffs in the lower canyon.

Descend from the knoll along the road through pinyon-juniper woodland to the east bank of the river and then head upstream on rocky road at a mildly rising grade, past willows, alders, and cottonwoods. Farther on, wild rose, currant, chokecherry, and desert peach contribute to the lush riparian foliage in the bottom of the canyon, along with a fine assortment of wildflowers, including columbine, paintbrush, lupine, bluebell, and penstemon.

By avoiding the initial stretch of mining road, you've also successfully avoided the numerous fords along the mining road. However, you're in for a change, as the route ahead crosses South Twin River ten times before arriving at a junction with a trail heading up the South Fork, 3.3 miles from the trailhead. A short distance prior to the junction, just before the ninth crossing of the river, you may notice a mining relic—an old mill wheel that utilized water power to process ore from a nearby mine—with the remnants of a couple of old cabins nearby.

Past the junction, you leave the mining road behind and follow single-track trail through lush foliage and across the river several more times. At 4.6 miles, you reach another junction, this one with the North Twin River Trail (see hike 28). Just before the junction the canyon starts to widen and sagebrush-covered hillsides replace the steep rock walls of downstream.

A gentle 0.8 mile hike from the junction of the North Twin River Trail brings you to the broad, moist meadow named South Twin Pasture. If you don't have to share the area with a herd of cattle, scattered campsites provide fine places to take a break or enjoy lunch before returning to the trailhead.

SINGLELEAF PINYON (*PINUS MONOPHYLLA*) The ubiquitous singleleaf pinyon pine appears in mid-elevation forests across the state. The term "pinyon" (or piñon) is from the Spanish *piñón* and refers to the large edible seeds that were a staple of the Paiute diet and are now a gourmet food item. The tree is the only single-needled pine in the entire genus. Hundreds of thousands of acres of pinyon pine woodland were cut down in the late 1800s to provide charcoal for the smelters and stoves during the mining boom.

HIKE 28 | NORTH TWIN RIVER

Hike along one of central Nevada's "rivers" through dense foliage and beneath striking cliffs to an aspen-covered flat.

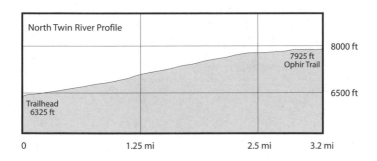

DISTANCE & ROUTE:	6.4 miles round trip
DIFFICULTY:	Moderate
SEASON:	Summer, fall
TRAILHEAD ACCESS:	All vehicles
WATER:	Available in North Twin River
GUIDEBOOK MAP:	19
USGS MAP:	Carvers NW, South Toiyabe Peak

Only by Great Basin standards can North Twin and South Twin be referred to as rivers, but what they lack in volume is more than made up for in vibrancy, drama, and scenic wonder. The deceptive characterization of these two streams as rivers was the creation of the Reese River Navigation

Upper North Twin River, Toiyabe Range

Company, a scam to separate unsuspecting Easterners from their pocketbooks. The company was seeking investment in order to develop a fleet of ships that would transport ore from a series of nearby mines along these "rivers" to processing plants. Despite the inability of these two watercourses to float anything larger than an inner tube, both tumble down impressive canyons and support a diverse assortment of riparian foliage.

The trail up North Twin River follows the course of a narrow, deep, and winding canyon. Dark volcanic spires and parapets tower over the churning river, which plunges down the canyon in a series of low waterfalls and turbulent cascades. The trail makes numerous fords of the river within the first couple of miles, crossings that could be dangerous in early season—check with the Forest Service about current conditions. Even in summer, wearing shorts and an old pair of tennis shoes for the first couple of miles is a good idea.

DIRECTIONS TO TRAILHEAD   Drive along the west side of Big Smoky Valley on S.R. 376 to a signed turnoff for the North Twin River trailhead, approximately 37 miles south of a junction with U.S. 50 and 63 miles north of a junction with U.S. 6. Head southwest and then west on F.R. 080, a single-track gravel road passable to the average sedan. Continue past a junction on your left with a road heading toward the South Twin trailhead at 3.5 miles, and continue another 0.3 mile to a large parking area near a pile of boulders. The actual trailhead is 50 yards farther, but a limited amount of parking there handles no more than a couple of vehicles.

DESCRIPTION   Cross the Arc Dome Wilderness boundary and follow the winding course of North Twin River, weaving back and forth through a narrow, twisting canyon. Proceed through cottonwoods, junipers, and pinyon pines to the first of many river crossings, a process you'll end up repeating fifteen times within the first couple of miles. Continue upstream alongside the river, which tumbles and churns beneath steep, rugged cliffs on a precipitous course toward its inauspicious end in the flat plain of Big Smoky Valley.

The canyon widens and the grade of the trail eases after the first 2 miles, where the river adopts a mellower demeanor, gliding past pinyon pines, wild roses, and willows. After a while, the canyon briefly narrows near a pocket of mature aspens, but soon widens again in an area of meadows. Beyond the meadows, the vegetation on the floor of the canyon becomes quite lush, so much so that the reality of being in the middle of Nevada is easily forgotten, at least for the moment. After fording the creek one more time, you break out into an extensive, aspen-covered flat carpeted with rich grasses. A few old logs

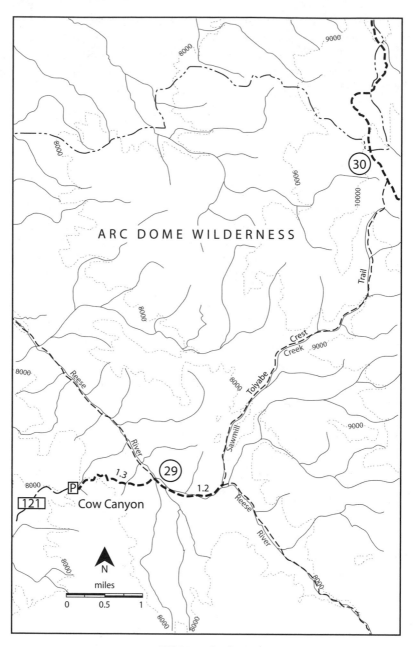

ARC DOME WILDERNESS

30

Trail

Crest
Creek
Toiyabe

Sawmill

Reese River

9000

9000

8000

Reese River

1.3

29

1.2

P

121

Cow Canyon

8000

8000

8000

8000

8000

8000

9000

9000

10000

9000

N

miles

0   0.5   1

MAP 20 | Cow Canyon

provide makeshift seats suitable for a picnic lunch. Nearby is a junction with the faint trail headed toward Ophir Summit.

UTAH JUNIPER (*JUNIPERUS OSTEOSPERMA*)   The other dominant member of the pinyon-juniper woodland besides the singleleaf pinyon pine is the Utah juniper, the most common conifer in Nevada. This drought-tolerant, round-topped tree rarely grows taller than thirty feet high, oftentimes with multiple trunks rarely larger than thirty inches in diameter. Within the Great Basin, the Utah juniper is common on mountain slopes between 3000 and 8000 feet.

HIKE 29 | COW CANYON

Scenery reminiscent of an old western movie and the lure of excellent fishing in the Reese River will tempt hikers and anglers alike.

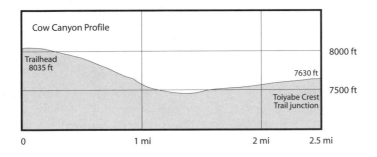

DISTANCE & ROUTE:	5 miles round trip
DIFFICULTY:	Moderate
SEASON:	Summer, fall
TRAILHEAD ACCESS:	All vehicles
WATER:	Available in Reese River
GUIDEBOOK MAP:	20
USGS MAP:	Bakeoven Creek

INTRODUCTION   A short hike in the Arc Dome Wilderness leads to the Reese River and a junction with the 66-mile-long Toiyabe Crest Trail. Impressive views of 11,773-foot Arc Dome and the Reese River country are nearly constant companions along the first mile of trail. The rolling terrain throughout the trip is wide open and the skies are as big as Montana, reminiscent of an old western movie—the only thing missing is a posse of white hats chasing some cattle rustlers. Anglers will enjoy the relatively easy access to good fishing in Reese River's eddies, pools, and beaver ponds. Interesting rock formations near the trailhead complete the captivating environment.

The trail loses 600 feet in the first 1.3 miles on the way to Reese River, before adopting a mildly rising grade following the river upstream for another 1.2 miles. Make sure you save some energy for the climb on the return trip. Pack along a pair of old tennis shoes or sandals for a ford of the river about halfway through the trip, at least until after midsummer, when the river may be low enough to cross without getting your feet wet.

DIRECTIONS TO TRAILHEAD   Follow the Reese River Valley Road (F.R. 018) south from S.R. 722 to a junction with F.R. 121 near Cloverdale Summit, approximately 17 miles south of the Reese River Guard Station. Head east on F.R. 121 and proceed 0.6 mile to a junction, where you turn left, following directions for Cow Canyon. Continuing on F.R. 121, you travel another 5 miles to the Cow Canyon trailhead, equipped with horse tie-bar, pit toilet, and primitive campsites.

DESCRIPTION   On well-defined trail, you cross into the Arc Dome Wilderness and climb a low formation of volcanic rock. Juniper and pinyon pine adorn the sagebrush-covered slopes, as you follow a nearly level track around a hill, where Arc Dome springs into view. With 4500 feet separating the summit from the Reese River Valley before you, Arc Dome towers over the open terrain. A steady descent across a sagebrush-covered hillside leads to the floor of a broad canyon, where the Reese River glides serenely northwest toward the plain of Reese River Valley. At 1.3 miles from the trailhead, you reach a T-junction with the Reese River Trail in a meadow above the west bank of the river.

North from the junction, an indistinct portion of the trail heads downstream along the river for 4.5 miles to the boundary between the Arc Dome Wilderness and the Yomba Indian Reservation. Turn south and head downstream on gently graded trail above the west bank, paralleling the alder- and willow-lined river through open slopes carpeted with sagebrush. Just past a large meadow, 2 miles from the trailhead, you pass through tall willows and alders to a ford of the broad river, where you should plan on getting your feet wet until late in the summer.

Beyond the ford, the trail climbs above the east bank and continues upstream. Where the path wanders away from the river, you stroll through sagebrush and widely scattered junipers. A number of beaver ponds provide anglers with excellent fishing opportunities. The Reese River Trail follows a sweeping bend of the river to a crossing of Big Sawmill Creek and an indistinct junction with the Toiyabe Crest Trail in a grassy clearing, 2.5 miles from the trailhead.

> **BIG SAGEBRUSH (*ARTEMESIA TRIDENTATA*)**   No plant is more closely associated with the Great Basin than the big sagebrush, and no fragrance so evocative of the area than the aroma from the plant after a sudden rain shower. The drought-tolerant plants have characteristically deep tap roots and a high degree of adaptability.

HIKE 30 | STEWART CREEK LOOP

A fine loop trip through the heart of the Arc Dome Wilderness offers hikers lush foliage along Stewart Creek and expansive views from the crest of the range.

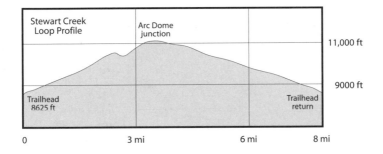

DISTANCE & ROUTE:	8 miles one way in loop
DIFFICULTY:	Strenuous
SEASON:	Summer, fall
TRAILHEAD ACCESS:	High-clearance vehicle recommended
WATER:	Available in Stewart Creek
GUIDEBOOK MAP:	21
USGS MAP:	Arc Dome, Bakeoven Creek, Corral Wash, South Toiyabe Peak

INTRODUCTION   The canyons that make up the Stewart Creek drainage are some of the most luxuriantly vegetated in the state. Dense stands of quaking aspen fill the canyons, a profusion of riparian vegetation lines the banks of the

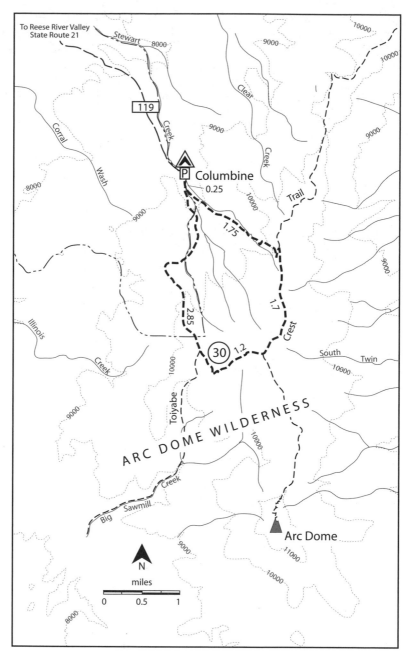

To Reese River Valley
State Route 21

Stewart   8000

Clear   9000

Creek

119

10000

10000

Creek

Corral

Wash

8000

9000

P Columbine
0.25

1.75

10000

Trail

9000

Illinois

2.85

10000

1.7

9000

Creek

30 1.2

Crest

South   Twin

10000

9000

Toiyabe

ARC DOME WILDERNESS

10000

Creek

Sawmill

Big

Arc Dome

9000

11000

N

10000

miles

0   0.5   1

8000

MAP 21 | Stewart Creek

streams, and wildflowers grace the hillsides with a palette of color in early and midsummer. At the upper elevations, wind-battered limber pines add a touch of character.

Lush foliage is not the only highlight found on this journey, as views from the Toiyabe Crest are excellent as well. Vistas are quite extraordinary of the neighboring ranges and valleys, including the Shoshone Mountains across Reese River Valley to the west, and the Toquima Range across Big Smoky Valley to the east. Arc Dome, the Toiyabe Range's highest summit at 11,773 feet, is equally spectacular as seen close up from various spots along the trail. Extremely hardy hikers could add a 6-mile round trip to the summit via the Arc Dome Trail.

This loop is not for the weak-hearted or inexperienced, as a stiff climb from the trailhead at Columbine Campground to the crest of the Toiyabe Range gains 2500 feet in a little over 3 miles. In addition, sections of the trail may be hard to follow, requiring that hikers have some rudimentary navigation and map-reading skills.

DIRECTIONS TO TRAILHEAD Follow the Reese River Valley Road to the Reese River Guard Station and a well-marked junction with F.R. 017, just south of the schoolhouse. Turn east onto F.R. 017, cross a bridge over Reese River, and reach a Y-junction at 0.4 mile.

From the junction, bear right onto F.R. 119 and travel 0.1 mile to a second Y-junction. After crossing Clear Creek, immediately encounter a third Y-junction, where you bear left. At 1.6 miles, turn right at yet another Y-junction. At each of these junctions, you remain on F.R. 119, following signs marked STEWART CREEK.

Near a fence line, 2.7 miles from Reese River Valley Road, bear to the right at a junction, still on F.R. 119. Farther on, at 5.6 miles, near a sign marked TOIYABE NATIONAL FOREST, follow the main road to the right and proceed to a crossing of Stewart Creek. The road climbs out of the drainage and continues another 3 miles into the narrowing, aspen-lined canyon of Stewart Creek. At 8.7 miles, just past a horse-loading area, you pass a sign reading TOIYABE CREST TRAIL, which is a lateral for equestrian use. Continue on F.R. 119, cross over a cattle guard, and enter Columbine Campground, 9 miles from Reese River Valley Road.

A sign marked CREST TRAIL near a pole gate on the right-hand side of the road designates the beginning of the hiker's trail. Parking is available around the campground loop road for about a half-dozen vehicles.

Columbine is one of the best Forest Service campgrounds in Nevada, a fine setting for a night's rest before hitting the trail. On the banks of Stewart Creek and shaded by aspens, the campground is equipped with picnic tables, fire pits, and pit toilets.

DESCRIPTION Follow the old track of a jeep road away from the campground through aspens, shrubs, and wildflowers. You briefly break out into the open to fine views of the canyon and mountains above, before returning to aspen cover. At 0.25 mile from the campground is a junction between single-track trail and the continuation of the Columbine Jeep Road. An old sign at the junction marked TOIYABE CREST TRAIL ½ is wildly inaccurate—as the actual distance is closer to 2 miles.

Veer left and follow the trail southeast through thick brush and tall aspens to a crossing of Stewart Creek. Beyond the crossing, wind your way uphill amid lush foliage to the top of a minor ridge, where you momentarily break out into the open. Follow the crest of this ridge, which separates two branches of the creek, and you will soon head under filtered shade from a light covering of aspens. Briefly back out into the open again, dramatic views of Reese River Valley with a backdrop of the Shoshone Mountains stretch out behind you to the west.

Continuing the ascent, crest a small knoll in a sea of sagebrush and scattered wildflowers, where the grade momentarily eases. Beyond, across a small, aspen-lined meadow filled with grasses and wildflowers, faltering trail leads to a curiously placed sign denoting an old junction with a now overgrown trail, which used to provide a 0.4-mile connection to the Columbine Jeep Road. A more defined track resumes beyond the meadow, as you continue climbing up the canyon through lush grasses, flowers, shrubs, and occasional stands of aspen. At 1.3 miles from the trailhead, you cross Stewart Creek to the north bank and continue up the narrowing canyon. As you progress, scattered limber pines and mountain-mahogany dot the slope. A steep, switchbacking climb takes you up the canyon and across a hillside. Just past some weather equipment with transmitter perched above the trail, you reach a junction with the Toiyabe Crest Trail, 300 vertical feet below the crest and 2 miles from the trailhead.

Turn south obeying signed directions for Arc Dome and follow the Toiyabe Crest Trail on a short traverse into the upper end of the north fork's canyon. You gain the crest at a low gap and make a short drop into the upper canyon of a tributary of North Twin River on the east side of the crest. Resume the ascent, on a 0.75-mile climb through the canyon on a return to the crest at the edge of a broad plateau, where Arc Dome dominates the skyline a mere 2 miles away. At 3.7 miles from the trailhead, you reach the junction with the 3-mile trail to Arc Dome's summit.

From the junction, the Toiyabe Crest Trail drops gently west across the mildly sloping plateau, before descending more steeply across a sagebrush-covered hillside. You reach an unmarked junction, at 4.9 miles, where the Toiyabe Crest Trail angles sharply south.

Leave the Toiyabe Crest Trail and proceed northbound on the Columbine Jeep Road, headed in the direction of the Shoshone Mountains across the broad plain of Reese River Valley. As the old road slices across the hillside, a large green meadow pops into view below. The trail wraps around some cliffs and follows a winding descent to a crossing of Stewart Creek. After the dry, barren slopes above, the lush riparian foliage lining the creek is nearly overwhelming.

A short way past the crossing, you reach the fringe of the meadow seen from above. If the lush, verdant meadow didn't have a fence around its perimeter that corralled a herd of cattle, you'd have a picturesque wilderness setting. The trail passes above the meadow on a nearly level course across a sagebrush-covered hillside to a gate at the far end. Pass through the gate, and descend the moderately steep path through sagebrush, grasses, and wildflowers. Soon dense stands of aspen begin to fill Stewart Creek canyon, a swath of sea green in summer that turns into a blaze of gold in autumn. Soon you pass the signed junction with the obscure and overgrown trail that connected the Columbine Jeep Road to the Stewart Creek Trail. Proceed past the nearly imperceptible junction on well-defined tread through lush foliage to a crossing of a tributary. After the crossing you pass through a sloping meadow and continue the descent to the junction at the close of the loop, 0.25 mile from Columbine Campground. From here, retrace your steps to the trailhead.

TOIYABE RANGE   At slightly over 125 miles in length, the Toiyabe Range is considered to be Nevada's loftiest mountain chain, with over 50 of those miles never dipping below 10,000 feet. The Toiyabe Crest Trail exposes backpackers to nearly 70 miles of the range's most dramatic topography.

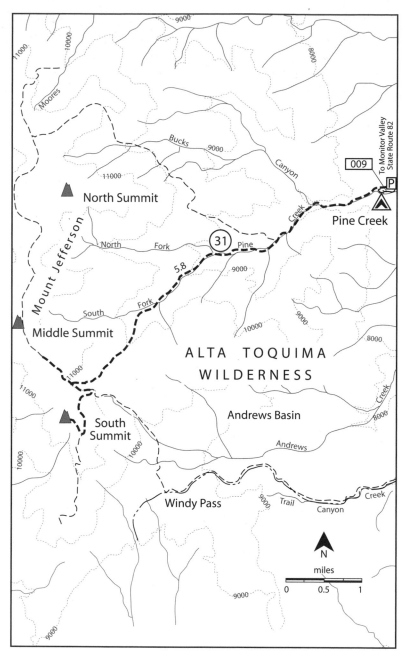

MAP 22 | Mt. Jefferson

Along with outstanding scenery, interesting botanical, geological, and archaeological features await diligent hikers who gain the unique summit environment atop Mt. Jefferson.

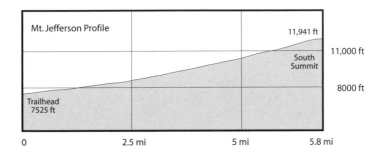

DISTANCE & ROUTE:	11.6 miles round trip
DIFFICULTY:	Strenuous
SEASON:	Summer, fall
TRAILHEAD ACCESS:	High-clearance vehicle recommended
WATER:	Available in Pine Creek
GUIDEBOOK MAP:	22
USGS MAP:	Pine Creek Ranch, Mt. Jefferson

INTRODUCTION   This trip offers hikers a diverse experience in the Alta Toquima Wilderness, following the Pine Creek Trail to a unique environment on top of Mt. Jefferson. Both Pine Creek and Mt. Jefferson have much to offer the visitor to this seldom-seen land. Beginning in pinyon-juniper woodland, hikers quickly encounter lush riparian foliage alongside tumbling Pine Creek, where fishing for brown, brook, rainbow, and cutthroat trout is reported to be quite good. As the trail gains elevation, quaking aspens and limber pines fill the upper canyon. Along the tableland crest of Mt. Jefferson, desert-like alpine flora make up a unique biological zone within the Mt. Jefferson Research Natural Area.

Near the head of Pine Creek's canyon, the Pine Creek Trail intersects the Mt. Jefferson Trail, which heads north-south along the lengthy crest of the mountain. Hikers turning south can climb South Summit, at 11,941 feet the highest of the three summits of Mt. Jefferson. The trail leads to a short, technically easy climb of the sixth highest peak in Nevada; the summit provides fine views in every direction. The trail to the north ascends to the Mt. Jefferson plateau, a long, narrow tableland above glaciated canyons. Views from the plateau stretch from one horizon to the other, offering long-range vistas that span the state.

DIRECTIONS TO TRAILHEAD Reach the Monitor Valley Road (S.R. 82) from the south via S.R. 376, which intersects U.S. 6 about 5.5 miles east of Tonopah. Drive on S.R. 376 for about 13 miles to a junction of Monitor Valley Road.

From the north, drive on U.S. 50 to the junction with S.R. 376, about 12 miles east of Austin. Head south on S.R. 376 and immediately turn southeast onto F.R. 100, following a sign marked TOQUIMA CAVE. Proceed for 28 miles to Monitor Valley Road.

Drive on Monitor Valley Road (S.R. 82) to the intersection with Pine Creek Road, approximately 47 miles north of the junction of S.R. 376 and 53 miles south of the junction of F.R. 100. Head south on Pine Creek Road (F.R. 009) for just short of a mile to a junction with a road to a ranch and bear right. After another mile the road bends southwest, entering Forest Service land at 2.9 miles from Monitor Valley Road, and continuing into Pine Creek Campground at 3.4 miles. Campsites are straight ahead, but the unsigned trailhead is up a short road to the right, where a wide clearing allows parking for several vehicles.

DESCRIPTION From the parking area, follow the continuation of the road for a short distance until reaching a single-track trail, where the road bends uphill. Proceed on the trail, soon passing a lateral from the campground, as you stroll above aspen-lined Pine Creek across a hillside dotted with pinyon pines. Step across a seasonal stream and reach the Alta Toquima Wilderness boundary, where a crude sign nailed to a cottonwood reads JEFFERSON 6.

Dense riparian foliage lines the banks of Pine Creek, which the trail fords three times before delivering you to a junction of the seldom-used trail 035 to Pasco Canyon, 1.1 miles from the trailhead.

Continue up the main trail through dense vegetation, fording Pine Creek four more times. At what appears on the ground to be a fifth crossing, remain on the north side of the creek, as newer trail climbs steeply up the hillside to surmount some cliffs. Soon the trail returns to the creek as you proceed upstream, making several more fords along the way. At 1.9 miles, you reach the poorly marked junction with trail 033 that provides a possible loop connection to the Mt. Jefferson Trail, although the unmaintained trail is in poor condition and difficult to follow in places.

Proceed upstream, as the trail wanders back and forth over the creek. Farther up the canyon, you ascend through lush aspen groves and grasslands decorated with blue lupine and red paintbrush. Eventually, you emerge from the trees and cross an open area of sagebrush and grasses, which allow good views

Crude sign at trail junction below Mt. Jefferson, Pine Creek Trail, Toquima Range

toward the sweeping slopes of upper Pine Creek canyon. Approximately 4 miles from the trailhead, the trail veers across the narrowing creek to a spring-fed meadow, where discernible tread temporarily disappears in the verdant grass—watch for ducks to help guide you to the resumption of trail.

The grade of ascent increases as you climb through a lush understory beneath the filtered shade of aspens and limber pines. Farther up the canyon, pass in and out of forest cover to a spring on the far side of the creek, about 4.5 miles from the trailhead. Leave the limber pines behind and climb across grassy slopes for another 0.3 mile to another set of springs that sends a trickle of water into the diminishing creek.

Now you ascend the wide open, sloping basin below the crest of the Toquima Range, where grassy slopes merge into austere, rock-filled hillsides. Once again, discernible tread disappears in the meadow grass; ducks will guide you to a more distinct junction of the Mt. Jefferson Trail near a large cairn, where a weathered tree limb supports a crude wood sign reading s. summit, north summit.

A couple of options face you at the junction. The trail to the southeast leads toward South Summit. To reach the top, follow the trail across a talus field to the crest of a ridge, where you meet the indistinct trail from Windy Pass. Bear west from the ridge and climb steeply below the east face of South Summit to milder climbing along an ascending traverse to the south side of the peak. Leave the trail and ascend easy slopes to the top, where a 360-degree vista awaits.

The second option is to reach the lip of the broad plateau that forms the top of Mt. Jefferson. Turn northwest from the junction and continue to climb out of the canyon to crest the low point in the ridge above. As you climb out of the canyon, the tread grows faint again, but ducks should successfully guide you past rock cliffs to where the track reappears. After a switchback, the trail curves around to gain the crest and then disappears. The long plateau atop Mt. Jefferson is before you, where expansive views stretch from eastern California to western Utah. Across Big Smoky Valley to the west, Arc Dome (11,773 feet) presides over the Toiyabe Range. Across Monitor Valley to the east, the vast mesa-like plateau of Table Mountain rises out of the Monitor Range. Within the Toquima Range, South Summit, Shoshone Mountain, and Spanish Peak dominate the foreground.

TOQUIMA HISTORY   The Toquima Range is rich in human history as well as natural history. "Toquima" literally means black backs, referring to the band of Mono Indians who once roamed freely in the lower Reese River Valley. In 1978, archaeologists discovered the remains of a village on top of Mt. Jefferson, which turned out to be the highest known settlement of Native Americans in North America. Archaeologists speculate that the area was used as a males-only hunting camp several thousands of years ago. Around A.D. 1300, entire families inhabited the area. In more recent times, John Muir explored the Toquima Range, deducing from his geologic observations that glaciers played an important part in the sculpting of mountains within the Great Basin.

Hikes in the eastern Nevada section are drawn from a national park, a wilderness area, and three state parks, which hint at the valuable recreation lands within the region. By now, describing areas of Nevada as remote starts to sound a bit redundant, but this region is far away from just about anywhere. Adding emphasis to this remoteness is the fact that the major highway (U.S. 50) providing the principal access to these lands has been dubbed "the loneliest highway in America."

Although setting aside the lands surrounding Wheeler Peak and Lehman Caves began as early as the 1920s, Great Basin National Park did not come into existence as we know it today until 1986. Despite the name, the park is composed of mountains and mountainous terrain, harboring subalpine lakes, flower-filled meadows, ice-sculpted canyons, bristlecone pine groves, and a completely unique feature in the Great Basin—a glacier. Comprising approximately 77,000 acres, the park straddles the crest of the southern Snake Range and includes seven named peaks over 11,500 feet in elevation, including the 13,063-foot crown jewel, Wheeler Peak, second highest summit in the state.

A variety of trails penetrate the park's hinterlands, leading to one rarity after another. The Alpine Lakes Loop leads hikers to a pair of subalpine lakes that seem more at home in the Rockies than a mountain range in Nevada. The Bristlecone-Glacier Trail climbs past an awe-inspiring grove of ancient, gnarled bristlecone pines to a dramatic cirque holding the glacier. A 3-mile, 3000-foot climb on the Summit Trail leads to the summit of Wheeler Peak, where summiteers enjoy extraordinary views that span across Nevada and Utah. If biodiversity strikes a chord, the Lehman Creek Trail passes through a wide range of Great Basin plant communities. In the southeast corner of the park, a short trail takes visitors to a six-story limestone arch standing guard over a narrow canyon. Rounding out the trail entries are a pair of forested trails leading to Johnson and Baker Lakes. Along with the hiking trails, visitors to Great Basin National Park should plan on taking a guided tour of Lehman Caves for a nominal fee.

A nearly forgotten neighbor to the north of Great Basin National Park, Mt. Moriah straddles the north end of the Snake Range, thrusting its summit above the surrounding basins as the fifth highest peak in the state at 12,067 feet.

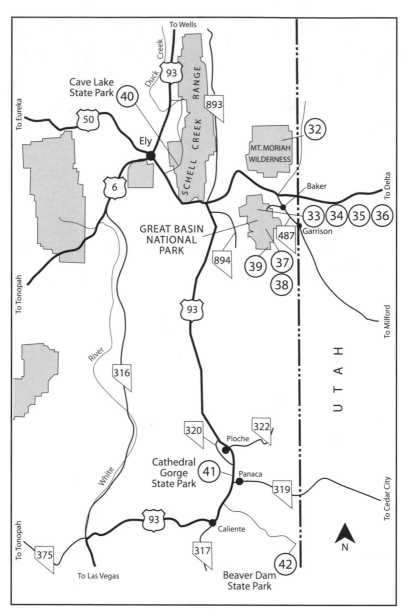

MAP 23 | Hikes of Eastern Nevada

A thousand feet below the peak, a broad, slightly sloping, square-mile table-land, aptly named The Table, offers grand views and interesting bristlecone pines. The Hampton Creek Trail travels through a scenic canyon filled with conifers, cottonwoods, and aspens before reaching the loftier heights of The Table and Mt. Moriah.

Paved roads access Cave Lake State Park, which helps make the area a relatively popular summer destination for campers, picnickers, boaters, and anglers despite the remote location. With an elevation near 7500 feet, the summer climate is quite nice and the 32-acre reservoir provides an excellent way to cool off after a stimulating hike along the Cave Springs Trail, a 5-mile romp through the pinyon-juniper woodland of the Schell Creek Range.

Cathedral Gorge State Park, adjacent to U.S. 93 and 2 miles north of Panaca, has some of the most interesting topography in the state. The long, narrow valley rimmed by cathedral-like towers of bentonite clay is truly an awe-inspiring place. Several short trails provide a wide range of views of Cathedral Gorge and the numerous formations composing the walls of the canyon. With an elevation just below 5000 feet, most visitors will find the best times for hiking to be in the spring and fall, although the park is open all year.

The 28-mile drive on a dirt road might be enough to dissuade most motorists from visiting Beaver Dam State Park just inside the Utah border, but the isolated park is well worth a visit for those who are striving to get away from it all. Four short trails visit perennial streams, hills covered by pinyon-juniper woodland, and a sizable reservoir that combine to provide excellent scenery. Despite the isolation, the park has developed campgrounds with running water.

FYI ■ As previously mentioned, the territory of eastern Nevada is remote and far away from any major population center. Ely is the nearest sizable town, offering a range of basic services. Despite the remote nature of the region, access to the trails is generally good, with routes over paved highways for many of the trails listed in this chapter.

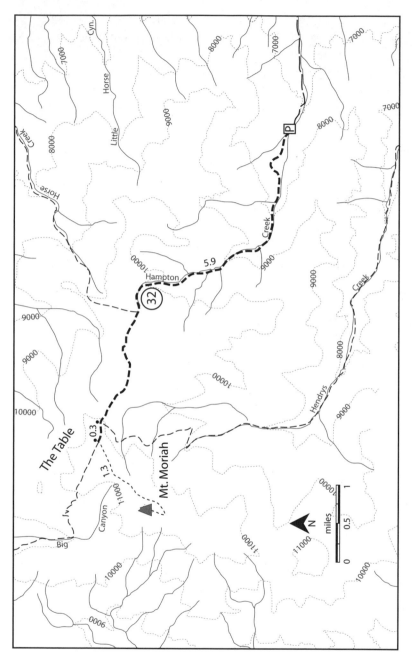

MAP 24 | Hampton Creek

Solitude is virtually guaranteed on the 7.5-mile-long journey to the top of Nevada's fifth highest mountain, where successful summiteers will be treated to an extraordinary vista.

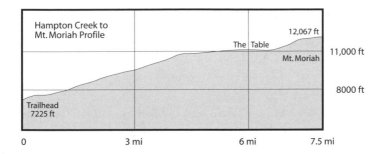

Hampton Creek to Mt. Moriah Profile

The Table

12,067 ft

Mt. Moriah

11,000 ft

8000 ft

Trailhead 7225 ft

0   3 mi   6 mi   7.5 mi

DISTANCE & ROUTE:	15 miles round trip
DIFFICULTY:	Strenuous
SEASON:	Summer
TRAILHEAD ACCESS:	High-clearance vehicle recommended
WATER:	Available in Hampton Creek
GUIDEBOOK MAP:	24
USGS MAP:	The Cove, Old Mans Canyon, Mount Moriah

INTRODUCTION The Mt. Moriah Wilderness is hidden along the extreme eastern edge of the state, hundreds of miles away from any sizable population center. Consequently, visitors can expect a reasonable dose of solitude while traveling the backcountry trails. The Hampton Creek Trail is the shortest route to Mt. Moriah and the heart of the wilderness with a trailhead accessible to vehicles without four-wheel drive.

The trail takes hikers on a climb through a steep canyon filled with a dense, mixed forest that impedes views of Mt. Moriah for the first 4.5 miles. Along the way, Hampton Creek is crossed several times before the trail veers away from the creek to climb toward The Table. Once on The Table, a broad, sloping plateau near 11,000 feet, spectacular vistas abound of Mt. Moriah, the surrounding wilderness, and Wheeler Peak and the rest of the Snake Range to the south. Hardy mountaineer types can follow a use trail another 1.3 miles and 1050 feet (one-way) for a climb of Mt. Moriah.

DIRECTIONS TO TRAILHEAD From U.S. 50 turn northeast onto paved Silver Creek Road opposite the junction of S.R. 487, which heads southeast toward the town of Baker and Great Basin National Park. This junction is approximately 58 miles east of Ely, Nevada, and 90 miles west of Delta, Utah. About 2 miles northeast of U.S. 50, the surface changes to gravel as you pass through Silver Creek Ranch. Cross the Utah border at 9.3 miles, pass the turnoff for Hendry's Creek at 10.7 miles, and immediately encounter a Y-junction with a prominent gravel road (Gandy Road) from the south. Continue northbound on this main road another 4 miles to the signed turnoff for Hampton Creek.

Head west toward the mountains on a narrow and rough dirt road, crossing into National Forest land near the 5.5 mile mark. Follow the road on a stiff climb alongside Hampton Creek, passing several mining operations along the way. At 6.25 miles, you pass a road on the left leading down to a small campsite near the creek, complete with picnic table and fire ring. The trailhead parking area is just past this road.

DESCRIPTION   Initially the route follows the continuation of the old road on a moderate climb through pinyon-juniper woodland to a short section of single-track trail. Make a switchbacking climb across the hillside before rejoining the road higher up the slope. At a Y-junction, follow the more traveled road on the right. Soon you encounter another road, where you veer left and reach the wilderness boundary after a mere 50 feet.

The grade abates for a while, as you wind around a hillside well above Hampton Creek. Approaching a seasonal stream, aspens, ponderosa pines, and white firs make their first appearances. A short way farther is an abandoned ditch, probably built to supply water for a nearby garnet mine. The grade of ascent increases, as you continue upstream amid mixed forest. After crossing two more seasonal streams the road merges with a single-track trail.

You leave the mixed forest briefly to cross drier slopes dotted with mountain-mahogany before wandering back into the trees and across Hampton Creek. Continuing upstream, step over two more seasonal streams and then climb a series of six switchbacks through Douglas-fir forest (with a smattering of white firs and ponderosa pines), which provides some welcome shade from the hot summer sun. Continue the climb up the canyon, crossing Hampton Creek several times along the way. The appearance of limber pines and then bristlecone pines herald the increase in elevation.

Progressing upstream, you pass through an extensive aspen grove and emerge onto a grassy meadow, where the track of the trail disappears. A few well-placed cairns should guide you across the meadow and back into mixed forest. Near the meadow is the unmarked junction with the primitive trail down Horse Canyon, 3.75 miles from the trailhead.

Mt. Moriah from The Table, Northern Snake Range

Follow cairns and ducks through a light forest of subalpine fir until the trail reappears. As you gain more elevation, bristlecone pines become the dominant conifer, intermixed with a smattering of subalpine fir. Farther on, a clearing allows the first view of Mt. Moriah to the west. You gain the crest of a ridge and then follow it to the east edge of The Table, a broad, sloping, rocky plateau, offering much better views of Mt. Moriah ahead and the Snake Range to the south.

Cairns delineate the route of the trail across The Table, where the contorted trunks and limbs of widely scattered bristlecone pines add a dash of character to the picturesque vistas. Sections of trail appear, disappear, and reappear across The Table, but the open terrain makes finding the route straightforward. At 5.9 miles is a junction with the Hendrys Creek Trail.

From the Hendrys Creek Trail junction, continue across The Table another 0.3 mile to the northeast ridge of Mt. Moriah. Leave the trail and follow cairns and ducks that lead up a steep slope to the crest of the northeast ridge, over the ridge, and then down to a small saddle. A distinct path away from the saddle traverses below a satellite peak northeast of the true summit to a larger saddle. From there, follow an ascending traverse across the east face of Mt. Moriah to where the well-defined path abruptly ends south of the summit, as if a trail crew decided to take a break and never returned. From here, head north over easy slopes to the top. Views from the summit are both incredible and far-reaching.

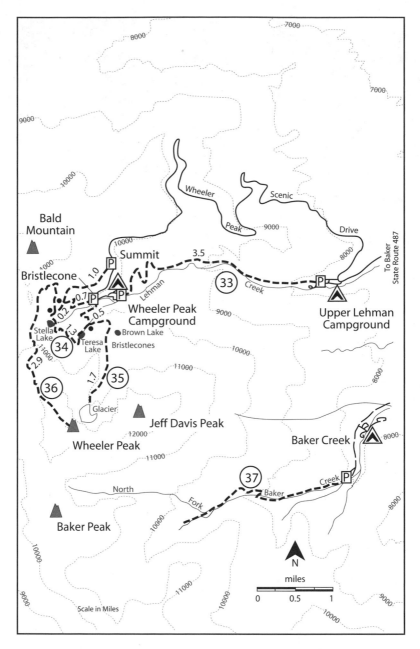

MAP 25 | Great Basin National Park (North)

HIKE 33 | LEHMAN CREEK

A short hike on an infrequently used trail exposes hikers to the biodiversity within Great Basin National Park.

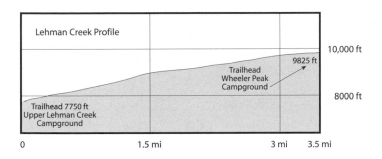

DISTANCE & ROUTE:	3.5 miles one way, shuttle for return
DIFFICULTY:	Moderate
SEASON:	Summer, fall
TRAILHEAD ACCESS:	All vehicles
WATER:	Available in Lehman Creek
GUIDEBOOK MAP:	25
USGS MAP:	Windy Peak

INTRODUCTION   The Lehman Creek Trail, connecting Upper Lehman Creek and Wheeler Peak Campgrounds, offers a steady climb through a diverse sampling of vegetation. In roughly ascending order, you will see such trees as pinyon pine, juniper, mountain-mahogany, aspen, Douglas-fir, white fir, limber pine, and Engelmann spruce. A wide variety of shrubs are seen as well, including the ubiquitous sagebrush, along with barberry, wild rose, and even some prickly pear cactus. Although the trail follows directly alongside the creek for only a short distance, you remain under the shade of riparian foliage or forest cover for most of the way, avoiding the direct rays of the hot summer sun. The Lehman Creek Trail provides a fine outdoor classroom for studying ecosystem diversity within the Great Basin environment.

While neighboring trails in the park see a good share of hikers, the Lehman Creek Trail is lightly used, offering a reasonable expectation of solitude for those in search of a little peace and quiet. The following description is from bottom to top—reverse the description if you prefer an easier downhill romp.

DIRECTIONS TO TRAILHEADS

START   From U.S. 50, approximately 58 miles east of Ely, Nevada, and 90 miles west of Delta, Utah, turn southeast onto S.R. 487, following signs for Baker and Great Basin National Park. Proceed on S.R. 487 for 5 miles to the town of Baker and turn west onto S.R. 488 toward Great Basin National Park.

Pass through the park entrance (no fee as of 2005) and turn right onto Wheeler Peak Scenic Drive, passing Lower Lehman Creek Campground on the way to the entrance for Upper Lehman Creek Campground, 2.4 miles from the junction. Follow the campground access road to the upper campsites and find the small trailhead parking area off a short turnoff on your right, where a sign marks the trail.

END   Continue on Wheeler Peak Scenic Drive from the entrance to Upper Lehman Creek Campground to Wheeler Peak Campground at the end of the 12-mile road. Proceed into the campground to the trailhead near the east end of the main loop, where parking is available for just a few cars.

DESCRIPTION   From Upper Lehman Creek Campground, start climbing along the course of an old road through mixed forest of mountain-mahogany, pinyon pine, juniper, and aspen, with a groundcover of scattered sagebrush and prickly pear cactus. Pass through a cattle gate and continue the mild climb, as the trail nears aspen-lined Lehman Creek and then soon veers away. You shortly reach the remnants of the Osceola Ditch.

The steady climb upstream takes you into the realm of Douglas-firs and white firs, interspersed with more aspens. Hike along the creek for a stretch and enjoy the fine display of wildflowers lining the banks, including a profusion of shooting stars. All too soon, you leave the tranquil creekside setting behind as a switchback leads into a seasonal drainage, where manzanita flourishes in the drier soils. Continue the ascent as limber pines begin to intermix with the Douglas-firs and white firs. The climb leads onto a broad, open flat, where you have your first glimpse of dramatic Wheeler Peak towering above the head of the canyon. Once across this clearing, dotted with an occasional sagebrush or mountain-mahogany, the trail reenters forest cover.

The sound of running water gets closer as you approach a wide, shallow stream coursing around moss-covered boulders, where a series of well-placed log rounds provides a trouble-free crossing. Away from the stream, the grade increases again as you follow periodic switchbacks across the hillside. Eventually the grade eases near a pocket of young aspens and, farther on, you pass through a cattle gate, which heralds your approach to Wheeler Peak Campground. A final clearing affords one more glimpse of Wheeler Peak before an easy stroll leads to the upper trailhead.

HIKE 34 | ALPINE LAKES LOOP

A relatively easy 2.7-mile hike passes by two lovely subalpine tarns.

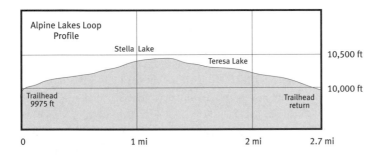

DISTANCE & ROUTE:	2.7 miles one way in loop
DIFFICULTY:	Easy
SEASON:	Summer, fall
TRAILHEAD ACCESS:	All vehicles
WATER:	Available in Stella and Teresa Lakes
GUIDEBOOK MAP:	25
USGS MAP:	Windy Peak, Wheeler Peak

INTRODUCTION   The Alpine Lakes Loop is one of the more popular trails within Great Basin National Park for good reason. At slightly less than 2.7 miles long with an elevation gain of less than 500 feet, the route is easy enough for just about anyone, young or old. The trail visits two picturesque subalpine tarns, Stella and Teresa, tucked into rock-rimmed basins scoured by ancient glaciers.

The lakes are particularly scenic in early season, when the lakes are full and wildflowers grace the shoreline. By late summer the water level of both lakes drops considerably, although the surrounding scenery is still quite pleasant.

Hardy hikers looking for a more rigorous challenge can combine a hike around the Alpine Lakes Loop with an extension to the Wheeler Peak Glacier (see hike 36).

DIRECTIONS TO TRAILHEAD From U.S. 50, approximately 58 miles east of Ely, Nevada, and 90 miles west of Delta, Utah, turn southeast onto S.R. 487, following signs for Baker and Great Basin National Park. Proceed on S.R. 487 for 5 miles into the town of Baker and turn west onto S.R. 488 toward Great Basin National Park.

Pass through the park entrance (no fee as of 2005) and turn right onto Wheeler Peak Scenic Drive. Follow Wheeler Peak Scenic Drive past the entrances to Lower and Upper Lehman Creek Campgrounds at 1.8 and 2.4 miles, the Osceola Ditch Exhibit turnout at 4.7 miles, Mather and Wheeler Peak Overlooks at 6.7 and 9.6 miles, and the Summit Trail parking area at 11 miles, reaching the Bristlecone trailhead near the entrance into Wheeler Peak Campground, 11.7 miles from the junction.

DESCRIPTION Across the paved campground road, the well-marked, well-graded, and well-used trail leads into a mixed forest of Douglas-fir, limber pine, and Engelmann spruce. After passing over the north branch of Lehman Creek on a wood bridge, you make a short climb to a signed junction. Turn right following directions for Alpine Lakes Loop Trail and wind through dense forest to the bridged crossing of a small, gurgling stream. Beyond the bridge, a clearing offers fine views of Wheeler and Jeff Davis Peaks. Briefly return to forest cover before reaching a large meadow and a junction with the Summit Trail. The two trails share the same path for the next 0.2 mile to a junction, where the Summit Trail veers north and the Alpine Lakes Loop heads southwest. Remaining on the Alpine Loop Trail from the Summit Trail junction, you pass through widely scattered spruces and pines to the shore of Stella Lake, 1 mile from the trailhead.

Shallow Stella Lake is a beautiful gem situated beneath steep rock walls. Early in the season, the spruce-and-pine-rimmed lake is full and a fine display of wildflowers is in bloom around the shoreline, creating a picturesque setting unrivaled in beauty, except for its exquisite neighbor, Teresa Lake. An old rock dam near the outlet seems largely ineffective at retaining the lake's waters, as by late summer the lake diminishes to the size of a large pond.

Continuing on the Alpine Lakes Loop, you pass Stella Lake above the east shore and gently climb through a forest of Engelmann spruce interspersed with an occasional limber pine. A 0.5-mile descent leads alongside a lushly lined, spring-fed creek to lovely Teresa Lake, 1.8 miles from the trailhead.

Rocky slopes dotted with pines and spruces encircle the symmetrical lake. Along the inlet is a verdant swatch of flower-carpeted meadow. Early in the season, Teresa Lake offers a picturesque scene; however, just like Stella, the lake level declines significantly by late summer.

Away from Teresa Lake, descend rocky terrain for 0.1 mile to a junction of the Bristlecone Trail (see hike 35). Take the left hand trail and continue descending toward the trailhead through thickening forest. You reach the end of the loop at the first junction, from where you should retrace your steps to the parking lot.

ENGELMANN SPRUCE (*PICEA ENGELMANNII*)   A high-elevation conifer common to the Rocky Mountains, Engelmann spruce is limited to four eastern Nevada ranges in Elko and White Pine Counties. The tree is most prolific in the Snake Range, where it appears in extensive forests with Douglas-fir and limber pine. Near timberline, stunted windswept trees often form tangled thickets known as *krummholz.*

HIKE 35 | BRISTLECONE GROVE AND WHEELER PEAK GLACIER

A short hike to a stunning grove of ancient bristlecone pines and a glacier makes this hike one of the most interesting walks in the Great Basin.

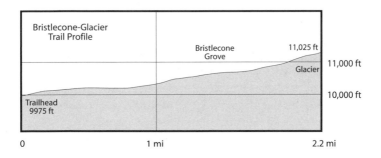

DISTANCE & ROUTE:	4.4 miles round trip
DIFFICULTY:	Moderate
SEASON:	Summer
TRAILHEAD ACCESS:	All vehicles
WATER:	None available
GUIDEBOOK MAP:	25
USGS MAP:	Windy Peak, Wheeler Peak

INTRODUCTION The Bristlecone-Glacier Trail lives up to its name by taking hikers first to a mature grove of stunning bristlecone pines, the oldest living things on the planet, and then 1 the only glacier within the entire Great Basin, set in a deep cirque beneath the rugged north face of 13,063-foot Wheeler Peak.

The trail provides the least difficult route within the state of Nevada for the average person to experience up close the magnificence of the bristlecone pines. Oddly enough, these trees thrive in the worst of conditions, living for thousands of years in harsh environments at high altitudes, while dying out after two hundred years or so in the seemingly milder conditions at lower altitudes.

Beyond the bristlecone pines lies an unmatched Great Basin experience, the Wheeler Peak Glacier. Almost incomprehensibly, a body of ice reposes beneath the steep north face of Wheeler Peak in a shady cirque basin. The lower section is referred to as a rock glacier, as glacial ice is buried beneath tons of rock debris. Noted by the U.S. Geological Survey in the 1800s but somehow forgotten until 1955, the glacier remains a mostly unknown entity to this day by the vast majority of people unfamiliar with Great Basin National Park. Not only is the glacier a unique geologic feature, but the cirque basin is one of the most strikingly dramatic canyons in the Great Basin.

DIRECTIONS TO TRAILHEAD From U.S. 50, approximately 58 miles east of Ely, Nevada, and 90 miles west of Delta, Utah, turn southeast onto S.R. 487, following signs for Baker and Great Basin National Park. Proceed on S.R. 487 for 5 miles into the town of Baker and turn west onto S.R. 488 toward Great Basin National Park.

Pass through the park entrance (no fee as of 2005) and turn right onto Wheeler Peak Scenic Drive. Follow Wheeler Peak Scenic Drive past the entrances to Lower and Upper Lehman Creek Campgrounds at 1.8 and 2.4 miles, the Osceola Ditch Exhibit turnout at 4.7 miles, Mather and Wheeler Peak Overlooks at 6.7 and 9.6 miles, and the Summit Trail parking area at 11 miles, reaching the Bristlecone trailhead near the entrance into Wheeler Peak Campground, 11.7 miles from the junction.

DESCRIPTION Across the paved campground road, the well-marked, well-graded, and well-used trail leads into mixed forest of Douglas-fir, limber pine, and Engelmann spruce. After passing over the north branch of Lehman Creek on a wood bridge, you make a short climb to a signed junction. Veer left and make a moderate climb, initially through dense pine and spruce forest, which becomes more scattered on the way to a signed junction, 0.5 mile from the trailhead.

Turn left at the junction and follow the Bristlecone-Glacier Trail east over a short hump and down into a dry, rock-filled swale, where the trail veers away to cross a talus field. After the talus, climb a slope covered with Engelmann spruce and bend south toward the canyon emanating from the glacial cirque below the north face of Wheeler Peak. Nestled beneath the trees, you see Brown Lake 0.1 mile east of the trail. Although bypassed by maintained trail, reaching the lake is easy via a short cross-country jaunt. After a brief descent across a seasonal drainage, you resume the climb through Engelmann spruce before encountering the first specimens of bristlecone pine.

Near the 1.3-mile mark, you reach a junction with the Bristlecone Interpretive Trail, which offers a worthwhile diversion, even if your ultimate destination is the glacier. The short nature trail takes you among some of the elder monarchs residing within the grove. Interpretive signs provide a bevy of interesting facts about the oldest living species on earth, including details on growth habits, cross-dating, and growth rings. One of the bristlecones has been dated as being 3,200 years old. The exhibits are very informative, and you will witness firsthand some of the most dramatic-looking bristlecones accessible by trail— don't forget your camera.

The main trail, signed GLACIER TRAIL, continues up the canyon, leaving behind the bristlecones and climbing toward the cirque basin below Wheeler Peak. Aside from a few tufts of grass and an occasional low-growing plant, the basin is filled with acres and acres of rock. After an interpretive sign about glaciation, the path becomes steeper, as you wind up the canyon into a dramatic amphitheater below pinnacled ridges and the strikingly vertical north face of Wheeler Peak. A sign near the base of the glacier's terminal moraine discourages further progress in the face of unstable rock and falling debris. Despite the warning, an unmaintained path surmounts the moraine and continues to the foot of the glacier. Proceed at your own risk, carefully observing the slopes above for rockfall. Jagged spires and pinnacled towers rim the quartzite cirque, potentially unstable from the continuous freeze-thaw cycle occurring at this elevation and exposure. If you're bold enough to proceed all the way to the head of the canyon, you may notice a *randkluft*, a large yawning chasm (like a *bergschrund*), where glacial ice has separated from the neighboring rock. Surrounded by the austere beauty of the cirque and the overwhelming stature of the vertical bulwark of the canyon walls, you can't help but develop a sense of personal insignificance.

Bristlecone pine, Bristlecone-Glacier Trail, Great Basin National Park

WHEELER PEAK GLACIER The Wheeler Peak Glacier is at the center of a mild controversy, which began in the 1950s: is this body of ice technically a glacier, or just an icefield? The main controversy boils down to whether or not the glacier is moving, or active. A glacier forms over a period of years when snow accumulates during the winter and then fails to completely melt during the following summer. The unmelted snow is covered by additional snowfall the next winter, compressing and transforming the underlying layers into a body of granular ice. As the ice continues to thicken, the glacier advances down the valley, plucking up the underlying rock material along the way. If snow accumulation fails to exceed or meet the rate of melting, the glacier retreats back up the valley. Most of the glaciers in the continental U.S. are classified as retreating. A rock glacier forms when an active glacier is covered by a significant layer of rock debris but otherwise exhibits the normal characteristics of a glacier.

HIKE 36 | WHEELER PEAK

The 13,063-foot summit of Wheeler Peak provides spectacular views and a grand sense of accomplishment for those who stand on top of Nevada's second highest mountain.

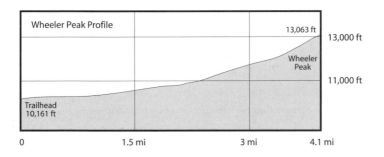

DISTANCE & ROUTE:	8.2 miles round trip
DIFFICULTY:	Strenuous
SEASON:	Summer
TRAILHEAD ACCESS:	All vehicles
WATER:	None available
GUIDEBOOK MAP:	25
USGS MAP:	Windy Peak, Wheeler Peak

INTRODUCTION   The ultimate climax to any hiker's visit to Great Basin National Park is the climb to the summit of Wheeler Peak along the aptly named Summit Trail. Thanks to a starting elevation near 10,000 feet, the ascent to the top of the 13,063-foot peak is not as overwhelmingly strenuous as it could be.

The first half of the trip climbs mildly through lush foliage before wandering through sparse stands of Engelmann spruce, limber pine, and bristlecone pine. The light forest allows excellent views of Wheeler Peak along the way. Beyond a broad saddle at the crest near the midpoint of the climb, harsh elements combine to create a less hospitable environment for the native vegetation. *Krummholz*, a German word meaning crooked wood, refers to the windswept, weather-beaten, and twisted forms of the limbs and trunks of the conifers just below timberline. Beyond timberline, the trail is steep, rocky, and nearly devoid of vegetation. After surmounting the rugged, boulder-strewn slopes, the summit provides extraordinary, 360-degree views through the clear skies of eastern Nevada and western Utah.

Wheeler Peak itself is one of the most dramatic-looking mountains in the Great Basin, towering some 8000 vertical feet above the surrounding valleys and dominating the skyline from both east and west. The vertical north face plummets 1500 feet from the summit to a cirque basin holding the only glacier in the entire Great Basin. The deep, glacier-carved cirque bordered by precipitous quartzite walls is a scene as magnificent as any alpine sight in the western United States.

Although the trail to the top of Wheeler Peak is considered easy by technical standards, a few concerns are worth noting. Always carry plenty of water, as aside from a couple of springs near the trailhead there is none along the trail. Keep an eye on the weather for developing thunderstorms, and realize that on the upper half of the climb you'll be the tallest object around. Be prepared to beat a hasty retreat when thunderstorms develop. Also, bear in mind that the temperature at the wind-prone summit may be substantially cooler than at the pleasant trailhead, so pack appropriate clothing. Make sure you're appropriately acclimated before embarking on this hike, as altitude sickness is a concern at these elevations. Be prepared for the intense rays of the sun at this altitude as well.

DIRECTIONS TO TRAILHEAD   From U.S. 50, approximately 58 miles east of Ely, Nevada, and 90 miles west of Delta, Utah, turn southeast onto S.R. 487, following signs for Baker and Great Basin National Park. Proceed on S.R. 487 for 5 miles into the town of Baker and turn west onto S.R. 488 toward Great Basin National Park.

Pass through the park entrance (no fee as of 2005) and turn right onto Wheeler Peak Scenic Drive. Follow Wheeler Peak Scenic Drive past the entrances to Lower and Upper Lehman Creek Campgrounds at 1.8 and 2.4 miles, the Osceola Ditch Exhibit turnout at 4.7 miles, Mather and Wheeler Peak Overlooks at 6.7 and 9.6 miles, on the way to the Summit Trail parking area at 11 miles from the junction.

DESCRIPTION   From the southeast edge of the parking lot, proceed on single-track trail through sagebrush, shrubs, and wildflowers, soon encountering a stand of mature aspens shading lush ground cover. Come alongside a small stream lined with beautiful wildflowers and small plants, then veer away from the stream into shrubby aspens. Further along the trail, springs feed more lush trailside vegetation. Head downhill into a clearing, where you'll find a signed junction of the Alpine Lakes Loop, 1 mile from the trailhead (by beginning and ending your trip at the Bristlecone trailhead, you could shave off 0.6 mile from the round trip—see hike 34).

For the next 0.2 mile, the Summit Trail and Alpine Lakes Loop share a common path to the next junction, where you veer uphill to the right and proceed northbound. A gradual climb wanders around the head of the canyon through widely scattered limber pines toward the crest above. Excellent views of Wheeler Peak and the surrounding terrain abound on this section of trail. As you near the crest, Stella Lake springs into view directly below. You gain the crest in a broad saddle, 2.3 miles and 800 vertical feet from the trailhead.

Now the rate of ascent increases as you climb steeply amid stunted limber pines that sporadically dot the slopes on the way to timberline. Climb through rocky terrain where the tread falters in places, although ducks should help keep you on the correct route. More distinct path returns as you gain elevation on a rising traverse across the east side of Wheeler Peak. A final switchback leads to the long and rocky summit ridge and to the top.

Constructed over the years, a plethora of rock towers, windbreaks, and manmade improvements dot the summit. Spectacular views are seen in all directions: to the south a cavalcade of summits parades across the southern end of the park, to the north lies remote Mt. Moriah, to the east a broad expanse of high desert rolls across western Utah, and across Spring Valley to the west is the Schell Creek Range, with linear rows of other ranges beyond it that march across the Great Basin. Hikers without an overwhelming fear of heights may want to peer down the vertical north face into the impressive glacial cirque below. Many notable landmarks within Great Basin National Park are visible from the summit, including Stella, Teresa, Brown, Baker, and Johnson Lakes.

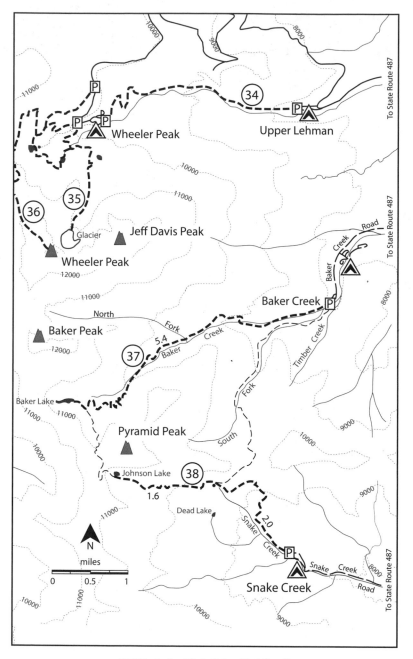

MAP 26 | Great Basin National Park (South)

HIKE 37 | BAKER LAKE

Follow alongside a tumbling stream to a pretty subalpine lake near the base of Baker Peak.

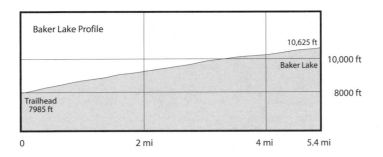

DISTANCE & ROUTE:	10.8 miles round trip
DIFFICULTY:	Moderate
SEASON:	Summer, fall
TRAILHEAD ACCESS:	All vehicles
WATER:	Baker Creek and Lake
GUIDEBOOK MAP:	26
USGS MAP:	Windy Peak, Kious Spring

INTRODUCTION   This trip offers a visit to a scenic lake near the crest of the Snake Range. Baker Lake reposes majestically near the head of Baker Creek canyon, beneath the rugged walls of a glacial cirque. The trail follows Baker Creek all the way to the lake, a delightful stream that tumbles down a forested canyon interspersed with flower-filled meadows.

DIRECTIONS TO TRAILHEAD   From U.S. 50, approximately 58 miles east of Ely, Nevada, and 90 miles west of Delta, Utah, turn southeast onto S.R. 487, following signs for Baker and Great Basin National Park. Proceed on S.R. 487 for 5 miles to the town of Baker and turn west onto S.R. 488 toward Great Basin National Park. Follow S.R. 488 past the park entrance and past Wheeler Peak Scenic Drive to a junction with Baker Creek Road on your left. Head south on well-graded, two-lane, graveled Baker Creek Road for 3.4 miles to the trailhead at the end of the road, which is 0.5 mile past the entrance into Baker Creek Campground.

DESCRIPTION   Begin hiking on the north side of Baker Creek near the transition between sagebrush-covered slopes to your right and thick forest to your left. Initially, the forest is composed of white fir, Douglas-fir, and aspen. Cross a wood bridge over a narrow rivulet coursing through verdant meadow grass and proceed across a large grassy clearing, where you pass through a cattle gate before entering back into thick forest. Continue through the trees until the path veers away from Baker Creek for a short time, entering an area of drier vegetation filled with pinyon pine, mountain-mahogany, sagebrush, and widely scattered fir. Return alongside the roaring creek and proceed upstream for quite a distance under the cool shade of the forest.

You reach a switchback and make a steep climb away from the creek before bending around in an upstream direction again through manzanita and mountain-mahogany. Farther along the trail, stroll through a scattered, mixed forest of mountain-mahogany, white fir, limber pine, and aspen with an understory of manzanita. The open nature of the forest allows partial views up the canyon, including the triangular-shaped Baker Peak.

You cross a strong-flowing tributary stream near a lovely pool, surrounded by a verdant assemblage of mosses, grasses, and wildflowers, including a bounty of columbines. This serene grotto provides a pleasant spot for a relaxing break before resuming the hike through mixed forest. Following the course of Baker Creek, you continue the steady climb up the trail, hopping over a twin-channeled tributary trickling down a narrow channel of rock. Farther on, a wood walkway bridges a patch of boggy meadow.

Briefly leave the shelter of mixed forest, as the trail passes through a small meadow bisected by a gurgling stream meandering through verdant grasses and wildflowers. Beyond the meadow, reach a switchback, cross another tributary on a four-log bridge, and then contour back toward Baker Creek. Farther upstream, the trail passes directly above a profuse spring, where water bursts out of the ground, tumbles over boulders, and courses through verdant grasses accented by a beautiful array of monkey flowers.

Beyond the spring, the canyon widens and you reach a series of switchbacks that climb a steep hillside covered with Douglas-firs. Above the last switchback, cross the outlet from Baker Lake on a four-log bridge, return to the main branch of Baker Creek, and proceed upstream to Dieshman Cabin. Near the cabin, the trail angles sharply right (west) and makes a switchbacking ascent through Douglas-fir, limber pine, and Engelmann spruce to a junction, 4.4 miles from the trailhead.

Proceed straight at the junction, obeying signed directions to Baker Lake and strolling through spruce forest until the grade becomes significantly steeper near a switchback. Follow the trail on a winding ascent to Baker Lake, cradled in a cirque near the head of the canyon, 5.4 miles from the trailhead.

Baker Lake is a shallow tarn, where talus slopes rise up from the water's surface toward dark, steep cliffs bordering the lake on three sides. Early in the season, icy-blue waters of the full-bodied lake reflect the rugged cliffs rimming the walls of the cirque basin, but by midsummer the lakeshore recedes considerably, exposing a wide band of bleached rock around the shoreline. Anglers can test their skills on the resident trout.

DOUGLAS-FIR (*PSEUDOTSUGA MENZIESII*) Despite being one of the most widely distributed conifers in North America, the Douglas-fir naturally occurs only in a handful of Nevada ranges. Outside of the Carson Range near Lake Tahoe, Douglas-firs are limited to four ranges on the extreme eastern edge of the state. Perhaps the easiest way to identify the tree is by the cones, which exhibit a scale pattern reminiscent of the tail end of a mouse heading into its hole.

HIKE 38 | JOHNSON LAKE

Step back into mining history on the way to picturesque Johnson Lake.

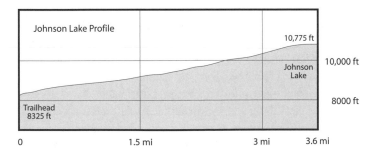

DISTANCE & ROUTE:	7.2 miles round trip
DIFFICULTY:	Moderate
SEASON:	Summer, fall
TRAILHEAD ACCESS:	All vehicles
WATER:	Baker Creek and Lake
GUIDEBOOK MAP:	26
USGS MAP:	Windy Peak, Kious Spring

INTRODUCTION   This trip follows the shortest route to Johnson Lake, a sublime subalpine lake cradled into a glacial cirque near the crest of the Snake Range. Exploring the operations of a defunct high-grade tungsten mine near the lake, including a tramway, stamp mill, numerous log cabins and some larger buildings, provides plenty of historical interest. If you decide to poke around these sites, leave everything in the same condition as you found it. Away from the bustling center of activity within Great Basin National Park, this trail holds plenty of promise for getting away from the crowds.

DIRECTIONS TO TRAILHEAD   From U.S. 50, approximately 58 miles east of Ely, Nevada, and 90 miles west of Delta, Utah, turn southeast onto S.R. 487, following signs for Baker and Great Basin National Park. Proceed on S.R. 487 for 5 miles to the town of Baker, continue for another 5 miles south of Baker, and then turn west onto Snake Creek Road at a sign reading SNAKE CREEK CANYON.

Head west on well-graded, gravel road to the Spring Creek Rearing Station at 3.7 miles from S.R. 487, after which the road narrows and becomes a bit rougher. After entering National Forest land at 4.1 miles and Great Basin National Park at 5.2 miles, the road comes alongside Snake Creek and passes some interesting cliff formations, including Standing Snake Pinnacle. Numerous informal campsites are passed along the way to Shoshone Campground at the end of the road, 12.6 miles from the highway. Nearby, a large sign marks the trailhead.

DESCRIPTION   Begin hiking on the continuation of the rocky road between aspens, white firs, and scattered ponderosa pines on one side and sagebrush-covered slopes on the other. You veer toward and soon cross Snake Creek on a wood plank-and-log bridge and then proceed upstream on the north side of the creek. A large clearing offers excellent views up the canyon. Beyond the clearing, a minor descent leads to the crossing of a seasonal drainage and into an open area of sagebrush. You veer away from the creek to make a steep climb of a sagebrush-covered hillside and then curve around through mixed forest to a junction, 2 miles from the trailhead. The trail on the right (east) is the Timber Creek Trail, which leads to the Baker Creek trailhead.

Head left (west) from the junction and proceed on the dirt track of the old road through dense forest. Reach a closed Park Service gate and continue under the cool shade of a mixed forest composed of white fir, limber pine, and aspen. Farther on, Engelmann spruce joins the forest. After a protracted stroll through the trees, you reach some of the old structures associated with the tungsten mine near Johnson Lake. The large, split-level building nearby housed the stamp mill, which concentrated the tungsten ore before wagons hauled it down the same road you just walked.

Beyond the first set of buildings, the road crosses the outlet stream from Johnson Lake and follows the refreshing brook upstream. The pleasant dirt track of the road from below is replaced by an extremely rocky surface, which makes for difficult hiking in places. You steadily climb through Engelmann spruce forest to a flat just south of the creek, where more historic cabins are located. A short walk from there leads to the south shore of Johnson Lake, 3.6 miles from the trailhead.

Along with the historical interest, Johnson Lake is perhaps one of the nicer lakes within the park. The surface level doesn't diminish over the course of the summer as rapidly as other lakes within the park. Miners attempted to raise the level of the lake by constructing a rock dam near the outlet, but their lack of success showed that they may have turned out to be better miners than dam builders. Steep, dramatic cliffs below the Snake Range crest ring the symmetrical lake, and rock outcroppings add character to the west shore. A small spring emanating from the hillside above the south shore sends a clear, cold stream of water toward the lake through a verdant hillside meadow filled with wildflowers. Whether you come to Johnson Lake to explore the remains of a bygone era, or to take in the enchanting scenery, you won't be disappointed.

JOHNSON MINE Tungsten was discovered in the Snake Mining District in 1913 and Alfred Johnson dug his mine high on the hillside above the west shore of the lake, where a short path still leads to the remains of a log cabin and several entrances to the abandoned mine. The area around Johnson Lake is filled with many other reminders of past activity. Still visible are remains of the old tramway that transported tungsten ore from the mine to a rock outcropping near the lakeshore, where pack mules would take it from there down to the stamp mill. Ultimately, wagons carried the ore all the way from the stamp mill to Frisco, Utah, from where it was transported by rail to a smelter in Salt Lake City. The mining operation continued until a massive snowslide destroyed the structure on the outcropping during the 1930s. Much of the wreckage ended up in the lake, some of which is still visible today near the outlet. Numerous other artifacts from the mining heyday are scattered around the basin.

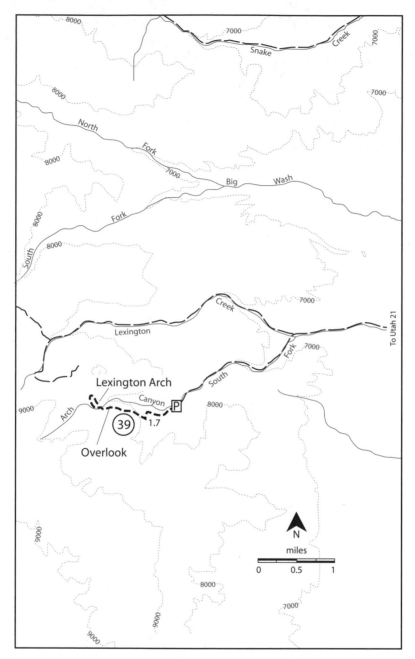

MAP 27 | Lexington Arch

Great Basin National Park is home to many unique natural wonders and Lexington Arch is another example of such uniqueness.

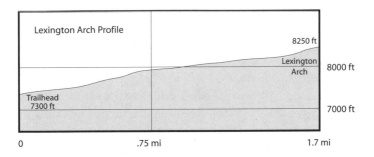

DISTANCE & ROUTE:	3.4 miles round trip
DIFFICULTY:	Moderate
SEASON:	Summer, fall
TRAILHEAD ACCESS:	All vehicles
WATER:	None available
GUIDEBOOK MAP:	27
USGS MAP:	Arch Canyon

INTRODUCTION   Tucked away into an obscure corner of Great Basin National Park is Lexington Arch, a six-story-high limestone span. While Lexington Arch is located within the park, most of the nearly 2-mile trail is on Forest Service land. Several years ago, the Forest Service wisely relocated the trail out of the usually dry wash of Arch Canyon. Nowadays hikers switchback up a wildflower-covered hillside to follow a mildly rising traverse to a vista point high above the wash, where the view of the arch is quite rewarding. The path continues a short way up the canyon and then switchbacks up to the base of the arch, providing picturesquely framed views of Snake Canyon. Pack along plenty of water, as there is no water along the entire route after snowmelt, and the relatively low elevation usually provides hot temperatures by midmorning.

Located well to the south of the Lehman Caves–Wheeler Peak center of activity in Great Basin National Park, access to the trailhead is via an 11-mile gravel road, which appears to be suitable for most passenger cars, although the Park Service recommends a high-clearance vehicle.

DIRECTIONS TO TRAILHEAD   Follow Nevada S.R. 487 south of Baker to the Utah border, where the road becomes Utah State Highway 21. Pass through the small community of Garrison and come to the Lexington Arch turnoff at milepost 6, just past Pruess Lake, about 12 miles from Baker. A large Great Basin National Park sign marks the junction.

Head westbound following a well-marked gravel road, arrive at a Y-junction at 9 miles from S.R. 21 and veer left, reaching the trailhead parking area at 11 miles.

DESCRIPTION   Proceed on single-track trail on a mild climb alongside a dry wash through typical pinyon-juniper woodland, with an understory of wild rose, chokecherry, and currant. After a short while, cross the wash and reach a trail register, beyond which the grade of ascent increases. Soon you follow a series of switchbacks up the hillside, eventually breaking out of the trees into open, shrub-covered slopes that offer good views of the surrounding topography and Snake Valley to the east. Early summer is blessed with a burst of color from the wild rose carpeting the slopes, along with a fine display of wildflowers, including sego lily, mule ears, lupine, penstemon, flax, and paintbrush. Beyond the final switchback you traverse across a hillside dotted with very widely scattered white firs.

The traverse ultimately takes you into Arch Canyon, high above the usually dry streambed. A light forest of firs shades the mildly graded trail on the way to a junction with a very short lateral on the right, which soon leads to the top of a cliff at the edge of the canyon. At this overlook, a well-placed park bench provides an excellent perch from which to enjoy a fine view of Lexington Arch, just a short distance up the canyon.

Back on the main trail, a forested descent leads to the bottom of the canyon, where a wood bridge spans the wash. Now on the north bank, you start to climb moderately steeply alongside the wash and past the base of the arch to a series of short switchbacks that zigzag up the slope through grasses, ephedra, currant, and mountain-mahogany. Clambering over a final set of rock steps, you stand beneath Lexington Arch.

Lexington Arch, standing 75 feet above the base and 125 feet across, seems much larger when viewed from directly below, as opposed to the previous view from the overlook. The arch frames an expansive vista to the east of Snake Valley.

LEXINGTON ARCH   Since most natural arches in the West are made up of sandstone, Lexington Arch's limestone composition makes it a unique natural feature. The origin of Lexington Arch has sparked a minor controversy among geologists: is the arch a natural arch formed in the traditional sense by erosional forces, is it all that now remains of an ancient cave, or is it really not an arch at all but a natural bridge instead? Whatever the origin, the landform is truly a scenic wonder.

Lexington Arch from Vista Point, Great Basin National Park

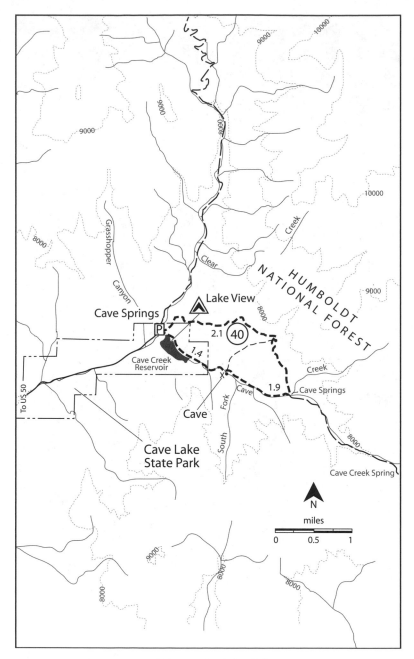

MAP 28 | Cave Springs Trail

A pleasant romp through pinyon-juniper woodland takes hikers to an interesting cave and a lovely reservoir within Cave Lake State Park.

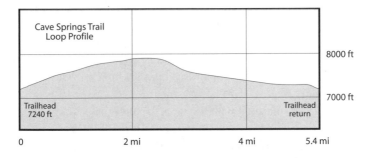

DISTANCE & ROUTE:	5.4 miles one way in loop
DIFFICULTY:	Moderate
SEASON:	Summer, fall
TRAILHEAD ACCESS:	All vehicles
WATER:	None available
GUIDEBOOK MAP:	28
USGS MAP:	Cave Creek

INTRODUCTION   Even with a location in the remote eastern part of the state, Cave Lake State Park is a popular summer playground for campers, anglers, boaters, hikers, and picnickers. The 5.4-mile Cave Springs Trail samples a variety of interesting terrain, including pinyon-juniper woodland, several riparian areas, and the park's namesake cave. A dip in the 32-acre reservoir and a meal at the nearby picnic area would provide a fine conclusion to the three-hour hike. Extra time would enable visitors the opportunity to hike the park's other maintained trail, the 1.5-mile-long Steptoe Creek Trail (3 miles round trip). The park has two developed campgrounds.

DIRECTIONS TO TRAILHEAD   Drive southeast: from Ely on U.S. 50 for approximately 8 miles to the signed turnoff for Cave Lake State Park. Follow Success Summit Road (S.R. 486) another 7 miles to the Cave Springs trailhead, immediately beyond the junction with the road to Cave Creek Reservoir and Lake View Campground.

DESCRIPTION   The trail drops to a bridge across Steptoe Creek and then intersects the Steptoe Creek Trail at a three-way junction. Turn left and make a moderate ascent through pinyon-juniper woodland along an old roadbed amid a smattering of wildflowers, including penstemon, aster, and paintbrush. Without notice you leave Cave Lake State Park and enter National Forest lands. With the subsequent gain in elevation Cave Creek Reservoir pops into view with the lightly forested hills of the Schell Creek Range in the background. With trailside mileposts to mark your progress, you continue the ascent through scattered to light woodland, encountering a trail register near the 1.4-mile mark. Gently graded trail followed by more climbing leads to a crossing of a seasonal stream canyon and then a junction with a twin-tracked jeep road beyond the far bank, 2.1 miles from the trailhead. A right turn at this junction provides a short cut to the reservoir.

Continuing straight ahead at the junction, the trail skirts a rock outcrop and then merges with an old jeep road from below. From this vantage point you have nice views of Steptoe Creek canyon and the surrounding hills. Soon a protracted descent begins on a steep and rocky section of road that leads down to a junction with the well-traveled four-wheel-drive road to Cave Mountain, 3 miles from the trailhead. The Cave Springs are just a short distance east.

Turn right and descend along the road, soon reaching a Y-junction near the banks of Cave Creek. Turn right again and follow gravel and dirt road on a downstream course along the north bank of the lushly lined creek, where willows, wild roses, and pockets of grassy meadow contrast sharply with the drier pinyon-juniper woodland away from the stream. A mile-long stroll along the road leads to a junction, 4 miles from the trailhead, with the twin-tracked jeep road you crossed previously. A short distance farther, within sight of Cave Rock, you cross the signed Cave Lake State Park boundary and continue a short distance to a use trail on the left. This path drops to a crossing of Cave Creek and then follows a short, steep climb up to the mouth of the cave.

Back on the main road, the grade of the descent eventually eases as the shimmering waters of Cave Creek Reservoir spring into view. Parallel the willow-lined creek to the northeast shore and then either follow paved road above the lake, or walk along the shoreline back to the trailhead.

SOUTH SCHELL PEAK   Hikers in search of a more challenging adventure than what is offered at Cave Lake State Park can opt for a climb of 11,735-foot South Schell Peak from Berry Creek Campground. From the campground, follow the trace of an old four-wheel-drive road up the canyon of North Fork Berry Creek to a large bowl below the peak. From there, leave the road and head directly toward the summit over rocky slopes. The climb is about 3 miles in length and gains approximately 3500 feet.

Dramatic canyonlands reminiscent of southern Utah provide exotic scenery on this easy loop trail.

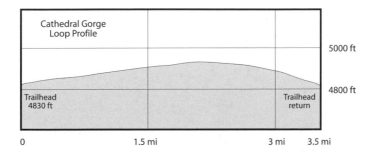

DISTANCE & ROUTE:	3.5 miles one way in loop
DIFFICULTY:	Easy
SEASON:	Spring, fall
TRAILHEAD ACCESS:	All vehicles
WATER:	Available at trailhead
GUIDEBOOK MAP:	29
USGS MAP:	Panaca

INTRODUCTION Bill Fiero in *Geology of the Great Basin* provides the following description of Cathedral Gorge: "Remember sitting on a beach or in a mud puddle as a youth and letting sand or mud filter through your fingers? With a little care, you learned to build spires and castles out of the liquid sand drops. Cathedral Gorge seems like a king-sized child's fantasyland." Cathedral Gorge, established as one of Nevada's first four state parks in 1924, is an incredibly scenic area and the Juniper Draw Trail is perhaps the best way to experience the majesty of the area up close. With negligible elevation change, you can stroll along the floor of the canyon amid statuesque spires and dramatic cliffs.

Cathedral Gorge State Park has a twenty-two-site campground equipped with shaded tables, grills, water, restrooms, and showers (April to November). Five other trails provide additional opportunities for hikers to stretch their legs. At this elevation and latitude, visitors to the park will find the most comfortable temperatures in spring and fall. Call (775) 728-4460 for more information.

DIRECTIONS TO TRAILHEAD The entrance to Cathedral Gorge State Park is on U.S. 93 between the towns of Caliente and Pioche, 1 mile north of the junction

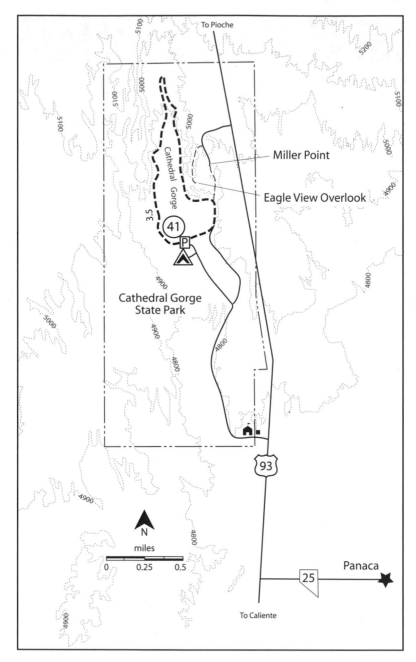

MAP 29 | Cathedral Gorge State Park

with S.R. 319, which heads east 1 mile to the town of Panaca (services). Enter the park (nominal fee) and follow the access road from the visitor center to the campground.

DESCRIPTION   The trail begins near the restroom, signed JUNIPER DRAW TRAIL. Begin hiking on a pea-gravel trail lined with rocks headed across the flat floor of the canyon toward buff-colored formations. Near a lone juniper you reach the first large formation. Pass along its base, and then follow alongside a dry wash. Soon the path veers sharply to cross the wash, travels a short distance to a second wash, and then follows the course of this wash on a meandering route up the canyon past yucca, barberry, greasewood, saltbush, shadscale, and the ubiquitous sagebrush. Being sandwiched between the towering, spire-rimmed walls of Cathedral Gorge creates a sense of reverent awe well suited to a sacred place with such an appropriate name. About 1.5 miles from the campground, you reach a marked junction. Although the loop trail heads back down the gorge from here, you can continue up the wash to the base of the cliffs at the north end of the gorge, a journey well worth the extra effort if you have the time.

Veering to the right toward the east wall of the gorge, what appears to be a succession of caves actually turn out to be a number of small, twisting slot canyons, eroded over time by rainwater and melting snow. About 0.4 mile from the junction a side canyon opens up on the left and sharp eyes may spy sightseers on the rim of the gorge strolling along the Eagle View Overlook Trail. Continue a southerly course until the trail bends sharply east to follow the edge

Rock formation in Cathedral Gorge State Park

of the widening gorge. After crossing a pair of washes, you encounter a narrow, picturesque side canyon to the north and intersect the Miller Point Trail, 2.6 miles from the trailhead.

Heading south again, you follow gently graded trail to the picnic area, where spires and towers provide fine scenery and a number of stone structures, built by the Civilian Conservation Corps in the 1930s, provide historical interest, including the oft-photographed water tower.

To return to your starting point, make a short walk down the road to the start of the signed nature trail and head across the floor of the canyon to the campground. Along the way a number of interpretive signs provide information on plants and animals.

MILLER POINT While visiting Cathedral Gorge, don't miss the opportunity to experience the breadth and depth of the valley from Miller Point, which provides a completely different experience at the gorge's rim than from the valley floor.

HIKE 42 | BEAVER DAM STATE PARK

Part of the adventure to this trip is just getting to Beaver Dam State Park. Once there, four short trails beckon the casual hiker to enjoy the scenery and seclusion.

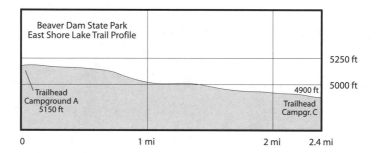

DISTANCES & ROUTES:	East Shore, 2.4 miles one way with shuttle; Interpretive Trail, 0.6 mile round trip; Waterfall, 1 mile round trip
DIFFICULTY:	Easy
SEASON:	Summer
TRAILHEAD ACCESS:	High-clearance vehicle recommended
WATER:	Available at trailheads, creeks
GUIDEBOOK MAP:	30
USGS MAP:	Panaca

INTRODUCTION   The wide-open spaces of Nevada are renowned for their remoteness, and Beaver Dam has perhaps the most remote location of all the state parks. A long way from nearly anywhere, just reaching the park requires a certain level of commitment. Deep canyons, perennial streams, a 15-acre reservoir stocked with rainbow trout, a waterfall, wildlife, and diverse plant communities are the chief attractions. Four short trails provide hikers with enough diversions to easily fill a weekend.

Despite the isolated location, developed campgrounds within the park are complete with running water from May to October. Rangers report that the only crowded time at Beaver Dam occurs during a Fourth of July weekend.

DIRECTIONS TO TRAILHEADS   As the saying goes, "if Beaver Dam State Park isn't at the end of the world, you can see it from there." Not only is the park located in a remote section of eastern Nevada near the Utah border, a long drive on a dirt road is necessary just to reach the park boundary. From U.S. 93, approximately 6 miles north of Caliente and 8 miles south of the Panaca junction, turn east and follow signs for 28 miles to the park. Plan on an hour-long drive from the highway to the park.

EAST SHORE LAKE TRAIL   From the main road, turn into Campground A and proceed through the campground to the end of the road and the day-use parking area (portable toilet, picnic tables).

INTERPRETIVE TRAIL   From the main road, turn into Campground B and park near the restroom.

WATERFALL TRAIL   Follow the main road past turnoffs for Campgrounds A and B and continue a short distance past the entrance road to Campground C. Park in a pullout large enough for a couple of cars. The trail is marked by a sign with a hiker symbol just off the road.

DESCRIPTIONS

EAST SHORE LAKE TRAIL   Follow a shady, single-track trail along Beaver Dam Wash through lush foliage. Soon the gently graded trail veers out of the vegetation and passes a beaver pond before a brief climb leads you high above Schroeder Reservoir. Beavers have been active along Beaver Dam Wash for quite some time, but the reservoir is a relative newcomer to the area; the dam was built in 1961 and the reservoir dedicated the following year. The reservoir was named after George Schroeder, who died at the construction site of a heart attack.

Toward the far end of the lake the trail dips down near the lakeshore, crosses the dam and then follows the creek downstream. A short distance south of the

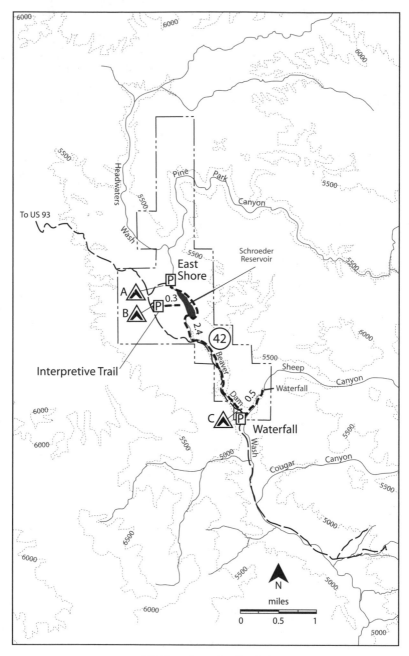

MAP 30 | Beaver Dam State Park

dam, you intersect the Oak Knoll Trail and then continue along the west bank of Beaver Dam Wash. The trail ends at Campground C, 2.4 miles from the day-use parking area.

INTERPRETIVE TRAIL   Climb away from the trailhead across a hillside through pinyon-juniper woodland. Periodically placed interpretive signs provide tidbits on some of the typical plants common to the region. Switchbacks take you up the hillside toward the crest of a hill, where you'll encounter a junction with a short loop around the top of peak 5570. By heading in either direction you'll soon reach the overlook with a fine view of Schroeder Reservoir and the surrounding terrain.

WATERFALL TRAIL   From the road, the trail drops into the riparian environment along Beaver Dam Wash and proceeds through willows and oaks to a boulder crossing of the stream. A short distance up the far bank, you pass over a ditch culvert and then follow a crushed-rock and stone-lined path on a mildly rising course paralleling Sheep Canyon Creek. Proceed upstream alongside the lush foliage of the streambed to a pair of crossings over the narrow and shallow creek. Beyond the second creek crossing, you reach a post marked with a number 2 and an arrow pointing to the left. The path to the left leads a short way to the site of some former swimming pools, which were filled with water diverted from the creek. By following the right-hand path you quickly reach the waterfall, a short cascade that spills over rocks into a small pool, where lush vegetation creates a cool grotto, which is especially fine on a warm summer day.

WILDLIFE   Beaver Dam is home to a wide variety of animals, including the namesake beaver that actually build dams in Beaver Dam Wash. Other mammals inhabiting the park include mule deer, antelope, and black-tailed rabbits. Watch for bats flying above the lake around dusk. The daytime skies may reveal golden eagles or red-tailed hawks. The reservoir is stocked with rainbow trout.

Contrary to the hordes of tourists who flock to the casinos like carrion-feeders to roadkill, the best thing about southern Nevada is not the artificial glitz and hype found on the Las Vegas Strip, but the natural beauty found in the surrounding mountains and canyons. For those people with images of Las Vegas as nothing other than a growing number of ostentatious gambling establishments, the attractions within the Spring Mountains, Red Rock Canyon, and Valley of Fire State Park remain virtually unknown. However, hikers, mountain bikers, landscape photographers, and climbers living in the fastest growing city in America are quite familiar with the prime recreation lands in their own backyard.

Valley of Fire State Park is an accurate appellation for this area an hour northeast of Las Vegas. The low elevation and southern latitude of this section of the Mojave Desert make this a place to avoid in the middle of summer. However, the awesome beauty created by the red sandstone formations, coupled with the more tolerable temperatures from autumn to spring make the park a fine place for a visit during the months outside of summer. Just miles west of Lake Mead, Valley of Fire offers hikers and scramblers several short routes through narrow canyons and up to vista points. Nevada's oldest and largest state park is home to many ancient Indian petroglyphs.

The Spring Mountains, so named for the abundant springs bubbling out of the characteristic limestone, rise from the desert floor several thousand feet to the top of the range at Charleston Peak's summit (11,918 feet). This lofty elevation provides summer recreation within the 56,598-acre Mt. Charleston Wilderness for Las Vegas residents attempting to escape the heat of the usual 100°F-plus temperatures in the valley. Although summer is the most popular time for use of the trails, other seasons have their appeal as well. Spring is the best time of the year to see the waterfalls and wildflowers; autumn can be quite pleasant with mild temperatures, changing colors, and fewer tourists; and with usually mild winters, Las Vegans have the occasional opportunity to experience a real rarity—snow.

The Spring Mountains are truly a hiker's paradise with an abundance of trails from which to choose for a variety of experiences. Whether the desire is for short hikes up picturesque canyons to waterfalls, visits to areas with limestone caves, easy climbs to wide-ranging vistas, full-blown assaults on the highest peaks, or a trip into a steep canyon so narrow that you could touch both walls with outstretched arms, the region has all this and more. The Spring Mountains also

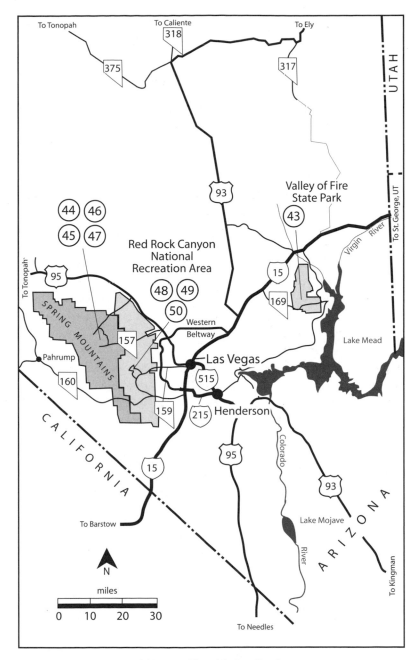

MAP 31 | Hikes of Southern Nevada

harbor the largest collection of bristlecone pines in the intermountain region, with many trails passing among the oldest living things on earth.

All the trails within the Mt. Charleston Wilderness and the surrounding lands are in very good condition thanks primarily to the maintenance provided by the Spring Mountain Youth Camp. Unlike more primitive areas in the state, hikers won't need to spend extra time hunting for trails that have disappeared, or find themselves staring in bewilderment at a map trying to determine the location of a trail junction. The trails in the Spring Mountains are probably the most civilized paths in Nevada.

Red Rock Canyon National Conservation Area is directly west of the sprawling subdivisions that creep ever farther from Las Vegas's core toward the area's boundary. The picturesque, multi-hued sandstone and limestone formations that characterize the topography lure scores of rock climbers and tourists alike from all over the world. With excellent access provided by the one-way scenic drive to the area's center of activity, recreationists have numerous opportunities for journeys that explore the canyons, scale the walls, or climb the peaks. More remote sections of Red Rock lure more adventurous souls into the untrammeled backcountry. The 196,810 acres protected within the limits of Red Rock insure that outdoor enthusiasts have plenty of terrain in which to enjoy their pursuits.

Managed jointly by the Nevada Division of State Parks and the Bureau of Land Management, Red Rock has been a model for resource protection and public enjoyment. Unlike the majority of Nevada's recreation lands, Red Rock experiences the pressures from increased visitation and suburban development. How the area survives these pressures will be the challenge for the future.

FYI ■ The majority of hikes described in this guide follow established trails into mountainous terrain. Red Rock Canyon and Valley of Fire differ from the norm, as the typical hike tends to follow a route instead of a defined trail all the way to a destination. Hikers can expect to follow the bottom of a wash, or a scramble route up a narrow canyon as part of their journey, especially the farther they travel from a road. Although such travel may sound ominous to those more accustomed to defined trails, these routes are generally straightforward. However, anyone wishing to veer away from established routes should be skilled in navigation and backcountry travel.

The low elevation and southern latitude make for unbearably hot temperatures during the summer months in both Red Rock and Valley of Fire. Hiking during this time of year should be confined to the early morning hours. Most recreationists prefer the milder climate of spring and fall, and at times a winter journey can be quite pleasant as well. Whenever you hike in southern Nevada, bring plenty of extra water, as very little is available in the backcountry and dehydration is always a concern in such a dry and hot climate. Rocky terrain and narrow canyons increase the chance for encountering flash floods during heavy rains. Keep an eye on the weather and avoid dangerous locales during rainy periods, as deaths from flash floods are periodic occurrences.

A short easy hike within Valley of Fire State Park leads hikers through a scenic sandstone canyon to a tank of water, or tinaja.

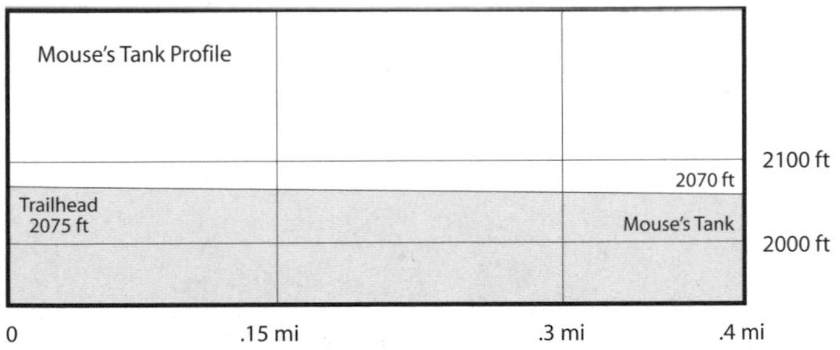

Mouse's Tank Profile

Trailhead
2075 ft

2070 ft

Mouse's Tank

2100 ft

2000 ft

| 0 | .15 mi | .3 mi | .4 mi |

DISTANCE & ROUTE:	0.8 mile round trip
DIFFICULTY:	Easy
SEASON:	Spring, fall
TRAILHEAD ACCESS:	All vehicles
WATER:	None available
GUIDEBOOK MAP:	32
USGS MAP:	Valley of Fire West

INTRODUCTION   Although a sign at the Petroglyph Canyon trailhead promises "many fine examples of prehistoric Indian petroglyph art" and trail markers that "identify many common desert plants and other natural features in the canyon," you may have a difficult time locating the hard-to-see petroglyphs, and gaining any information about plants and natural features will be impossible unless the missing signs are replaced. Despite these unfulfilled promises, the hike to Mouse's Tank is both easy and scenic. Strolling along a nearly flat wash that passes through a narrow, picturesque sandstone canyon with steep red walls takes travelers to a *tinaja,* a natural rock tank or depression that holds rainwater after storms. Experienced hikers in search of a more challenging trip can follow narrow canyons beyond the tank, but they should be skilled in basic navigation and scrambling.

While the sandstone formations of Valley of Fire State Park are stunningly picturesque at any time of the year, most visitors will appreciate the milder temperatures from October to April. Summers are unbearably hot with over 100°F days the norm and highs of 120°F not uncommon. Winter temperatures

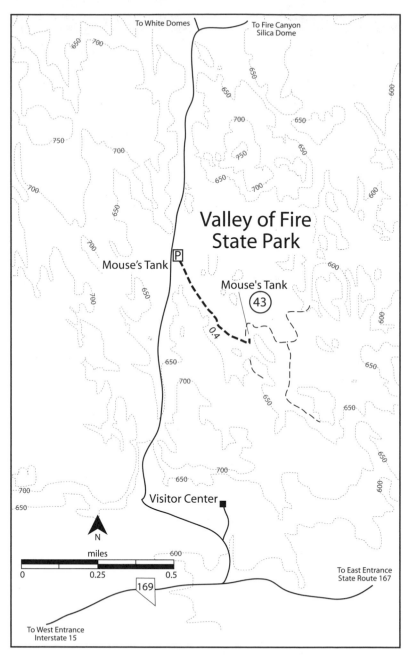

To White Domes

To Fire Canyon
Silica Dome

Valley of Fire
State Park

P

Mouse's Tank

Mouse's Tank
(43)

0.4

Visitor Center

N

miles

0   0.25   0.5

169

To East Entrance
State Route 167

To West Entrance
Interstate 15

MAP 32 | Mouse's Tank

can vary from freezing to 75°F. The area boasts several fine trails in addition to the Petroglyph Trail to Mouse's Tank. Campsites with shaded tables, restrooms, running water, showers, and grills are available at nearby Atlatl Rock Campground. A nominal fee is charged for entrance into Valley of Fire State Park, and additional fees are collected for use of the campground. For more information call (702) 397-2088.

DIRECTIONS TO TRAILHEAD　Take I-15 northeast from Las Vegas to the signed turnoff for Valley of Fire State Park, approximately 35 miles from the city center, and turn southeast onto S.R. 169. Follow the highway to the park entrance and continue toward the Valley of Fire Visitor Center. Approximately 18 miles from I-15, turn left onto the visitor center access road and continue past the visitor center to the signed trailhead (pit toilet), 1.25 miles from S.R. 169.

DESCRIPTION　Follow a very short paved path away from the parking area onto the red, sandy surface of a wash through a narrow canyon carved between scenic sandstone formations. While you will pass several pictographs on your way to Mouse's Tank, a watchful eye is necessary to see the faint, unsigned markings. Continue the easy stroll past mesquite shrubs to a point where the canyon divides and an arrow on a sign directs traffic to the left. Shortly after turning up this narrow side canyon, you find Mouse's Tank hidden in a cleft of rock on the right-hand side. The best time to view Mouse's Tank full of water is after periods of significant winter rainfall.

From Mouse's Tank a very short climb over sandstone slabs leads to the sandy floor of a small flat at the head of a slender wash below the tank. Further exploration of this wash is possible, but it will eventually require some scrambling to negotiate travel through the narrow and steep parts. Another alternative proceeds straight up the canyon where the arrowed sign leads left to Mouse's Tank. Initially travel is easy, but eventually steep climbing is required for further progress.

MOUSE　Mouse's Tank was named for a renegade Paiute Indian who used the labyrinth of canyons in Valley of Fire to elude several groups of pursuers. A number of varying legends have sprung up to explain how Mouse got into trouble in the first place, but following his initial misdeeds he met his end in July 1897. After raiding an Indian woman's garden, Mouse fled to Valley of Fire and evaded a posse for five days before they tracked him down near Muddy Spring. Refusing surrender, Mouse fired upon the posse and was subsequently shot and killed.

Narrow canyon on Mouse's Tank Trail, Valley of Fire State Park

One of the Spring Mountains' most picturesque springs provides a refreshing oasis following a steep climb along a section of the North Loop Trail.

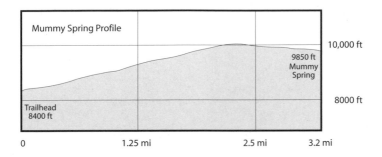

DISTANCE & ROUTE:	6.4 miles round trip
DIFFICULTY:	Moderate
SEASON:	Summer, fall
TRAILHEAD ACCESS:	All vehicles
WATER:	None available
GUIDEBOOK MAP:	33
USGS MAP:	Angel Peak, Charleston Peak

INTRODUCTION   A short but stiff climb leads to a unique spring in a cool canyon filled with lush foliage. Although the route to the spring follows part of the North Loop Trail to Charleston Peak, the trail is lightly used and offers something of a secluded oasis away from the crowds. As an added bonus, the trail leads past several gnarled, ancient bristlecone pines that will delight photographers and naturalists alike.

DIRECTIONS TO TRAILHEAD   Head northbound from downtown Las Vegas on U.S. 95 approximately 15 miles to a junction of S.R. 157 (Kyle Canyon Road). Head west on S.R. 157 for 17 miles and turn right (north) at a junction with S.R. 158 (Deer Creek Highway). Follow S.R. 158 for 4.6 miles to the trailhead on the left (south) side of the highway, 0.2 mile beyond the entrance to Hilltop Campground.

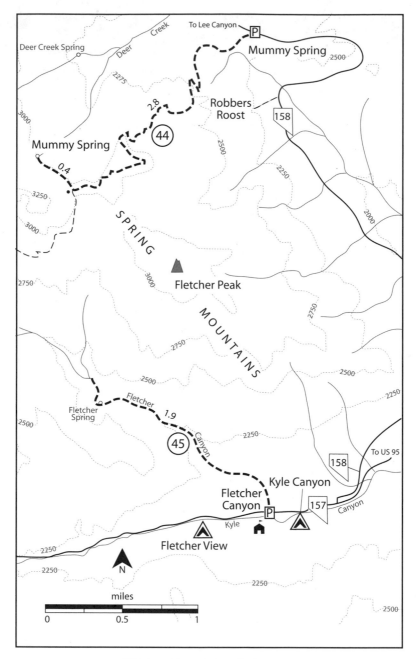

To Lee Canyon

P

Deer Creek Spring

Deer Creek

Mummy Spring
2500

Robbers Roost

158

2275

2.8

44

3000

Mummy Spring

0.4

2500

3250

2250

3000

2000

SPRING

2750

3000

Fletcher Peak

2750

MOUNTAINS

2750

2500

2500

Fletcher

1.9

Fletcher Spring

2250

45

Canyon

2500

2250

2500

2500

158

To US 95

Kyle Canyon

Fletcher Canyon

157

P

Canyon

Fletcher View

Kyle

2250

2250

N

2250

2250

2500

miles

0   0.5   1

MAP 33 | Mummy Spring & Fletcher Canyon

DESCRIPTION   For nearly the first 3 miles, the trail to Mummy Spring shares the route of the North Loop Trail on a stiff climb toward Charleston Peak. Leave the parking area and follow wide dirt-and-gravel tread above the highway through mountain-mahogany and ponderosa pine. Following the first of many switchbacks to come, you cross the Mt. Charleston Wilderness boundary and make a steady ascent up the hillside. With the gain in elevation, first white firs and then bristlecone pines become the dominant conifers. At 1.3 miles from the trailhead, you reach a knob covered with a number of old, gnarled bristlecone pines that are quite photogenic.

The rate of ascent moderates briefly near a dry campsite with an excellent view of Mummy Mountain, but soon resumes the steep climb through mixed forest. A series of a dozen switchbacks lead you into exclusively bristlecone pine forest at the top of a ridge dividing Kyle and Deer Creek Canyons. Climb along this ridge to a saddle, where you're blessed with a commanding view of the massive limestone face at the south end of the Mummy Mountain massif, which offers a shape reminiscent of a 1950s vintage diesel train engine. The grade mercifully eases for the next 0.5 mile, as you traverse over to a saddle directly below the imposing limestone face. In the saddle is a three-way junction between the continuation of the North Loop Trail on the left and the trail to Mummy Spring on the right.

Turn northwest from the junction and follow mildly descending trail for nearly 0.4 mile to Mummy Spring. The area around the spring is filled with lush foliage, including aspens, gooseberries, ferns, grasses, wildflowers, and other thirsty plants. The northeast-facing ravine tucked into the deeply forested slopes of Mummy Mountain produces a cool microclimate that appears to be quite conducive for such verdant vegetation. Just below the spring, a wall of limestone covered with travertine deposits provides a dramatic fall for the dancing waters of nascent Deer Creek. Delightful in any season, Mummy Spring is particularly stunning in autumn, when golden aspens contrast with ice-covered formations on the limestone wall.

MUMMY MOUNTAIN   Mummy Spring takes its name from the profile of Mummy Mountain, which when viewed from the northeast resembles an Egyptian mummy lying on its back.

A narrow limestone canyon with towering walls offers hikers a unique experience in the Spring Mountains.

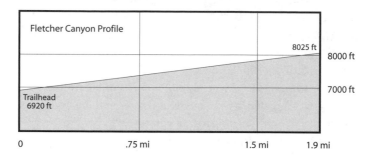

Fletcher Canyon Profile

8025 ft

8000 ft

7000 ft

Trailhead
6920 ft

0   .75 mi   1.5 mi   1.9 mi

DISTANCE & ROUTE:	3.8 miles round trip
DIFFICULTY:	Moderate
SEASON:	Spring, summer, fall
TRAILHEAD ACCESS:	All vehicles
WATER:	Seasonally available in creek
GUIDEBOOK MAP:	33
USGS MAP:	Angel Peak, Charleston Peak

INTRODUCTION   The Fletcher Canyon Trail is a short, fairly easy hike into one of the most unusual environments in the Mt. Charleston Wilderness. Diverse vegetation borders the trail for the entire length, and the steep, narrow limestone walls of the canyon suggest scenery more reminiscent of a slot canyon in southwest Utah than the typical terrain found in the Spring Mountains. This little-used trail will provide plenty of discoveries for the ardent hiker. If photography is your passion, pack a tripod and speedy film for the low-light conditions in the shady canyon.

DIRECTIONS TO TRAILHEAD   Head northbound from downtown Las Vegas on U.S. 95 approximately 15 miles to a junction of S.R. 157 (Kyle Canyon Road). Head west on S.R. 157 for 17.5 miles to the trailhead on the north side of the highway, 0.5 mile past the junction with S.R. 158 (Deer Creek Highway). Keep a careful watch for the trailhead, as driving past the narrow gap of Fletcher Canyon is quite easy. Parking is extremely limited, but more space is available on the opposite shoulder.

DESCRIPTION   The signed trail begins in the gravel of the streambed, occasionally sharing the course with the bottom of the wash. A bona fide trail leads out of the stream channel to the north side, crossing twice more before you reach the wilderness boundary, 0.5 mile from the highway. The diverse nature of the surroundings is striking, with numerous species of plants and trees residing in the canyon, including shrub live oak, mountain-mahogany, manzanita, pinyon pine, ponderosa pine, and Utah juniper.

Spout and pool in Fletcher Canyon, Spring Mountains

Continuing up the canyon, water may appear briefly in the stream channel only to quickly disappear again, seemingly with the same regularity that the course of the trail crosses from one side of the canyon to the other. Where the canyon starts to narrow, the grade of ascent increases. Vertical limestone walls grow taller and closer together as you go farther upstream. The foliage changes as well, responding to both an increase in shade, which produces cooler temperatures, and an increase in moisture. About 1.5 miles from the highway, the canyon begins a sweeping bend to the north and narrows even more; soon you can almost span the canyon walls with your outstretched arms.

Eventually the path all but disappears, forcing you along the floor of the slim canyon. The canyon becomes even steeper and splits into two branches, approximately 1.9 miles from the highway. In the left-hand canyon, a spring cascades down a steep, narrow cleft, climaxing in an eroded chute carved out of a limestone boulder that spills into a gravel basin.

Travel beyond this point up the steep left-hand canyon is very difficult without climbing gear. However, you can head up the right-hand canyon another 50 yards or so before being faced with a similar dilemma.

> **FLORA AND FAUNA** The Spring Mountains chain is one of the most biologically diverse ranges in the United States. Along with forty-eight endemic plant species, the range has twenty-one unique animal species as well, including the Palmer's chipmunk, spotted bat, flammulated owl, and Mexican spotted owl. As Las Vegas development continues at an alarmingly rapid rate, protection of the plants and animals of the Spring Mountains is of vital concern.

HIKE 46 | MARY JANE FALLS

Hikers will enjoy the falls in spring, while more adventuresome souls will enjoy exploration of limestone caves later in the year.

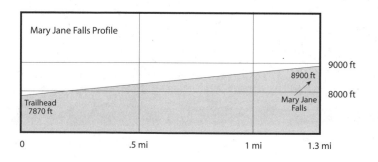

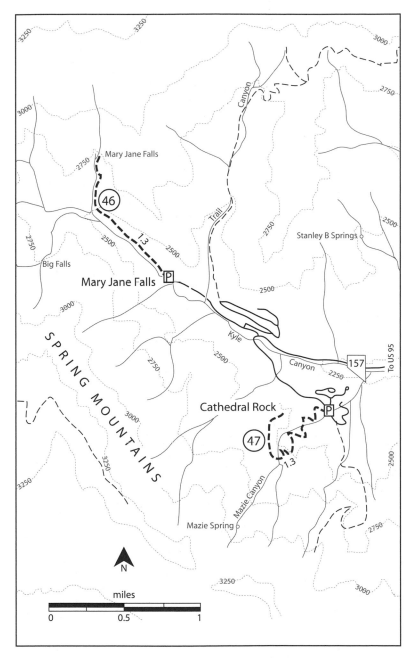

MAP 34 | Mary Jane Falls & Cathedral Rock

DISTANCE & ROUTE:	2.6 miles round trip
DIFFICULTY:	Easy
SEASON:	Spring, summer, fall
TRAILHEAD ACCESS:	All vehicles
WATER:	Seasonally available in creek
GUIDEBOOK MAP:	34
USGS MAP:	Charleston Peak

INTRODUCTION A dramatic waterfall and limestone caves provide the main attractions of this short hike into the upper reaches of Kyle Canyon. Spring is the best time to view the falls, while low water conditions in summer and fall offer excellent times to explore the caves. This trail is quite popular, so don't expect to have the place to yourself. However, the upper part of the canyon offers plenty of off-trail opportunities for those who want to leave the crowds behind.

DIRECTIONS TO TRAILHEAD Head northbound from downtown Las Vegas on U.S. 95 approximately 15 miles to a junction of S.R. 157 (Kyle Canyon Road). Head west on S.R. 157 for 20 miles to the turnoff for Mary Jane Falls, 3 miles past the junction of S.R. 158 (Deer Creek Highway). At the beginning of a hairpin turn, veer right onto Echo Road and travel 0.4 mile to a gravel road on the left. Follow this gravel road another 0.2 mile to the trailhead, where there is plenty of parking and pit toilets.

DESCRIPTION The Mary Jane Falls Trail follows the continuation of the road beneath the shade of some ponderosa pines, and the occasional pocket of aspens. You reach the end of the road at 0.9 mile and proceed on single-track trail that switchbacks up the hillside. White firs join the forest as you continue switchbacking, heading up a canyon rimmed by precipitous limestone cliffs. Eventually the trail leads you below vertical cliffs and over to the falls.

The falls appear in a dramatic setting near the head of Kyle Canyon, rimmed by a horseshoe of steep limestone cliffs. Located about halfway up the headwall, the area around the falls provides you with impressive views down the canyon. During peak flow, Mary Jane Falls puts on a stunning display of watery splendor, but at drier times of the year diminishes to a wisp of light spray. Fall compensates for the lack of water with vivid autumn colors. The force of water spilling across the limestone face has produced a deep cleft in the rock near the base of the falls. A large opening reveals a shallow cave just past the falls and is well worth the little extra time to reach. For the more adventurous, the upper part of Kyle Canyon is ripe for further off-trail exploration.

PONDEROSA PINE (*PINUS PONDEROSA* VAR. *SCOPULORUM*) The ponderosa pine found in the Spring Mountains is of the Rocky Mountain variety, which scientists theorize migrated into the Great Basin from the southern Rockies. This normally three-needled pine will appear with some regularity as having only two needles. Found at elevations between 7000 and 8500 feet, ponderosa pine is part of a montane forest that also Includes such conifers as pinyon pine, white fir, juniper, limber pine, and bristlecone pine.

HIKE 47 | CATHEDRAL ROCK

Beautiful views down Kyle Canyon and out to the desert floor are fine rewards for the short but steep climb to the top of Cathedral Rock.

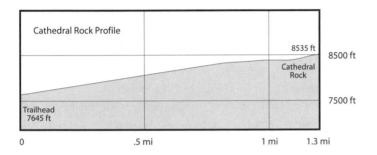

DISTANCE & ROUTE:	2.6 miles round trip
DIFFICULTY:	Moderate
SEASON:	Spring, summer, fall
TRAILHEAD ACCESS:	All vehicles
WATER:	Seasonally available in creek
GUIDEBOOK MAP:	34
USGS MAP:	Charleston Peak

INTRODUCTION Autumn color, spring waterfalls, and impressive views lure the hiker to the Cathedral Rock Trail. A short, moderate climb leads to the top of Cathedral Rock and one of the grandest views in the entire Kyle Canyon area. Spring is a fine time to make the trip, when wildflowers are peaking and the falls are full. Autumn is also a prime time, when the expansive stand of aspens in Mazie Canyon splashes the slopes with a blaze of golden yellow. No matter what time of year you climb Cathedral Rock the views are always superb.

DIRECTIONS TO TRAILHEAD Head northbound from downtown Las Vegas on U.S. 95 approximately 15 miles to a junction of S.R. 157 (Kyle Canyon Road). Head west on S.R. 157 for 20.25 miles to the Cathedral Rock Picnic Area, 3.25 miles past the junction of S.R. 158 (Deer Canyon Highway). Turn right into the picnic area and proceed along the road for nearly 0.4 mile to the trailhead on the right. Just prior to the trailhead, paid parking is available in turnouts on the left side of the road. The gate closes at 8 p.m. in the summer and 6 p.m. in spring and fall, so plan your hike accordingly.

DESCRIPTION Follow a continuation of the road on a climb up Mazie Canyon beneath the scattered shade from ponderosa pines and white firs. At a bend in the trail, approximately 0.25 mile from the trailhead, you reach an unsigned junction with a trail headed northwest. Bear left, remaining on the Cathedral Rock Trail, and climb through an extensive stand of aspens. The abundant groundwater allows a spectacular display of wildflowers in early season, and the autumn show of color from the turning aspens is equally as stunning. About midway through the aspens, where the road curves again, a side road heads a short distance off to your left and over to a delightful waterfall, which spills in three steps into small punch bowls. This scene is quite stirring in spring, but by late in the season the falls have diminished to a trickle.

Continue on the old roadbed, winding back and forth up the canyon through more aspens, until you reach a hillside covered with pines and firs. Views of Kyle Canyon begin where the road makes a nearly level traverse across the slope. You reach an unsigned junction at a saddle, 1.2 miles from the trailhead, where the road continues toward a spring above Little Falls in the next canyon to the northwest.

From the junction, follow the foot trail branching to the right, heading slightly downhill. After a short descent, the trail arcs around to a knob. From here, the grade increases at a switchback, as you climb around the back side of the knob and then to the summit.

Cathedral Rock offers a commanding view of Kyle Canyon all the way out to the desert floor. Impressive limestone cliffs ring the gorge, as you gaze toward Mary Jane Falls. To the west is Charleston Peak, at 11,918 feet the highest peak in the Spring Mountains.

KYLE CANYON The canyon was named for the Kyle brothers, who operated a sawmill in the area during the 1870s and were later murdered in 1883. While considering their untimely deaths, exercise caution on top of Cathedral Rock, as the steep cliffs have claimed other lives in the past.

Hike through a classic red sandstone canyon to a trio of natural water tanks and an impressive view across the desert floor.

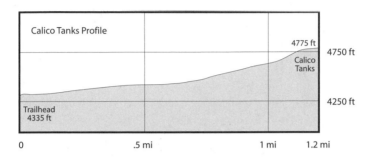

DISTANCE & ROUTE:	2.4 miles round trip
DIFFICULTY:	Moderate
SEASON:	Fall to spring
TRAILHEAD ACCESS:	All vehicles
WATER:	Seasonally available in tanks
GUIDEBOOK MAP:	35
USGS MAP:	La Madre Mountain

INTRODUCTION A short moderate hike leads to one of the desert's most important features—a *tinaja,* Spanish for earthen jar. Capturing and holding rainwater for an extended time, these rock depressions provide a vital water source for wildlife. This popular trip leads hikers through some of Red Rock Canyon's characteristically picturesque sandstone formations on the way up a narrow and steep canyon to the Calico Tanks, a trio of *tinajas.* The first tank is the largest and most impressive and will satisfy the desires of most hikers; the other two tanks are smaller, more difficult to locate, and require an extra bit of scrambling to reach.

With a location in the desert west of Las Vegas, hiking in Red Rock Canyon is best appreciated between the months of October and April.

DIRECTIONS TO TRAILHEAD The traditional way to reach Red Rock Canyon was to follow West Charleston Boulevard (S.R. 159) through Las Vegas and continue to the Scenic Loop. Although this route will still get you to Red Rock Canyon, nowadays it's an interminable drive encountering innumerable traffic lights through an ever-expanding succession of subdivisions built to house the rapid influx of new residents to the fastest growing city in America.

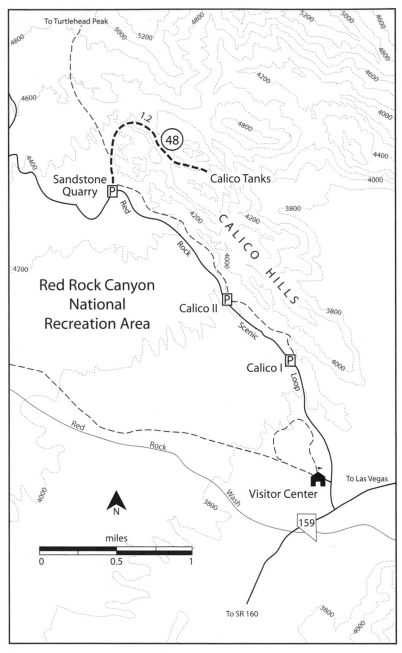

To Turtlehead Peak

4800
5000
5200
4800
5200
5000
4600
4800
4600
4200
4600
4000
4400
1.2
(48)
4800
Sandstone
Quarry P   Calico Tanks
4400
4000
4000

Red
CALICO HILLS
3800
4200
4200
4200
4200
Rock
4000

Red Rock Canyon
National
Recreation Area

Calico II P
3800

Scenic

Calico I P
4000

Loop

Red
Rock

Visitor Center   To Las Vegas

N

4000
3800
Wash

159

miles
0   0.5   1

To SR 160
3800
4000

MAP 35 | Calico Tanks

You can avoid most of the stop-and-go-traffic on West Charleston by following the Las Vegas Beltway (Clark County Road 215). Accessible from I-215 in the south and U.S. 95 in the north, the beltway takes you to S.R. 159 west of the city. From there a short drive leads to the beginning of the one-way Scenic Loop.

Once on the Scenic Loop, pay the nominal fee at the entrance station and continue about 3 miles to the signed turnoff for Sandstone Quarry (restroom).

DESCRIPTION From the parking area, follow the wide path of an old gravel road north to a flat near the site of the quarry. A small sign on the left-hand side of the flat designates the beginning of the Calico Tanks and Turtlehead Peak Trails. The route immediately crosses a wash and continues on gravel tread to a signed Y-junction. Turn right at the junction, soon reaching a second signed junction, where you veer to the right to follow single-track trail about 100 yards to a dry wash. Walk along the wash briefly before single-track trail leads out of the wash and quickly into another wash composed of red sand.

Now heading southeast, you follow the wash into a canyon that soon narrows and becomes steeper. Climbing rock steps and scrambling over sandstone slabs takes you higher up the picturesque canyon. Periodically placed cairns will help keep you on track where the route crosses extensive sections of sandstone. The grade eases for a stretch, followed by more rock steps, and then another short section of gentle grade, before you climb to the first and largest of the Calico Tanks. The first *tinaja* resembles more of a small pond rather than a typical tank, but it is certainly an impressive natural feature way out here in the midst of the desert. Two smaller tanks are above the first tank, hidden in the sandstone. By climbing all the way to the top of the ridge, you'll get a good look at the backside of the vividly red Calico Hills and a grand vista across the desert floor toward Las Vegas.

WILD BURROS Motorists headed for the Sandstone Quarry trailhead may see wild burros roaming through the Red Rock area. The burros were brought here back in the mid-1800s when prospectors flooded the area following the discovery of gold in the Colorado River basin and in neighboring California. After the boom, many of the burros were turned loose or wandered off, left to fend for themselves in the harsh desert environment. After decades of mistreatment, wild burros and horses received federal protection through the Wild Free-Roaming Horse and Burro Act of 1971. Proving to be quite adaptable to the desert environment, the population of wild burros and horses increased dramatically. Nowadays, to prevent widespread destruction of the fragile desert habitat, many of the wild animals are removed from sensitive lands through an adoption process.

This easy loop trip is an excellent way to get acquainted with the trails in Red Rock.

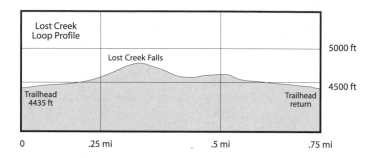

Lost Creek
Loop Profile

Lost Creek Falls

5000 ft

4500 ft

Trailhead
4435 ft

Trailhead
return

0   .25 mi   .5 mi   .75 mi

DISTANCE:	0.75 mile one way in loop
DIFFICULTY:	Easy
SEASON:	Fall to spring
TRAILHEAD ACCESS:	All vehicles
WATER:	Seasonally available in creek
GUIDEBOOK MAP:	36
USGS MAP:	La Madre Mountain

INTRODUCTION By connecting the Lost Creek Canyon Trail with the Children's Discovery Trail, you can follow a short 0.75-mile loop through some diverse topography and vegetation. A year-round spring provides refreshment and nourishment for the riparian foliage lining Lost Creek Canyon, and seasonal rains produce an intermittent but dramatic waterfall farther up the canyon. Pictographs and an agave roasting-pit site provide historical and cultural interest.

With a location in the desert west of Las Vegas, hiking in Red Rock Canyon is best appreciated between the months of October and April.

DIRECTIONS TO TRAILHEAD The traditional way to reach Red Rock Canyon was to follow West Charleston Boulevard (S.R. 159) through Las Vegas and continue to the Scenic Loop. Although this route will still get you to Red Rock Canyon, nowadays it's an interminable drive encountering innumerable traffic lights through an ever-expanding succession of subdivisions built to house the rapid influx of new residents to the fastest growing city in America.

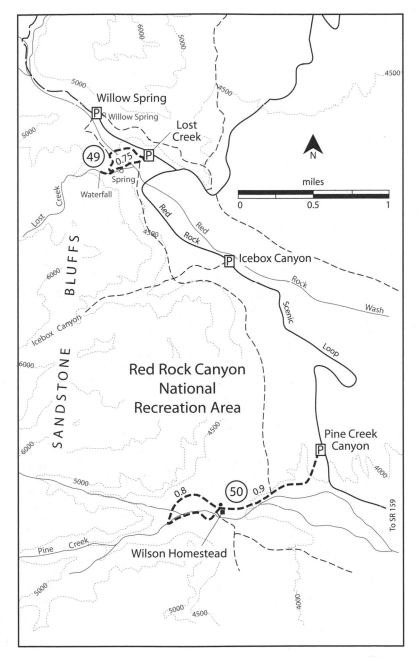

Willow Spring

Willow Spring

Lost Creek

49 0.75

Spring

Waterfall

Lost Creek

S A N D S T O N E   B L U F F S

Icebox Canyon

Red Rock

Red Rock

Icebox Canyon

Rock Wash

Scenic Loop

Red Rock Canyon National Recreation Area

Pine Creek Canyon

0.8 50 0.9

Wilson Homestead

Pine Creek

To SR 159

N

miles

0   0.5   1

5000
6000
4500
4000

MAP 36 | Lost Creek & Pine Creek

You can avoid most of the stop-and-go-traffic on West Charleston by following the Las Vegas Beltway (Clark County Road 215). Accessible from I-215 in the south and U.S. 95 in the north, the beltway takes you to S.R. 159 west of the city. From there a short drive leads to the beginning of the one-way Scenic Loop.

Lost Creek Falls, Lost Creek Canyon Trail, Red Rock Canyon

Once on the Scenic Loop, pay the nominal fee at the entrance station and continue about 7.5 miles to the signed turnoff on your right for Willow Spring. Drive paved road a short distance to the Lost Creek parking area on the left (restroom).

DESCRIPTION　From the parking lot follow the rock-lined Lost Creek Canyon Trail southwest toward the base of some sandstone bluffs. Approximately 100 yards up the trail is a signed Y-junction with the Spring Mountain Youth Camp Trail, which provides a 2.2-mile connector to the Icebox Canyon Trail. Veer to the right at the junction, cross willow-dotted Red Rock Wash, and then ascend a set of rock steps to a shrub-covered hillside sprinkled with pinyon pines, junipers, and ponderosa pines. Past several fenced restoration areas you come alongside trickling Lost Creek and soon reach a boardwalk, built in 2002 by Friends of Red Rock to minimize environmental degradation of the riparian area along the creek. An informational sign clues visitors to the presence of two species of freshwater snails found only in the Spring Mountains.

Away from the boardwalk you enter the wilderness study area and come to a three-way junction with a trail on the right, which will be the return route after a visit to the waterfall. Continuing ahead, you cross the rocky creek channel, pass a park bench perched beneath the shade of a ponderosa pine, and climb through lush foliage and huge boulders to the base of the waterfall. If you time your visit during or just after a storm, the fall may actually be running.

From the fall, return to the junction and turn left. A wood rail fence heralds your approach to a degraded cultural site that used to provide untarnished examples of some ancient Indian pictographs. Proceed to a three-way junction with a connector to Willow Spring and veer to the right. Soon the dense vegetation is left behind as you cross Red Rock Wash and follow gravel trail back to the trailhead.

WATER　Water is a very precious commodity in Red Rock that is usually in very short supply. The region receives only four to ten inches of precipitation per year, most of which falls between the months of January and March. To appreciate the wonder of Lost Creek Falls, you'll have to time your visit during or just after a significant rainfall.

One of Red Rock's classic hikes, the Pine Creek Canyon Trail leads hikers into the heart of the backcountry.

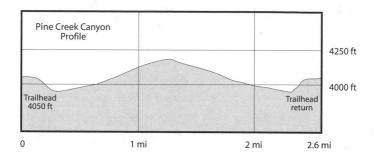

DISTANCE & ROUTE:	2.6 miles round trip including short loop
DIFFICULTY:	Moderate
SEASON:	Fall to spring
TRAILHEAD ACCESS:	All vehicles
WATER:	Seasonally available in creek
GUIDEBOOK MAP:	36
USGS MAP:	Blue Diamond, La Madre Mountain, Mountain Springs

INTRODUCTION   The Pine Creek Canyon Trail follows a seasonal stream to the base of the western escarpment of the Spring Mountains, where Mescalito, a towering sandstone formation, stands guard over the twin branches of the upper canyon. Along the way you'll see numerous ponderosa pines lining the banks of the stream, somewhat of a rarity at this low elevation, and the foundation of the old Wilson homestead. The official trail ends at the base of the escarpment, but experienced hikers can follow a scramble route up the south branch of the canyon to a picturesque pool.

DIRECTIONS TO TRAILHEAD   The traditional way to reach Red Rock Canyon was to follow West Charleston Boulevard (S.R. 159) through Las Vegas and continue to the Scenic Loop. Although this route will still get you to Red Rock Canyon, nowadays it's an interminable drive encountering innumerable traffic lights through an ever-expanding succession of subdivisions built to house the rapid influx of new residents to the fastest growing city in America.

You can avoid most of the stop-and-go-traffic on West Charleston by following the Las Vegas Beltway (Clark County Road 215). Accessible from I-215 in the south and U.S. 95 in the north, the beltway takes you to S.R. 159 west of the city. From there a short drive leads to the beginning of the one-way Scenic Loop.

Once on the Scenic Loop, pay the nominal fee at the entrance station and continue about 10 miles to the signed turnoff for Pine Creek Canyon.

DESCRIPTION Follow dirt and rock trail on an angling descent toward the floor of Pine Creek Canyon and then turn west to head upstream. Pass by twin junctions with the Fire Ecology Trail and continue the mild ascent toward the mouth of the canyon through typical desert scrub. The perennial creek is lined with lush, riparian foliage, including the canyon's namesake ponderosa pines. Reach a junction with Dale's Trail, a 2-mile connector to the Icebox Canyon Trail, at 0.4 mile from the trailhead.

Continue up the trail toward the mouth of the canyon. At 0.9 mile you reach a junction with the Arnight Trail and the Pine Creek Canyon Loop. Beneath some shady cottonwoods, between the trail and the creek, lies the foundation of the old Wilson homestead.

Veer to the right at the junction and proceed upstream toward the triangular-shaped formation known as the Mescalito, which divides the canyon into two branches. Soon you cross into the wilderness study area and continue to an unmarked junction, where the loop trail bends left and crosses Pine Creek. The use trail straight ahead provides access to a scramble route up the north branch of the canyon.

After crossing Pine Creek, you encounter another use trail. Experienced hikers can follow this scramble route 0.75 mile up the south branch to a picturesque pool. The Pine Creek Loop heads downstream along the south bank of the creek for 0.25 mile to a signed junction with the Arnight Trail. From the junction, hop across the creek, make a brief ascent past the Wilson homestead, and reach the loop junction. From there retrace your steps back to the trailhead.

WILSON HOMESTEAD Horace and Glenna Wilson built their home here in the early 1920s, also planting a large garden and an orchard nearby. The Wilsons lived here until 1933, leaving Red Rock for Las Vegas. After their departure the house was abandoned and subsequently vandalized. Nowadays all that remains of the Wilsons' presence is the stone foundation and a grove of apple trees, which are happily consumed by the wild burros that frequent the canyon. The area around the homestead provided the setting for *The Stalking Moon,* a 1969 film starring Gregory Peck. A photo of the intact house hangs in the Red Rock Canyon Visitor Center.

NORTHWESTERN NEVADA

U.S. FOREST SERVICE

Santa Rosa Ranger District
1200 Winnemucca Blvd. East
Winnemucca, NV 89445
(775) 623-5025
www.fs.fed.us/htnf/

BUREAU OF LAND MANAGEMENT

Winnemucca Field Office
5100 E. Winnemucca Blvd.
Winnemucca, NV 89445
(775) 623-1500
www.nv.blm.gov/Winnemucca/

NORTHEASTERN NEVADA

U.S. FOREST SERVICE

Jarbidge Ranger District
1008 Burley Avenue
Buhl, ID 83316
(208) 543-4129

Humboldt-Toiyabe National Forest
Supervisor's Office
976 Mountain City Highway
Elko, NV 89801
(775) 738-5171

Ruby Mountain Ranger District
428 South Humboldt
P.O. Box 246
Wells, NV 89825
(775) 738-3357

LAKE TAHOE REGION

U.S. FOREST SERVICE

Carson Ranger District
1536 So. Carson Street
Carson City, NV 89701
(775) 882-2766

NEVADA DIVISION OF STATE PARKS

Lake Tahoe Nevada State Park
P.O. Box 8867
Incline Village, NV 89452
(775) 831-0494

CENTRAL NEVADA

U.S. FOREST SERVICE

Austin Ranger District
100 Midas Canyon Road
Austin, NV 89310
(775) 964-2671

Tonopah Ranger District
PO Box 3940
Tonopah, NV 89049
(775) 482-6286

EASTERN NEVADA

U.S. FOREST SERVICE

Ely Ranger District
825 Avenue E
PO Box 539
Ely, NV 89301
(775) 289-3031
www.fs.fed.us/htnf/

NATIONAL PARK SERVICE

Great Basin National Park
100 Great Basin National Park
Baker, NV 89311
(775) 234-7331
www.nps.gov/grba/

Beaver Dam State Park
HC 64 Box 3
Caliente, NV 89008
(775) 726-3564
www.parks.nv.gov/

Cathedral Gorge State Park
P.O. Box 176
Panaca, NV 89042
(775) 728-4460
www.parks.nv.gov/

Cave Lake State Park
PO Box 151761
Ely, NV 89315
(775) 728-4460
www.parks.nv.gov/

SOUTHERN NEVADA

NEVADA DIVISION OF STATE PARKS

Valley of Fire State Park
P.O. Box 515
Overton, NV 89040
(702) 397-2088
www.parks.nv.gov/vf.htm

U.S. FOREST SERVICE

Las Vegas Ranger District
2881 S. Valley View Blvd., Suite 16
Las Vegas, NV 89102
(702) 873-8800
www.fs.fed.us/htnf/

BUREAU OF LAND MANAGEMENT

Red Rock Canyon National Conservation Area
HCR 33, Box 5000
Las Vegas, NV 89124
(702) 515-5350
www.redrockcanyon.blm.gov/

NEVADA WILDERNESS AREAS

WILDERNESS	ACREAGE	MANAGEMENT AGENCY	LOCATION	YEAR ESTABLISHED
Alta Toquima	38,000	USFS	Central	1989
Arc Dome	115,000	USFS	Central	1989
Arrow Canyon	27,530	BLM	South	2002
Black Canyon	17,220	NPS, BLM	South	2002
Black Rock Desert	315,700	BLM	Northwest	2000
Boundary Peak	10,000	USFS	Central	1989
Bridge Canyon	7,761	NPS	South	2002
Calico Mountains	65,400	BLM	Northwest	2000
Currant Mountain	36,000	USFS	Central	1989
Death Valley National Park Nevada Triangle	44,000	NPS	South	1994
East Fork High Rock Canyon	52,800	BLM	Northwest	2000
East Humboldt	36,900	USFS	Northeast	1989
El Dorado	31,950	NPS, BLM	South	2002
Grant Range	50,000	USFS	Central	1989
High Rock Canyon	46,600	BLM	Northwest	2000
High Rock Lake	59,300	BLM	Northwest	2000
Ireteba Peaks	32,745	NPS, BLM	South	2002
Jarbidge	113,167	USFS	Northeast	1964, 1989
Jimbilnan	18,879	NPS	South	2002
Jumbo Springs	4,631	BLM	South	2002
La Madre Mountain	47,180	USFS, BLM	South	2002
Lime Canyon	23,233	BLM	South	2002
Little High Rock Canyon	48,700	BLM	Northwest	2000
Mount Charleston	56,598	USFS, BLM	South	1989, 2002
Mount Moriah	82,000	USFS, BLM	East	1989
Mount Rose	28,000	USFS	Northwest	1989
Muddy Mountains	48,019	BLM, NPS	South	2002
Nellis Wash	16,423	NPS	South	2002
North Black Rock Range	30,800	BLM	Northwest	2000
North Jackson Mountains	24,000	BLM	Northwest	2000
North McCullough	14,763	BLM	South	2002
Pahute Peak	57,400	BLM	Northwest	2000
Pinto Valley	39,173	NPS	South	2002
Quinn Canyon	27,000	USFS	Central	1989
Rainbow Mountain	24,997	USFS, BLM	South	2002
Ruby Mountains	90,000	USFS	Northeast	1989
Santa Rosa–Paradise Peak	31,000	USFS	Northwest	1989
South Jackson Mountains	56,800	BLM	Northwest	2000
South McCullough	44,245	BLM	South	2002
Spirit Mountain	33,518	NPS, BLM	South	2002
Table Mountain	98,000	USFS	Central	1989
Wee Thump–Joshua Tree	6,050	BLM	South	2002
TOTAL LEGISLATED ACREAGE:	2,051,482			

Note: Great Basin National Park contains 77,180 acres.

Friends of Nevada Wilderness
P.O. Box 9754
Reno, NV 89507
(775) 324-7667
e-mail: fnw@nevadawilderness.org
www.nevadawilderness.org/

The Nature Conservancy
Nevada Field Office
1 E. First St., Suite 1007
Reno, NV 89501
(775) 322-4990
e-mail: nevada@tnc.org
www.nature.org/

Sierra Club–Toiyabe Chapter
Great Basin Group
P.O. Box 8096
Reno, NV 89507
(775) 323-3162
e-mail: webmaster@toiyabesierraclub.org
www.nevada.sierraclub.org/gbgroup/

Sierra Club–Toiyabe Chapter
Southern Nevada Group
P.O. Box 19777
Las Vegas, NV 89132
(702) 732-7750
www.nevada.sierraclub.org/sngroup/

Tahoe Rim Trail Association
DWR Community Non-Profit Center
948 Incline Way
Incline Village, NV 89451
(775) 298-0012
e-mail: info@tahoerimtrail.org
www.tahoerimtrail.org/

Truckee Meadows Trail Association
P.O. Box 265
Reno, NV 89504
(775) 786-8154
e-mail: info@truckeemeadowstrails.org
www.truckeemeadowstrails.org/

BIBLIOGRAPHY

Carlson, Helen S. 1974. *Nevada Place Names: A Geographical Dictionary.* Reno: University of Nevada Press.

Charlet, David Alan. 1996. *Atlas of Nevada Conifers: A Phytogeographic Reference.* Reno: University of Nevada Press.

Clark, Jeanne L. 1993. *Nevada Wildlife Viewing Guide.* Helena, Mont.: Falcon Press.

Cline, Gloria Griffen. 1988. *Exploring the Great Basin.* 1963. Reprint, Reno: University of Nevada Press.

Fiero, Bill. 1986. *Geology of the Great Basin.* Reno: University of Nevada Press.

Graf, Michael. 1999. *Plants of the Tahoe Basin.* Sacramento: California Native Plant Society Press.

Hart, John. 1992. *Hiking the Great Basin: The High Desert Country of California, Oregon, Nevada, and Utah.* Rev. ed. San Francisco: Sierra Club Books.

Hauserman, Tim. 2002. *The Tahoe Rim Trail: A Complete Guide for Hikers, Mountain Bikers, and Equestrians.* Berkeley: Wilderness Press.

Kelsey, Michael R. 1999. *Hiking and Climbing in Great Basin National Park: A Guide to Nevada's Wheeler Peak, Mt. Moriah and the Snake Range.* 3rd ed. Provo, Utah: Kelsey Publishing.

Lanner, Ronald M. 1984. *Trees of the Great Basin.* Reno: University of Nevada Press.

McPhee, John A. 1982. *Basin and Range.* New York: Farrar, Straus and Giroux, The Noonday Press.

Mozingo, Hugh N. 1987. *Shrubs of the Great Basin.* Reno: University of Nevada Press.

Nicklas, Michael L. 1996. *Great Basin: The Story Behind the Scenery.* KC Publications.

Stone, Irving. 1982. *Men to Match My Mountains: The Opening of the Far West 1840–1900.* 1956. Reprint, New York: Berkeley Books.

Taylor, Ronald J. 1992. *Sagebrush Country: A Wildflower Sanctuary.* Missoula, Mont.: Mountain Press Publishing Company.

Twain, Mark. 1962. *Roughing It.* 1871. Reprint, New York: Penguin Books.

White, Michael C. 1997. *Nevada Wilderness Areas and Great Basin National Park.* Berkeley: Wilderness Press.

———. 2004. *Top Trails Lake Tahoe.* Berkeley: Wilderness Press.

Whitney, Branch. 1999. *Hiking Las Vegas: 60 Hikes Within 60 Minutes of the Strip.* Las Vegas: Huntington Press.

———. 2000. *Hiking Southern Nevada.* Las Vegas: Huntington Press.

Wuerthner, George. 1992. *Nevada Mountain Ranges.* Helena, Mont.: American & World Geographic Publishing.

Zdon, Andy. 2000. *Desert Summits: A Climbing & Hiking Guide to California and Southern Nevada.* Bishop, Calif.: Spotted Dog Press.

INDEX

Note: Italic page numbers refer to illustrations.